ESCAPE FROM VENEZUELA'S DEADLIEST PRISON

NATALIE WELSH

SPELLING DIFFERENCES: UK V US

This book was written in British English, hence US readers may notice some spelling differences with American English: e.g. color = colour, meter = metre and = jewelry = jewellery

CONTENTS

FOREWORD

Thank you for buying this book. I really hope that you enjoy the story and can hear the message that I am trying to convey: please think hard before choosing certain paths in life. No matter what you think, you always have a choice. I hope my story inspires you to transform your life and to avoid the temptation of venturing down the path of criminality. It never works out the way you think it will – especially with drugs.

Big thanks to my publisher Shaun Atwood at Gadfly Press, for his encouragement and support with the republication of this book, and a massive thanks to John a.k.a. Lion-eye and Robo for always being by my side in good and bad times; for never judging me when the rest of the world did, and for always encouraging me and reminding me of the true power I have inside to achieve anything I want – the same power we all have inside.

PROLOGUE

'Well, this is going to be the hardest ten years of my life, but I will take it as a learning experience, and I will come out a stronger person. The question on my lips is, Will there be a happy ending?'
Letter from Natalie to her friend Eve, August 2001

I trembled as I walked towards the international departures entrance at Margarita Airport. It was July 24, 2001, and I was twenty-one. With one hand, I held my four-year-old daughter Nikita's little fingers and with the other, I clutched my freshly glued suitcase. The palm trees swished in the breeze and the strong Venezuelan sun beat down on my back, burning through my T-shirt. I looked up at the intensely blue, cloudless sky one last time and felt sad that tomorrow I'd be back in grey, drizzly England.

At least I'll be four-grand richer, I said to myself.

Cars pulled up outside the departure area and families jumped out, unloading gigantic suitcases and speaking to each other in agitated Spanish. There was lots of hugging and kissing as family members who were not travelling bade fond farewells to those who were. I couldn't fathom what they were saying, but during my fortnight's holiday, I'd got used to the cadence of the language, which sounded much more exotic than English.

'Wave bye-bye to Venezuela. We'll be back home tomorrow,' I said to Nikita.

She waved and looked sad. 'Can't we stay a bit longer, Mummy?' She'd had a great holiday and didn't seem in any hurry to go home.

'Not this time, darling. You'll be able to see all your friends again tomorrow and you can tell them about all the exciting things you did here.'

She gazed up at me with her huge brown eyes, nodded and smiled. She was such a good, happy little girl. During this trip, I had been able to devote every second to her and she had blossomed. Her tanned skin glowed and her hair was freshly plaited. I looked at her and felt a rush of love. She was the most precious thing in the world to me. Her dad and I were no longer together, but Nikita and I made a good team.

Margarita Airport was a low, modern building. As I walked through the doors, it seemed eerily quiet. A few passengers were checking in, nobody queuing at the car-hire offices or at the fast-food outlets.

I gripped the handle of my suitcase. The smell of glue seemed to be overwhelming and I was terrified that one of the officials would march over and poke an accusatory finger into my chest. Al had said that the National Guard stationed at the airport had been alerted to the contents of my suitcase and had been paid hush money to allow me to board the plane with my suitcase intact, but his words hadn't reassured me. I was getting increasingly edgy. I wondered if there were sniffer dogs at the airport. If there were, I was sure they'd make a beeline for the strong-smelling glue.

It was unusual for me to feel so anxious. Most of the time, I had an unassailable belief that everything I did would somehow work out fine, as if I wore some invisible lucky charm that protected me from lousy outcomes, an invincibility that would pull me through any disaster great or small.

Yet, as I walked towards the Alan Air check-in desk, I felt as if this protective charm was slipping away. My head was screaming, 'Don't do it. Dump the suitcase in the loo, get on the plane and forget about the whole thing.' Even though I wouldn't get the money I had been promised, at least I'd still have had a free holiday, I reasoned. *But this is such easy money*, another voice in my head piped up.

Something more powerful than my reason propelled me

towards the check-in desk. I beamed at the woman who was processing passengers for the flight to Holland and tried to act nonchalant as I lifted my suitcase onto the conveyor belt.

The woman, immaculately turned out in a navy suit with her dark hair in a chignon, smiled at Nikita. I allowed myself a small sigh of relief. She didn't seem to have noticed the smell of the glue, nor had she suspected that there was anything untoward lurking in my suitcase. But still, I had a sick feeling in my stomach that things weren't quite right.

Airport security at that time was lax, and so after we'd checked in, we walked straight through to the departure lounge. I looked around nervously, but everything seemed normal. Holidaymakers were chatting to each other and were showing one another trinkets that they'd bought at local markets. I didn't have much money left, but realised I'd bought nothing for my friend Eve or her daughter Mara. There was a stall in the departure lounge selling pretty necklaces made of shells and glass beads, so I bought a couple for them. I had a strong sense of foreboding but thought that if I put all my energy into looking like an ultra-normal mum, it might ward off any unwelcome attention, particularly regarding the contents of my suitcase.

Nikita and I sat down at a table and I showed her the necklaces I'd just bought. She chattered away, full of all the things she'd done at the beach and in the pool. Although my gaze was fixed on her, I was suddenly aware of two men in uniform entering the departure lounge and looking around, slowly and deliberately. I allowed myself a quick glance at them and recognised their uniforms as being those of the National Guard. Both wore combat trousers, had big, bushy moustaches and carried guns. I inhaled sharply. I'd been expecting them, but when I saw them, the hairs on my skin stood on end and panic raced through my veins. They were obviously looking for someone. I turned back to Nikita, willing them not to come up to us. The guards approached a woman sitting at the next table with two children. I watched her show them her ID, but this didn't reassure me at all. The voice in my head that had told me to dump the suitcase was now shouting out that it was me they wanted, not her.

They flicked open her passport, nodded to her and then came over to me. They couldn't speak English, but through a combination of hand gestures and Spanish, with the occasional English word thrown in, I understood that they wanted to see my passport. This time, they didn't nod and hand it back. They gestured to me to stand up and, taking me firmly by the arm, led me out of the departure lounge. Nikita held my hand. She wasn't scared because she had no idea what this was all about, but she was puzzled.

'Where are these big men taking us, Mummy?' she whispered.

'Don't worry, darling, they're just doing some checks on our passport and tickets. We'll be on our way soon.' She seemed satisfied by this explanation and didn't ask any more questions.

Al had explained that I would probably be questioned by the National Guard, but he had assured me that these questions would just be a formality because they had been paid off. However, the looks on their faces told me that this wasn't just a case of going through the motions. This was serious.

My heart started to beat fast and I was overwhelmed by a strange sensation. I felt like a character in a film where everything in the background drops away into a blur while I moved across the polished floor of the departure lounge in slow motion. We were led into a bare, windowless room with a naked light bulb hanging from the ceiling. More guards were waiting there, standing with their muscular arms folded across their chests. If this was all just a formality, why were there so many of them here? And why was the atmosphere so icy? The guards were giving me such piercing stares that I felt they were X-raying me with their eyes. I was by now shaking with fear, but tried to stop my knees from knocking together as I sat on a hard-wooden chair. There were six guards in the room and the way they towered over me made me feel young and weak.

My God, what have I done? I said to myself.

In the middle of the room was a wooden table, with my suitcase perched on it. Straight away I could smell the glue, which had been used to seal the false bottom of the suitcase after the packages of cocaine had been put in. I would have given anything to have flung it out the window of the departure lounge, and to be walking onto the plane with the rest of the holidaymakers, my head held high.

Deep down, I knew that everything had gone wrong. I screwed up my eyes, thinking that if I prayed hard enough, God would turn back time for me. I clung on to the tiny, illogical hope that they were going to say, 'Don't put this in the hold. What you've got in there is too precious: carry it on board.'

I told myself that things might still be all right. *Please hurry this up so we can get on that plane*, I said silently. Nikita started to whimper. I cuddled her close and told her that everything was going to be fine.

'Your suitcase?' one of the guards barked in heavily accented English.

I nodded.

He gestured to me to open it and empty out the contents. Each moment that passed without me being waved on to the plane made my heart sink further. I glanced at my watch and knew that it wasn't long until the flight would be taking off. The room had no air conditioning. I felt as if I were suffocating from the heat and tension. A guard left the room and returned with a member of the Alan Air staff, who explained in English that he would be translating.

'They want to know if you've got anything else in your suitcase,' he said.

'No,' I squeaked.

'Did anyone give you the suitcase?'

'No.'

One of the guards whipped something out of a holder in his belt. The few remaining shreds of hope I'd clung onto disappeared when I saw the glint of the blade.

This isn't part of the plan. This isn't supposed to be happening, I screamed silently. I tried my best to keep my expression calm in the hope that he'd change his mind and put the knife away. He didn't, of course. Instead, he plunged it into the false bottom of the suitcase, then sighed contentedly as twelve fat, neat packages plopped out onto the table. I had made the most foolish decision of my entire life when I had agreed to carry five kilos of cocaine – with a street value of £325,000 – all tidily wrapped in black plastic bags.

I lowered my eyes, then dared to look up at the guard with the knife. He shook his head.

They can't do anything to me, I'm English … it will be OK, I thought. *Maybe I'll have to go to prison in England for a few months, but I'll get through that. Just let me get on that damn plane.*

'You'll be going to prison for ten years,' the guy from the airline said flatly. 'Everybody gets the maximum sentence for carrying drugs.'

I looked at him hopelessly, unable to absorb what he'd just said. I was determined not to believe him.

'What's happening, Mummy?'

'It's OK, darling. Someone put some stones in my suitcase, and it makes it too heavy for the plane, so this man is just taking them out for me.'

'Why are they cutting up your suitcase?'

'They're just checking everything, because the stones shouldn't be in there.'

She had no concept of drugs, and the last thing I wanted to do was enlighten her. She believed everything I said and remained calm. As I looked at the packages laid out on the table, and then back at Nikita, I was overwhelmed with guilt and despair.

For God's sake, Natalie, you've got a four-year-old daughter. What on earth did you think you were doing, putting everything at risk like this? I yelled silently at myself. I knew that I was completely out of my depth. I was young and gullible and had believed the drug smugglers, knowing how desperate I was for money, when they had promised I wouldn't get caught.

'We've missed this plane but maybe we'll get the next one,' I said to Nikita, struggling to control my trembling voice. I hoped I could explain as much as possible to her without telling her the truth.

By now, quite a congregation had gathered in the room. I couldn't understand what was being said but, judging by their animated tones, I guessed it was something along the lines of, 'Oh yes, we've got someone!' The guard with the knife stabbed one of the parcels of drugs. White powder trickled onto the table. He raised the knife to his lips and put it onto his tongue. I didn't need the airline guy to translate him confirming 'Cocaine!'

After they'd finished dismantling my suitcase, they started checking my flight details. I watched them numbly, still hoping against hope that they'd let me go.

'Is someone waiting for you at the other end?' I had always prided myself on not being a grass, and so didn't want to reveal the identity of Tony, who'd recruited me in England.

'No, there won't be anyone waiting for me at the other end,' I replied shakily.

The Alan Air guy was pleading with me to tell the truth. 'In the end, it will be easier for you if you just tell them everything,' he said sadly.

I was still hoping the embassy would ship me off to London and that everything would be sorted out over there.

I repeatedly said, like a robot, 'The embassy will sort it out.'

'You'd be better off cooperating with them,' said the translator.

I shrugged and said nothing.

By now, I had resigned myself to not getting the plane back that day, but I still believed that once someone from the British Embassy got involved, I would be on a flight tomorrow. I longed to be back in grey and grimy England. I didn't care what would happen to me when the plane touched down on British soil. All I wanted was to get out of that room, that airport, that country.

I vowed that, however much I struggled to provide for Nikita, I would never do anything like this again.

'Please let me speak to the embassy,' I said, trying to sound as calm as I could. One of the guards nodded, looked up a number and dialled it on a phone in the corner of the room. A woman with a clipped, upper-class accent came on the line. 'Can you arrange for me to get a plane out of this place? Let the British authorities deal with me,' I pleaded. She sounded unsympathetic and was obviously not going to commit herself to getting me onto a plane anywhere, anytime soon.

'You're in a lot of trouble – you have to go with the guards. Someone from the embassy will come and see you tomorrow.'

Then the line clicked, and she was gone.

It was evening and I'd obviously interrupted this woman. I imagined her sipping drinks on a terrace, like in those films about Brits in the colonies a century ago. It was clear from the tone of her voice that I was inconveniencing her.

'Let's go,' said one of the guards abruptly. He pulled a pair of handcuffs out of his pocket and locked himself to me. I felt ashamed as I stared down at the metal shackles but tried to remain expressionless. I didn't want to give the guards the satisfaction of seeing how scared and humiliated I felt, and I managed to fight back the tears. I was led out of the main airport building and taken in an army truck to the airport police station. I put my free arm around Nikita, to try to shield her from as much of what was going on as possible.

I knew that our flight had gone, and my heart sank, thinking of all the other passengers carefree and airborne. I felt like a circus freak, on display to the world as I was marched out of the truck.

Lots of airport staff had come out to see the English drug mule, and the way they all stared at me, open-mouthed, made me feel as if I was a serial killer rather than a bit-part player in a global operation.

The two guards escorting me to the police station were kinder than those in the airport. I realised that I was a novelty to them, with my blonde hair and blue eyes, and it was a relief not to have to deal with any icy stares, for the moment at least.

I sat on a hard bench in the police station, shutting my eyes and trying to make sense of everything that was happening. I'd suspected that something wasn't right from the moment I got on the plane to Venezuela and, unhappily, I'd been proved right. The more I thought about it, the more convinced I was that I'd been set up. The smugglers knew that I was young, and that I had no idea what I was getting myself into, and so they had taken full advantage of that. In short, I'd been duped.

I'd heard of smugglers putting several mules on the same plane and making it obvious to customs officials that one of them was carrying drugs. Arresting one person would satisfy them that they were doing their job properly and would divert attention from the others. Al, my contact in Margarita, obviously saw me as someone who could be dumped in the rubbish bin in order to keep the operation running smoothly.

Fear started to give way to anger that Al had set me up and that I had been stupid enough to let him. *How could I have been so gullible?* Furious with myself and with him, I took a few deep breaths to try to calm myself down. I still had faith that somehow this mess would be sorted out and that by tomorrow Nikita and I would be on our way home.

1 THE ROOT OF THE PROBLEM

My early years held no clue to the dramatic events that unfolded a decade or so later. A neat, three-bedroomed house in the heart of suburbia was my first home. The house belonged to my mother's parents. I loved living there with my grandparents, Granny and Grampy, and my mum. Life was calm, ordered and conventional. I was a happy child.

Granny worked in an office and my mum had a good job as a personal assistant at a prestigious law firm. It fell to Grampy, who had retired from the RAF, to take care of me.

The other member of the household was Leo, my mum's ginger and white cat. Leo harboured a strange passion for being vacuumed. Grampy oversaw the vacuuming, and the cat insisted on being vacuumed before he started on the carpets, which always made the two of us collapse into fits of giggles.

Grampy adored chess and before I started infant school, he'd achieved his mission of teaching me how to play. He studied the game, read books about it and played against a computer.

He assured me that I'd never beat him and when I finally did, at the age of twelve, he vowed never to play another game against me. 'There's no point in me playing you anymore because I've got nothing left to teach you,' he said with a smile. My mum had split up from my dad before I was born. She was a slim, attractive woman with blonde hair – people sometimes told her she looked like Michelle Pfeiffer. My dad was tall, of medium build, with brown hair and a moustache, and had a tattoo of a heart, sword and eagle on top of each other on his left forearm. He ran several pubs and had a reputation as a womaniser. His roving eye was the reason why he and my mum split up. I think she had thought she could tame him, but he just wasn't designed for lifelong fidelity.

I thought my dad was wonderful. He lived nearby and I saw him regularly. One of my earliest memories is of him walking into the bathroom at Granny and Grampy's, carrying a little pink bunny rabbit. I clung onto that bunny for years, until it only had one ear and half a nose left. I even went to my dad's funeral clutching the rabbit.

My dad always had plenty of girlfriends, often at the same time, and when he looked after me, we often met up with one or other of them. I loved the fact that my dad didn't try to hide anything from me; it made me feel grown up. Sometimes he took me to see his mum, my nan, a woman I adored. She was small with curly black hair, and my special treat was to make toasted sandwiches in her sandwich maker whenever I visited her. She had a long back garden and I used to love running around in it with my cousins Tom and Helen.

My stepfather Alan was a different kettle of fish. I don't remember him ever not being around, although he didn't move in with us until I was five. Alan was a tall, slim man with a receding hairline. His face was long and nondescript, and I couldn't understand what Mum saw in him: he was nowhere near as good-looking as my dad. When my mum decided to move out of my grandparents' house, she bought a maisonette and Alan moved in soon afterwards. He then persuaded my mum to give up her job with the firm of solicitors. One day, he and my mum got married in secret. They didn't tell any family, or any of their friends, and just pulled two witnesses off the street.

For the first few years, Alan and I got along well. I remember being proud when both he and Mum came on a school trip to the Forest of Dean with me. He often helped me with my homework and took me swimming. But by the time I was ten, and in my final year at primary school, Alan and I had started to argue about anything and everything.

As these arguments increased, I felt more and more wretched. It seemed that, however hard I tried to be good, I couldn't do anything right, so after a while I gave up trying. While it seemed perfectly acceptable for the adults to shout at me, I was always expected not to show anger and to take whatever was thrown at me without complaint.

Sometimes, Alan was kind to me, gave me pocket money and helped me with my homework, but at other times, he and my mum were excessively strict, sometimes grounding me for six months when I stayed out too late. For a ten-year-old, six months is forever, and their sanctions only made me more rebellious. I felt that neither Alan nor my mum were treating me fairly. This triggered a vicious downward spiral in which I didn't respect them, and they didn't respect me. Whenever I went to friends' houses, I was conscious that they had much better and more relaxed relationships with their families than I did.

Their parents were less strict than mine, and because they had greater freedom, they listened to their parents more and there were fewer tensions. I wasn't unhappy at primary school, but perhaps because of my troubles at home, I never felt that I quite fitted in there.

Despite the arguments, I was still basically a good girl. I loved drawing, played the clarinet and was involved in lots of sports at school, like netball. Being good at sport helped me to be accepted by the other kids, but I still felt like an outsider.

I worked hard and passed an exam to get into the local grammar school. I was keen to go there, and my mum and Alan rewarded me with a bike when I found out I'd got a place. But, once again, I didn't feel that I fitted in. Early on, a girl in my class was asked to read out an essay she had written. I gasped because the standard was so high, and I felt that I'd never be able to produce anything of that quality. I felt useless and inferior at the grammar school – if I'd gone to an ordinary comprehensive school, I would have probably felt more at ease and could have done well.

I had friends at school but was never as popular as I wanted to be. None of the boys fancied me: they all made for blonde-haired china dolls with names like Lorna and Lisa.

I began to look for friendships elsewhere and started to spend time with a group of teenagers my mother and Alan thought were undesirable, who lived on some of the nearby council estates. I hung around with this group more and more, and for the first time in my life, I really felt that I fitted in. Like me, they were all outsiders, kids who didn't slot neatly into any group.

One night, I'd been grounded. Even though I usually tried to stay out as late as possible to avoid spending time at home, I had had no intention of breaching my ban and going out. But when I went downstairs to get myself a drink, Alan assumed I was about to sprint out, so I leapt across the hallway, bolted the door and grabbed the key.

Right, that's it, I said to myself, storming upstairs. *If that's what they think I'm going to do, I might as well do it.*

I was filled with hurt and rage. Impulsively, I grabbed the pair of compasses I used for maths and began to scrape out the sealant around the glass in my bedroom window. The pane I silently prised out of the frame was about two foot by one. I placed it on my bedroom floor, feeling the wind on my face. I carefully lowered myself through it onto the corrugated plastic roof underneath my bedroom window, and climbed over the fence of the house next door.

My adrenalin was pumping. I'd never run so fast, and I was jubilant that I'd outwitted Alan and my mum. I continued running until I reached the phone box where I usually hung out with my friends. My heart was banging hard against my chest and I couldn't catch my breath, but I felt euphoric.

'I've just escaped from Fort Knox,' I panted to my friends, who were lounging against the phone box and couldn't understand what all the fuss was about. My friends seemed impressed by what I'd done. Although we rarely talked about what was going on at home, many of them were involved in similar conflicts.

My mother and Alan had of course called the police as soon as they realised that I'd pulled off a great escape of sorts. I hadn't been in trouble with the police before, but because the phone box we chose to hang around – for reasons I couldn't fathom – was right outside the police station, we were all on first-name terms with the police.

A couple of hours after I'd made my bid for freedom, two police officers walked out of the station and headed towards me. My heart started to jump around in my chest. I hadn't been expecting to get away with it, but now I wondered just how much trouble I was going to get into.

'Come on, Natalie, time to go home,' said one. I was relieved to see that he was smiling. He was accompanied by a female officer, who was also smiling. I nodded and allowed myself to be led to the police van. The officers weren't hostile because I wasn't causing any trouble.

They probably thought I was just a good kid who'd got in with the wrong crowd. The phone box where I'd been picked up was just a few minutes' drive from home and as I sat in the back of the police van, I braced myself for a huge telling off. I was approaching the age when I thought I knew much better than adults what was right and what was wrong, and I wasn't prepared to accept that my mum or Alan knew what was best for me.

Alan appeared at the front door. What happened next stunned me. I'd run through various scenarios – being grounded for six months, having my window padlocked, being told off for days on end – and decided that they couldn't do anything worse to me than what they had done before.

I could see Alan talking to the police officer. It was clear from his demeanour that he was angry. Then my mum appeared and, timidly, stood behind him. Although I strained my ears, I couldn't hear what was being said. The front door closed, and the policeman walked back to the van scratching his head. I couldn't understand what had happened. Why had they shut the door? I knew I wasn't being arrested, because the police officer had told me he was taking me home.

He climbed back into the van and looked at me kindly. 'I'm

really sorry, Natalie, but your mum and stepdad don't want you to come home now.'

I couldn't believe what I was hearing. I fought back the urge to burst into tears. There can be no greater rejection than to be thrown out of your home by the people who are supposed to be caring for you.

'Don't worry, love, we'll take you back to the station and sort out a place for you to stay tonight. Your stepdad seemed pretty mad with you but I'm sure he'll have calmed down by morning, and we'll take you back home then.'

While part of me was devastated by what had just happened, another part of me was relieved that I didn't have to go home and face the music. It was getting late and I felt completely exhausted. All I wanted to do was curl up in bed and forget the whole thing.

I was taken to the lounge where the officers had their breaks and ended up playing pool with one of the officers, which took my mind off things for a while. Then I sat down in an armchair and waited.

My eyes filled up with tears, but I was determined to be strong. I was still in shock that I'd been turned away.

'Come on, Natalie. We've found a children's home that has space to take you for tonight. Off we go,' said the police officer who had spoken to Alan.

I hadn't considered that I'd be taken to a children's home and had no idea what to expect. I felt scared but at the same time I was too tired to worry about it. I followed the police officer out to one of the patrol cars. In the car, I kept blinking to try to stay awake. After a twenty-minute drive, the officer turned off the main road down a private drive with overhanging trees on both sides. An enormous building loomed out of the darkness.

A skinny man with curly, mousy hair greeted us. It was after midnight and all the children seemed to be in bed. I was shown to my bedroom, a plain but not unpleasant room with bland, oatmeal carpet, and wearily undressed. The second my head touched the pillow, I fell into a deep sleep.

2 EXPERIMENTS WITH WILDNESS

The next morning, I saw lots of children of all ages running around. None of the staff told them off and the general atmosphere was relaxed. I had imagined children's homes to be grim and terrible places, but this one wasn't. I took an instant liking to it.

After breakfast, my mum and Alan appeared to discuss me returning home. My mum's face was streaked with tears and she looked crumpled, as if she'd been crying for most of the night.

Alan was stony-faced. I felt so guilty when I saw what I'd put my poor mum through. I knew that I'd been reckless and hadn't thought any further ahead than 'getting even' with Alan.

It was decided that I'd return home in a few days, when things had settled down a bit. But by then, I had adapted to life in the children's home and asked to stay there. As far as I was concerned, it was a fantastic contrast to all the restrictions imposed on me at home. I was immature and instead of trying to work through my differences with Mum and Alan, all I could think about was that, at long last, I'd be able to do exactly as I pleased. It didn't cross my mind how much my decision would hurt them.

The social workers agreed that I could stay for a while with a view to returning home when things became more stable, and life changed dramatically for me. At last, I had the kind of freedom that I could only have dreamed about before. I continued to go to school but felt more than ever that I didn't fit in with the grammar school scene. I noticed that the kids in the children's home who had been expelled from school were having an absolute ball. Staff took them ice-skating, ten-pin bowling and to Alton Towers. This seemed a much better way to spend the day than sitting behind a desk, so I began missing school in the fervent hope that I too would be expelled.

Although the headmistress was supportive and gave me lots of chances, the point came when I had missed so much school that she reluctantly had to expel me. A member of staff at the children's home broke the news to me casually – it was obviously a scenario she was familiar with. Observing that I didn't look in the least bit upset by the news, she said, matter-of-factly, 'Right, there's an ice-skating trip tomorrow. Do you want to come?'

My heart leapt. I was overjoyed to be free from school at last: I could now concentrate on enjoying myself. Now I look back sadly at my eagerness to abandon my studies. If I could have my time over again, I would have stayed at school and tried to get some qualifications. But at the age of fourteen, I was in such a tearing hurry to be an adult, and I thought I knew all the answers.

We got up to all sorts of pranks at the children's home. One time, a girl called Carly climbed up a ladder onto the roof and refused to come down. The police were called and climbed the ladder to try to coax her down. Eventually, she agreed to come down, descended at lightning speed and then cheekily picked up the ladder and ran off with it, leaving the police stranded on the roof.

We laughed so much we thought our stomachs were going to split open.

There was a lot of scope for all of us to be who we wanted to be, yet at the same time none of us had to put on continuous tough-guy acts.

Once a week, we had a meeting with our key worker. This was an opportunity to unburden ourselves, to talk about family relationships and to feel safe and supported. Now and again, returning home was discussed, but because I was so happy and settled in, it was never seriously pursued.

It was when I met a new key worker, Delroy, that my life changed forever. After two blissfully happy years at the children's home, when I was sixteen the social workers decided that I should move to a smaller place because I risked becoming institution-alised. I didn't understand what they were talking about when they said that: as far as I was concerned, I was well adjusted, and life felt normal to me.

Delroy had been assigned to me to help me make the transition from the large children's home to a small group home with places for eight or nine teenagers. I took an instant dislike to him. When Delroy took me to the ordinary red-brick house in an anonymous cul-de-sac that was to be my new home, my heart sank, but I knew that I had no choice but to settle down and make the best of life in my new surroundings.

I was deeply unhappy to be away from the children's home I loved so much. I cheered up a bit when I was shown around – there was a larder there where we could help ourselves to snacks, something that was a great novelty to me. At home, my mum and Alan had been strict about food and rarely allowed snacks. At mealtimes, I had been expected to eat everything on my plate, whether I liked it or not.

The idea of this place was that it was a halfway house between the security blanket of the children's home and independent living.

At first, I recoiled from Delroy, but gradually I found myself opening up and looking forward to our sessions more and more. He was kind and attentive, and he seemed to understand what I was saying. I was sixteen, and I craved affection. This was what Delroy was giving me, though without laying a finger on me. His words wrapped themselves around me, making me feel safe and understood. I found that I could talk to him about absolutely everything and I loved the way he treated me like an adult, which none of the other staff did.

He encouraged me to go to college, which I was keen to do because I thought I'd be treated like adult there. I enrolled to do GCSEs in Maths, English, Sociology and Child Psychology, and settled in quickly. I started going out with a nice boy of my own age, but I increasingly found myself thinking about Delroy.

There was an exciting tension in the air when we were together.

In his company, I felt special, as if I was bathed in a soft, warm light.

Over the next couple of months, my feelings for him intensified, and eventually I felt that I was going to burst if I didn't confess the thoughts whirring around my head to him. He was my main confidant and the obvious person to tell. The only problem was that, unlike most of the secrets I shared with him, this one was about him.

'There's something I need to tell you,' I blurted out at one of our sessions. I met his steady gaze with difficulty and felt electricity surge through me.

'Sure, you know you can tell me anything,' he said reassuringly.

I lowered my eyes. I assumed the 'anything' he referred to didn't include a declaration of my feelings for him. I shook my head and said, 'Oh, don't worry, it's nothing.'

I just couldn't tell him.

He shrugged and let it go. I wondered if he knew what was on my mind. We chatted about mundane things until it was time to go back to the halfway house and drove back in silence. I could feel the strain and I was sure he could, too.

We got out of the car and, as we walked past the big industrial bins at the side of the house, I suddenly turned to him, looked him boldly in the eye and said, 'I like you.'

A slow smile spread across his face. He looked entirely unsurprised by my confession.

'I like you, too,' he said softly. My heart was racing. I had imagined many different reactions from Delroy, but not that one. Then he cupped my face gently in his hands and gave me the softest, gentlest kiss I'd ever had. My head was spinning. I felt as if I'd died and arrived in heaven.

Delroy should have gone straight to the supervisor and flagged up my declaration of passion. This was why I'd told him: I believed that the right thing would be done. Of course, I too should have gone straight to the supervisor, alerted her to my growing obsession with Delroy and asked to have a new key worker assigned to me.

But neither of us did anything of the sort. We were frenzied. After that first kiss, Delroy sneaked into my bedroom whenever the coast was clear and kissed and caressed me. I didn't think about the possible consequences for both him and me. I was incapable of anything other than living for the moment. As far as I was concerned, I was in love and nothing else mattered.

Eventually, things got to a point where I felt that both of us would spontaneously combust if we continued snatching relatively chaste kisses but nothing more.

Delroy kept telling me how much he wanted to be alone with me and told me that he knew of a place a few miles away where we could meet. He gave me the address and told me to get a taxi there the following evening. The day dragged and I couldn't wait to be properly alone with Delroy at last. The place he'd chosen was an old derelict house. He answered the door beaming and I stepped over the threshold hesitantly.

It was squalid but Delroy had lit candles and a fire was roaring in the hearth. A grubby mattress had been laid out by the fire. Looking back, I can't understand why I found this sordid scene enchanting, but somehow, I did. As far as I was concerned, he had brought me to the most perfect love nest. He ordered some takeaway food and opened a bottle of wine. As we sat by the fire eating and drinking, I felt that I might burst with happiness.

Then, at last, we consummated our relationship. We had been together for just a month, yet I had never felt more certain that I was doing the right thing. I no longer thought about the fact that Delroy was old enough to be my father, nor of his wife and children, nor that he was in serious breach of his role as a responsible carer. I was completely and utterly in love.

I'd had boyfriends before, and had had unremarkable sex with them, but for the first time in my life, I was making love. It was slow and passionate and tender. The physical and the emotional had merged into a perfect whole. I felt as if fireworks were exploding in my soul.

After that first night, we tried to snatch time together as often as we could. It was torture for me to have to pretend that there was nothing going on between Delroy and me when I was at the children's home, and then falling into his arms as soon as we were off the premises.

Eventually, I confessed what was going on to a social worker I bumped into from my old children's home. I couldn't cope with the torrent of different emotions I was feeling. I was completely infatuated with Delroy, but I knew that what we were doing was wrong. I didn't know which way to turn.

She, of course, reported it to the social workers at my current place and all hell broke loose. Delroy was suspended and I was told not to contact him, but when I was by myself, I called him and told him how much I loved and missed him. An inquiry was launched and Delroy was sacked for gross misconduct. We continued to see each other, which was easier as I had moved into a bedsit. Delroy tried to be with me as often as he could, though I was getting frustrated with the relationship because although he had promised to leave his wife, he was still with her.

Julie, a friend from the first children's home I was in, lived in the bedsit next door to mine. Together, we started experimenting with ecstasy and a form of speed we called base. Unsurprisingly, my college work really suffered, and I ended up abandoning my studies.

I hardly saw my mum and Alan anymore, and they weren't really involved in my life. By the time I'd moved to the small children's home, the social workers no longer focused on returning me home and instead worked to help me find some stability.

I got a job working on a hot pork roll stall in the town centre, and soon after started to feel sick in the mornings. I'd been using contraception with Delroy, but decided to do a pregnancy test just in case. To my amazement, I was pregnant. I was delighted, even though the baby was unplanned, but neither my mum nor Delroy shared my happiness when I broke the news to them.

Mum looked aghast and said, 'Why can't you just behave yourself and stay out of trouble?' She did her best to persuade me to have an abortion, but I was appalled at such an idea and refused to consider it. I stopped using drugs while I was pregnant and looked forward to the birth.

Delroy sneaked away from his wife and family as often as he could to see me, but I never felt it was enough.

'I love you so much; I wish it could just be me and you. I've never loved anyone as much as I love you. It hurts me so much that things can't be straightforward between us,' Delroy often said.

Foolishly, I believed every word he said and was convinced he was telling the truth when he said it was only a matter of time before he would leave his wife.

When I went into labour, Delroy was by my side. He was kind and mopped my brow. The pain was unbearable but when the baby, a girl, finally arrived, all memories of what I'd just endured vanished. I was overwhelmed with joy at having produced such a perfect creature.

Delroy spent a few minutes with me after the birth and then said distractedly, 'I've got to get back,' gave me a quick kiss and disappeared. I was gutted that he was leaving so quickly, and that he didn't seem as besotted with our new arrival as I was. Sitting in the hospital bed cradling my daughter in my arms, I felt alone. I decided to call her Nikita, a Russian name. I liked the name because it was so unusual. Although the baby had an ugly, scrunched-up face, I was instantly filled with love for her.

While I was pregnant, I had decided to breastfeed, as I'd read that this intensifies the connection between mother and child. I wanted to do everything right by Nikita, and to make sure that she had the best of everything.

As I lay back on the pillows, exhausted, I thought about my family. I knew how much I'd disappointed them and felt bad for once again having forced my mum into a situation she would have done absolutely anything to avoid. All she wanted was a well-behaved, conventional daughter who worked hard at school and grew into a well-balanced, productive adult. I knew I'd let her down badly and wished that things had turned out differently for her sake.

I hadn't planned to move into the children's home, to begin the relationship with Delroy or to have Nikita, but somehow these things had just happened. I now know that life isn't just a series of experiences that you fall into, and that you can choose which path you follow, but I certainly didn't understand that then.

My mum and Granny came to visit me in hospital the day after the birth. Mum cuddled Nikita, and had bought her a dress, but after I returned home from hospital, she didn't offer much help with childcare, something that made me feel hurt. I was young, inexperienced and isolated, and I would have welcomed some hands-on support.

I was still madly in love with Delroy and thought the baby would change our relationship for the better. I dreamed that now we had a child, he'd finally leave his wife for me.

I'd been given a new council flat when I fell pregnant, although it wasn't ready for me to move into until a couple of weeks before the birth. While we were in the hospital, Delroy had prepared the flat for Nikita and me, and he came over as often as he could once we went home. As a father of two other kids, he knew more about babies than I did, and understood what to do when Nikita got colic.

Often, he came around in the evenings, the time of day that I couldn't get her to stop crying and the time at which I was at my most exhausted. He used that well-known trick – popular with the desperate parents of new-borns – of driving her around the neighbourhood to lull her to sleep.

By the time Nikita was three months old, the colic had passed, and she became a delightful, easy baby. She was pretty, and strangers cooed over her when I took her out in her pram. I adored her and felt like she had become part of me, like an extra limb. Her unconditional love soothed my disappointment with my family. I met other new mums, and, unlike me, they all had the support of their families.

I longed for my mum to have a change of heart and to start getting involved in Nikita's life, but for her there were simply too many things she wasn't happy with: I was just seventeen and was with Delroy, who she considered to be an unsuitable partner. I tried not to think too much about my mum giving Nikita and me the cold shoulder, but I was hurt. I longed for her acceptance and approval.

I stayed off drugs while I was breastfeeding Nikita, but suddenly my milk dried up. I didn't realise that she was sucking away but getting no nourishment until, one day, she screamed for hours on end. I had no idea what was wrong, but my neighbours heard her cries, recognised that they were wails of hunger and went out and got her some formula milk. She guzzled it down and then cooed contentedly. My breastfeeding days officially over, I went back to taking drugs.

I often got a babysitter for Nikita so I could go clubbing with a group of friends, and I took ecstasy while I was out. I started selling the tiny pills to earn a bit of money, because I wasn't working. I had fun but my drug taking wasn't out of control. I was starting to grow up and was hanging out with people of my own age. Gradually, I realised that I was no longer in love with Delroy. I was happy spending time with friends and didn't feel the same desperate need for protection that I'd felt in the children's home.

Although none of my friends had jobs, I was determined to try to do something with my life, so got a job in an Internet café when I was eighteen. The staff also designed websites and I learnt about computer technology there. I was proud of myself for not just sitting at home on benefits, but nothing I did ever seemed to earn me the praise I craved from my mum.

'Hmmm,' she said, when I told her I'd got a job. 'It's only part-time.' I longed for her to say 'well done' just once, but she never did.

I tried to inoculate myself against this distress by immersing myself in my job and by going clubbing, where I could lose myself in ecstasy and music. I was still selling about two hundred Es a week, which didn't make me much money but, added to my wages from the Internet café, I had just enough to get by.

My father had married a woman called Pauline, who was a civil servant working for the Ministry of Defence, and they had settled at an army base in Germany a few months before Nikita was born.

He seemed happy with her, but one night, out of the blue, I got a call from her. 'Natalie, your father has killed himself. He was found in a car on the base.'

I was flabbergasted. My dad had seemed so happy; I couldn't imagine why he would suddenly kill himself. I was so shocked that I couldn't take in what Pauline was saying.

'It's true, Natalie. He left a suicide note,' she said, sounding almost irritated by my disbelief.

'Well, can I see it?'

'I'm afraid not. He left it on the computer screen and the military police have taken the computer away to investigate the note.'

I put the phone down, shaking from head to toe. I couldn't believe that my dad would take his own life. I phoned my mum who, like me, was devastated. Although my parents' relationship hadn't worked out, on some level my mum had carried on loving him. We cried together about his death.

'I can't believe he'd kill himself,' I kept saying, repeatedly. Eventually, I phoned the police and asked them to investigate his death, but they said they could do nothing, as they had no jurisdiction over incidents on Ministry of Defence land. To this day, I've never been able to uncover the exact circumstances of my dad's death.

I tried to push my sadness as far away as I could, because it was just too painful to deal with, and I threw myself into a new social circle. I met a group of people who were always laughing and having fun, and who drove nice cars. It all seemed sociable and I was keen to be part of their circle.

A guy called Michael was in this group. He'd been a heroin addict and had been in and out of prison for twelve years. We became friends and he spent a lot of time at my house. He was proud of himself because when he got his Giro, he went out and bought tracksuits rather than drugs. Later, I would understand why this was such an achievement, but at the time his boasts about his new tracksuits baffled me. His friends who weren't using heroin were supportive of him, though he was destined to continue mixing in the world of drugs.

Dealers saw the potential in him because he was wired into all the right social networks and asked him to start selling pills for them. I abandoned my fledgling drug-dealing business because Michael overtook me. I didn't really mind, though, because I liked his company. He introduced me to his friends, and I felt like I was the queen bee because suddenly lots of them came knocking on my door. As I had my own place, and they lived with their parents, my flat became a popular place to hang out.

My relationship with Delroy continued to go downhill. We weren't sleeping together anymore but he was still clinging on. One day, he turned up at my flat with all his belongings. I assumed his wife had thrown him out. If he'd announced he was leaving his wife and moving in with me straight after Nikita's birth, I would have been overjoyed, but by the time he did leave, I had fallen out of love with him.

When I was nineteen, I finally split up with him. I felt regret because he had been my first proper love and the father of the baby I adored, but at the same time I felt enormous relief.

I often went to the pub with my new friends in a convoy of three or four carloads. We had a laugh and a really good time, and when the sun shone these outings were perfect. There was something exceptional about that summer: I still consider it to be the best of my life. I was out all the time with Nikita at my side and she was readily accepted as part of the group.

It was at this point that I started taking far too many Es.

Through Michael, I met a woman who wanted to buy lots of pills. She was ten years older than me, was married and had three kids. She was daring and didn't seem to care about anything. Both she and her husband were having relationships with other people, and she made her husband pick up her boyfriends and bring them back to their home. She lived in a smart house and had plenty of money, but none of it meant anything to her. All she wanted to do was seek bigger and bigger thrills. I recognised parts of myself in her and she encouraged me to take more and more ecstasy, although I didn't need much persuading.

Then I met Tim, a man of my own age. He was attractive and seemed to be a genuinely nice guy. He told me he'd never had a proper girlfriend before. On our first date, we went out in the afternoon then spent the night together, cuddled up on the sofa. He said that because he'd never been in a proper relationship before, he didn't want things to move too fast.

After a few weeks together, he took me home to meet his parents. I had really fallen for him and his parents seemed lovely. I wasn't used to harmonious family relationships like his and I thought, *wow*. His family was the kind I had always longed to have.

I was convinced that I was in love, although the reality was that I was caught up in the moment with the sun, the drugs and the heady feeling of being with a nice, attractive man.

Sadly, it didn't last long. Suddenly, to my horror, he didn't want to be around me anymore and I felt I was losing control. I had become used to things always going my way and couldn't cope with being rejected.

One of the guys I went to the pub with was a crack smoker. I had tried the drug once before, but it had had little effect on me. He and his friends came to my house and gave me some to smoke. This time, the effect was completely different: I had never experienced such an intense, euphoric buzz before, and at that moment, I fell in love with the drug. The sensation it gave me was extremely pleasurable and I wanted more.

For a while, I smoked it and enjoyed it, but never craved it. Then I met a girl called Sabrina who had a reputation as a crackhead. Sabrina was a well-built black girl with an Afro that she didn't look after properly, usually pushing it out of sight under a denim hat. She had a musky, unpleasant smell about her because she didn't wash often. All her time, money and energy were poured into getting money for crack and then smoking it.

In a matter of weeks, everything came tumbling down around me. I was distraught about the end of my relationship and that the group of friends I went to the pub with, who I adored, no longer seemed to want to spend time with me. They only smoked crack occasionally, as a 'treat', and they disapproved of me because they thought that my drug use was out of control. Nikita's godmother had the flat above me and the group started flocking to her flat instead of mine. I felt hurt and abandoned.

Why is everyone round at her house and not at mine? I asked myself, overwhelmed with jealousy. It was at that moment, when I had reached a real low point of despair, that Sabrina knocked on my door. People like her seem to have an extraordinary radar and can detect the sort of misery that will find solace in drugs.

'Have some of this,' she said soothingly, seeing how distressed I was. That was when I started falling into a bottomless pit. I inhaled the drug, and the fact that my relationship had broken up no longer mattered; the fact that my friends were giving me the cold shoulder no longer mattered; the fact that after I'd bought Nikita's food, every penny I had was spent on crack no longer mattered – crack was worth more than gold to me now. I was lost.

3 CHEMICAL SLAVERY

When crack wraps you in its embrace, you fall hard and fast. Once Sabrina had given me a real taste for the stuff, there was no stopping me. I became a slave to the little glass crack pipe. I made sure that Nikita was washed, clothed and fed, but beyond that, my thoughts were only for crack. Crack removed most human emotions: I no longer felt hurt that my friends had stopped calling round, I no longer minded my mum's critical remarks and I no longer cared about trying to make something of my life. Crack filled the spaces where all those other things had been.

I later found out that two notorious dealers had paid Sabrina in crack to get me hooked. It was cynical and immoral, and, like a fish, I blindly jumped up to the bait. It never occurred to me not to take what was being offered to me. Sabrina came with crack for me every day and, for some reason that I couldn't understand, didn't seem to want anything in return.

Then, almost imperceptibly, things shifted. I began to buy crack myself, as well as smoking what Sabrina brought. Most people who use crack can never get enough of it to satisfy their deep, nagging ache for the stuff. It's a drug that makes you greedy. Suddenly, my Giro vanished before I'd bought any food or paid the gas bill.

Sabrina seemed to have no problem looking herself in the eye and saying, 'I'm a crackhead. So what?' But I was in denial about what I'd become. I felt ashamed of smoking crack and tried to hide my addiction. I knew this wasn't the real me, but somehow, I couldn't stop myself sleepwalking into a bigger and bigger nightmare. I started to visit a crack house and, although I tried to conceal it, I found myself going more and more often.

When I first started using it regularly, crack made me chatty, but that changed fast. I got to a point where I couldn't communicate with people because it felt as if my mouth had sealed itself shut. I developed terrible paranoia and began peeping through the curtains to look for the people I was sure were coming to get me.

When I'd first starting smoking crack, I'd seen other people behaving in the same way and I'd been scornful of their irrational behaviour. But now, as soon as I'd had my hit, the same sensations drenched me.

Looking back at that period now, as a rational, drug-free person, I don't know why I smoked crack for so long, because doing so made me extremely unhappy. At the time, though, it all seemed to make perfect sense. Feebly, I often thought about giving up, but never actually got around to it. Every morning, when I woke up, I told myself that today was going to be my last day on crack. But every day, I trudged up the stairs to the flat of a Yardie dealer I knew and bought more.

Addiction to crack is characterised by a dizzying succession of highs and lows. At one particularly desperate point, I called my mum and started sobbing down the phone. I felt I no longer had the strength to continue the insane merry-go-round I'd jumped on. I rarely saw my mum at that point, and she didn't know much about drugs, but even she must have known something was up.

I called her at midnight, begging, through my tears, to come home. 'Mum, please. My life is in a complete mess, I'm a mess. Please, please can I come home?' It was the first time I'd ever asked her for help.

'Do you know what time it is? It's twelve o'clock,' she said curtly, putting the phone down. I really think that if I had gone home, things would have turned out differently. My mum never referred to that phone conversation ever again. Wounded by her rejection, I headed to the crack house to blot everything out.

I knew I wanted out of that miserable life. I had hoped that my mum would offer me that route out but, looking back, I can understand why she took a step away from me, fearful of the malign influence I might have on her two children that she had had with Alan. I was a complete mess and I suppose she thought that with some tough love, I might eventually sort myself out.

Sabrina was one of several British women who had married Yardies in exchange for money for crack. Wayne, Sabrina's husband, was the meanest of the bunch.

One day, when I was sitting in the crack house looking particularly wrecked, Wayne said, 'How'd you fancy a sun, sea and sand holiday in Jamaica? If you bring some cocaine back, I'll pay you well.'

'How does that work?' I asked, interested immediately.

'We'll pay for everything and we'll give you a cover story. You have to take Nikita with you.'

'Fine, I'll do it.' When you're addicted to crack, you don't really think about consequences. Life is lived in the present tense and all roads that lead to crack look appealing.

It was just a week after Wayne first mentioned Jamaica that I was on my way. Before I went, I had to go to London to get a passport – I didn't have one because I'd never been abroad before.

Apart from that, I didn't think any further ahead than sorting out what clothes Nikita and I would need for our unexpected break in the sun. It didn't occur to me that I could be getting into trouble. I had a deep-seated belief that somehow, I could sail through any tricky situation in life.

Wayne warned me not to tell Sabrina, but I couldn't see any reason not to and so told her about the trip Wayne had lined up for me. She encouraged me, knowing that I'd spend all the money I earned doing the drug run on crack, and that she would cling, leech-like, to me to make sure that she could share in my windfall.

On my way to the airport, I felt excited because I'd never been on a plane before. I'd seen photos of Jamaica's palm-fringed beaches and turquoise sea in holiday brochures and couldn't wait to get there.

As soon as the door of the plane was opened, I was hit by a wall of heat. Not even the hottest day in England felt like this.

Wayne had told me to get a taxi to the hotel he'd booked me into. It was an extremely bumpy ride because the roads had great big holes in them. If a car had got stuck in one of these holes, it would have certainly have seriously damaged it. Although it was a beautiful island, I was shocked by the poverty. All along the roadsides were run-down shacks which skinny, barefoot children skipped in and out of.

Wayne had booked me into a shabby hotel in Montego Bay. The walls were supposed to be white but were almost black. Huge cockroaches scuttled across the floor of my room, and the swimming pool was filthy. I had wondered how I'd manage without crack but to my surprise it was a relief not to be smoking it.

Because I was out of my usual environment, with all its triggers, I didn't even have any cravings. My focus was on Nikita, and I dedicated all my time to playing with her. She looked up at me adoringly, but I felt a pang of guilt when I looked into her innocent, trusting eyes. She was blissfully unaware of just how chaotic my life was back home and was just enjoying the moment.

After struggling with the mysteries of international dialling codes for almost an hour, I finally managed to get through to Wayne. He told me to wait at the hotel and said that some people would come to see me, although he was vague about when they'd arrive. A few hours later, two men appeared. Both seemed nice and friendly, and had short, cropped hair.

'How's Wayne doing?' one of them asked.

'Oh, we call him Smallhead, for obvious reasons,' I said. Both laughed. They had a smart white jeep and took me to another hotel, down the coast at Runaway Bay. This hotel was even worse than the first: it wasn't in a tourist area, and was miles away from anywhere, out in the Jamaican countryside. The car was constantly swerving to avoid massive holes in the road.

It turned out that the hotel that the two men had deposited me at wasn't really a hotel at all. It was just a big house with lots of rooms, and all the guests were expected to do their own cooking. I was a lousy cook and had no clue how to prepare Jamaican food.

There was a scruffy lounge full of battered armchairs that nobody ever sat in, no air conditioning and even more cockroaches than in the last hotel, sprinting along the bottom of the walls. The crickets screeched at night and the sound drove me mad. Later, in Venezuela, I grew to love that noise and found it hard to get off to sleep unless the sound of crickets was buzzing in my ears.

I hung around this grim hotel for two days, getting bored.

There was a Manumission party a couple of miles away and I could hear the distinctive bass line of the music drifting towards the hotel. *I'm in the wrong life. Right now, I'd love to be dancing with all the other ravers, without a care in the world*, I thought wistfully.

I phoned Wayne and begged him to move me somewhere nicer. He agreed and his friends took me to Discovery Bay, the next town along the coast. The hotel there was better, with a swimming pool that Nikita and I could swim in, and some edible food.

One evening, Wayne called me at the hotel. He told me, agitatedly, that I didn't need to bring any drugs back with me.

'You fucking idiot, you told Sabrina and she's blabbed to all sorts of people about it. Police and customs have got wind of it and they're going to be waiting for you at the airport. She told that Yardie dealer you buy crack from and he tipped off the police because he doesn't want a competitor bringing stuff in.'

The dealer, Fitz, was Wayne's arch-rival and, unwittingly, Sabrina had done me a big favour. I was relieved not to have to bring any drugs back with me. Going to Jamaica had provided me with some space to think. *What on earth am I doing here, prepared to smuggle cocaine into the UK?* I asked myself. *You must be mad, Natalie.* I had barely considered the consequences, not only for me but for Nikita, if I got caught smuggling drugs.

After I'd finished speaking to Wayne, loneliness washed over me. I wanted to go home. I hadn't thought about them for ages, but suddenly I had a craving to be with my nice pre-crack friends again.

A few days later, I flew home. As soon as I got off the plane, the customs people fell on me like a pack of dogs who'd found a particularly appetising piece of meat.

'Where have you been and what hotels have you stayed in?' one of them barked. He was a small man with a mean pencil moustache. The customs men said they were going to take me to hospital for an X-ray, to see if I'd swallowed drugs.

'No way,' I said firmly. 'I've got my daughter with me and I want somebody from social services here for her. If you're going to take me away, I want to make sure she's properly looked after. I'll only release her into the care of a social worker.'

In the end, they allowed Nikita to stay with me. I was X-rayed at the local hospital and allowed to go when nothing showed up. They had obviously been certain I was meant to be bringing drugs in, because one of the customs officials looked completely dumbfounded.

When I got home, the first thing I did was rush off to buy a rock of crack. I don't understand why I did this. I was happy not to be smoking the drug while I was in Jamaica and hadn't even missed it, yet as soon as I was home, I raced back to the crack house. Crack is not a rational drug. Once I was settled back in, I was more hooked than ever before.

After my abortive mission to Jamaica, I hadn't given much thought to smuggling drugs. But my ears pricked up when a friend of Wayne's said that a big player in London wanted someone to do a run to Venezuela. He told me that Wayne wanted me to set him up, and to pretend I was going to do the run for him.

It all sounded far-fetched, but I didn't have anything better to do, so thought that I might as well meet the guy. He came up from London to see me. I had half-expected him not to turn up and was amazed when he did. He was a black British man with a London accent and seemed like a nice guy. He told me his name was Leroy and that he was one of a mysterious Mr Big's foot soldiers. He chatted to me for half an hour or so, satisfied himself that I wasn't a police plant, then said he was going to escort me down to London by train with Nikita. I didn't know it at the time, but I was about to embark on a new and even more disastrous period of my life.

4 A PACKAGE HOLIDAY WITH PACKAGES

Leroy had a nice flat that he shared with a Jamaican woman called Marcia. He also had a girlfriend, who thought he was a music scout. Marcia told me that they quite often had people staying at their flat, and Leroy had apparently told his girlfriend that I was a singer.

That evening, I went out with Marcia. She knew that I was being briefed to go on a drug-smuggling mission, although she didn't know I'd been instructed to double-cross Tony, the Mr Big of the operation.

Soon after we returned to Leroy's flat, Tony arrived. He was Jamaican and could switch between a Jamaican and an English accent with ease. He wore a low-key Nike tracksuit and had curly black hair. He obviously didn't use crack and seemed to be a nice guy.

I'd brought some crack with me and had secretly been smoking it in the bathroom. Because I'd just had a hit, I couldn't hold a proper conversation, but I tried my best to make out that I was clean.

Tony didn't say much and seemed keen to get to the point. After I'd been introduced to him, he said, 'You're going to go on a nice holiday and bring a suitcase back. Here's some money now and we'll give you the other half when you get back.' I nodded eagerly. It all sounded too good to be true.

'Let's go,' he said to me. 'We've got a couple of other people to pick up.'

I confessed to Tony that I was supposed to be setting him up but that I really wanted to do the drug run. He laughed when I told him what Wayne had planned.

'Obviously you can see that this is the better option,' he said with a smile. 'I'd like to see someone try to con me,' he added, making it clear that the guys I knew were amateurs compared with him. He was laughing and joking, and I didn't feel at all intimidated. He told me he didn't like Yardies, and that he thought they were giving Jamaicans a bad name.

First, he picked up a man called Joe, a tall, skinny twenty-three-year-old who emerged from an anonymous block of flats. Then we collected a woman called Angie who was in her thirties. She was a plump, well-groomed black woman.

I didn't know London and had no idea which part of the capital we were in, but Angie clearly lived in quite an upmarket neighbourhood. After we'd picked up Joe and Angie, we stopped at a hospital. Tony's partner had just had a baby and he went in to see her. While we waited in the car, Angie explained that Tony had kids all over the place but was a responsible dad who provided for all his children, even when he was no longer with their mothers. He wasn't a Yardie or a joker like Wayne, he was a serious businessman. I hadn't come across people like him or Angie before, and for the first time, a whole new dimension to the crack world opened itself up to me.

Every day, I thought about giving up crack and perhaps the opportunity to become like Tony or Angie was just the incentive I needed. 'I'll be a better mum to Nikita, and I'll stop smoking,' I vowed, as I sat in the back of the car, my mind racing as I considered my various options. 'Even more importantly, this work will give me a good steady income so that I can provide for her. I'll just do it for a little while, until I've got myself on my feet, and then I'll go to college and get some training.'

I cuddled Nikita, who was sitting by my side, as ever gazing up at me with her trusting, innocent eyes. 'Everything's going to be OK,' I whispered to her.

I was busily planning my new crack-free life and my urge to smoke another rock drained away. It was an enormous relief to be with people who didn't smoke the stuff, and not to even have to think about it. When I wasn't around all the people and places that triggered my craving for the drug, I seemed to be able to manage without it.

Tony spent about fifteen minutes at the hospital, then jumped back into the car and we sped off. I had no idea which direction we were heading in. It isn't the done thing to ask where you're going in these situations. Tony had chosen an anonymous family car that was a few years old, rather than a flashy dealer's car. It proved to me how serious he was. He always behaved in a quiet and humble way, and had no interest in flaunting his wealth the way some of the Yardies did, with their BMWs and chunky gold chains.

I finally plucked up the courage to ask where we were going.

'We're nearly there. I'm taking you to a house,' he said. I shouldn't have bothered asking, as I was none the wiser.

A few minutes later, we arrived at a bungalow. It was around seven in the evening and the light was starting to fade.

'The port of Harwich is about twenty minutes down the road,' Tony explained, seeing how baffled I looked. There was a huge gravel driveway with a separate entrance and exit, and statues in the garden. It was beautiful, but as soon as we walked through the door, I sensed that no one lived there permanently. It was obviously just a stopgap for people going to and from the port.

The house was spacious and contemporary, with cream leather sofas in the lounge. Nikita and I were given a lovely bedroom with an en suite bathroom. There was a kitchen with marble worktops, a swimming pool with a plastic cover over it, a garage with a pair of Jags in it and an outhouse with a sauna and steam room. To top it all off, there was an impressive home cinema system instead of a normal TV.

I loved everything about the place. My brain was whirring ahead of itself, thinking that one day I could live somewhere like that.

Tony bought us all a Chinese takeaway, then he explained what was going on. 'You're going to do a practise run to Holland. You'll pick up some stuff from there.' He told me that he was going to pay me three thousand pounds, then calmly reached for his wallet and handed over a third of it.

Angie said that she and Joe were going to be together on the ferry, but that I shouldn't speak to them. The drugs I would be given were to be strapped to me, so I needed to wear baggy clothes. I didn't ask what I'd be carrying and instead said, 'I don't have any baggy clothes.'

'Don't worry, we'll sort that out over there. You can buy whatever you need.'

I slept soundly that night, completely exhausted from the travelling and the excitement of entering a different world. I was convinced that my luck had changed and that my life was going to be transformed.

The next morning, Tony took us all to the boat which was going to the Hook of Holland. I loved being on the ferry and spent a lot of time with Nikita in the children's play area. I ached with love for her as I watched her clamber up and down the plastic slide. I loved Nikita more than I could say.

I hadn't smoked the drug since my secret hit in Tony's bathroom and the drug-addled film that covered my brain was starting to dissolve. I realised that I couldn't love both crack and Nikita at the same time, and promised myself that from now on my daughter would always come first. The money I was going to earn from my drug missions would ensure that she had the best of everything.

While the boat docked, Joe and Angie waited for us on the shore. We went down a street and stopped at a pub. I was surprised that everyone spoke English. In the pub, Angie gave me some advice and told me a little bit about herself. 'People think I'm a high-flying businesswoman,' she said with a laugh. 'I'm more than happy for them to think that. You'll be OK with Tony, he's a decent guy. Better than a lot in the business.'

Tony had told her about my plan to rip him off and she also found it amusing. I was becoming increasingly aware that the

Yardies were seen as amateurs, and that I was now mingling with the professionals.

A Moroccan man named Hamid who spoke a little English met us down the road from the pub and took us to a Holiday Inn in Rotterdam. He checked us in, then I phoned my friend Eve to tell her where I was and what I was doing. I was paranoid that Tony, Joe or Angie were listening at the door of my room and so spoke in an undertone.

Eve went mad when she heard what I was doing. 'You fucking crackhead. What do you think you're doing?'

'Don't worry, Eve, I know exactly what I'm doing,' I said, trying to sound confident and in control of the situation.

Then I phoned my mum and told her I was in Holland. 'What are you doing there? Where did you get the money? Be careful,' she cautioned.

Angie, Joe and I went down to the restaurant for something to eat. Joe told me he was going off and that I wouldn't be seeing him again. I found it hard to believe that he was involved in trafficking drugs. He was a quiet, studious type. He wore little round glasses and carried a pile of textbooks under his arm. I knew better than to ask him where he was going to.

When I went to Jamaica, I had sometimes felt jittery because I was mostly by myself and had no idea what to expect. But I felt much more relaxed in Holland. I was being properly looked after and had Angie to reassure me.

After dinner, I went back up to the hotel room. I didn't feel at all worried about taking drugs back to Britain, and felt confident that my tourist act wouldn't arouse any suspicions among the customs officers. The next morning, Hamid picked us up from the hotel and paid the bill. He didn't bat an eyelid when my account showed that I'd made international calls and had plundered the minibar.

'Now we buy nice things,' he said, grinning.

He took me shopping for the baggy clothes I needed. Angie

was there to cast her expert eye over the best things for me to buy. I was skinny then, because of all the crack I'd been smoking.

I kept looking at the price tags, but Angie said, 'Just pick whatever you want, don't worry about the price.' She helped me choose a loose but tailored jacket and told me that this would cover the drugs well. I also bought some clothes for Nikita, and a gold watch. I loved every minute of my shopping spree.

Hamid took us to a flat, and a young woman with blonde hair and a pleasant smile opened the door. Angie explained that this was where I would have the drugs strapped to my body.

'Are you bringing anything back?' I asked.

'No, not this time.'

Hamid and the woman who owned the flat took Nikita into the other room to watch TV.

I went into the bedroom with Angie, then Hamid came in and put a pile of packages wrapped in black plastic on the bed. Angie got a big roll of industrial tape and began attaching packages to me: two on my stomach, two on my back and one on each side of me.

I felt no sense of danger, just excitement. It never crossed my mind that I might get caught. Looking back, I can't imagine how I could have done that. I had a young daughter in the next room who was totally reliant on me. What on earth was I thinking of, allowing fat packets of drugs to be strapped to my body?

Angie told me the packages might dig in, and that they would get more uncomfortable the longer they were strapped to me. I couldn't adjust them or show that they were hurting me while I was on the boat.

'You're going to do a big trip to Venezuela after this,' she added. Venezuela had been mentioned once, but then I'd heard nothing more about it. 'The guy we work with there, Al, will love you. When I did a trip there, he was sleazing all over me. I look forward to hearing what happens to you when you meet him.'

Angie and I got on the ferry. I was so sure that I wouldn't get caught that I strode confidently up the gangplank, making small talk with the crew.

Whenever I stopped smoking crack, I became ravenous. I felt as if there was a deep hole in my stomach, created from going for months on end without proper food. However much I ate, I didn't seem to be able to fill it. There was an all-you-can-eat restaurant on the boat, and I spent several hours in there, gorging myself.

As Angie had advised, I also spent lots of time playing with Nikita. The packages were digging in under my ribs and bruising me, but I managed not to touch them or to wriggle around in an obvious way. Angie had said that it would hurt when they were removed, but I couldn't wait for the moment the tape was ripped off – anything would be better than being attached to those fat sausages of drugs.

I was one of the first people off the boat. I chatted casually to the customs people and had no problems getting through. Angie called Tony and he picked us up and took us back to the house, where he paid me the rest of my money. My first mission as an international drugs smuggler couldn't have gone more smoothly.

Angie was singing my praises, saying how much Al was going to love me, but there were no congratulations from Tony.

Nonetheless, I felt proud that everything had gone without a hitch and was incredibly relieved when Angie took me into the bedroom to remove the packages. My skin was sore from the tape and I winced as it was ripped from my skin, but I decided that the three thousand pounds I'd earned was excellent compensation for a few hours of physical discomfort.

Tony took the drugs and told me that he'd come and pick me up the next day, to take me to the airport. He spoke calmly, as if jumping onto a flight to Venezuela to pick up drugs was as ordinary as popping to the supermarket. Everything was happening at breakneck speed, but I was loving this new existence and didn't want to do anything to slow things down.

When I wasn't at home, I lost my appetite for crack and I reasoned that anything that kept me away from it was a good thing, even if I was switching my addiction from smoking crack to trafficking the stuff. Angie left, leaving Nikita and I alone in the house. I began dreaming again of a wealthy future and I decided that my luxury pad would have similar décor to this house, with minimalist, cream-coloured furniture and thick carpets.

Tony had told me to help myself to food in the kitchen and to order whatever I wanted, so I phoned for a Chinese takeaway.

As darkness fell, I began to feel uneasy about the trip to Venezuela and wondered if I was getting involved in something out of my league. I pushed the thought away and went to bed.

When I woke up the next morning, I felt lonely in the perfect house. It was too quiet and sterile. It desperately needed to have some real life breathed into it, rather than just what I assumed to be an anonymous stream of people passing through, staying for a day or two at a time.

I didn't know anyone in the area and didn't have Tony's phone number. He hadn't said what time he'd be coming. Anxiously, I walked to the shops with Nikita, leaving the door on the latch.

I felt that I had been waiting for Tony forever. He didn't call and I wondered if he had abandoned me. Eventually, he turned up in the early evening. When I heard the key turning in the lock, I was flooded with relief. For the first time since I'd met him, Tony talked to me properly and explained what we were going to do.

'Tomorrow, we'll go to Holland to buy your tickets to Venezuela, then I'll drop you and Nikita off at the airport in Amsterdam and you'll fly direct from there to Margarita – it's an island where lots of tourists go on holiday.'

There would be someone waiting for me at the airport in Venezuela, and Tony told me to enjoy myself.

'The day before you're due to fly home, the drugs will be put in a suitcase for you, and then I'll be waiting at the airport in Holland.'

He said that it would be easier to get the drugs into the UK via Holland rather than straight from Venezuela, but Tony didn't try to push me into doing a drug run for him.

'Are you happy with all this?' he asked. 'Remember, you don't have to do it.' I nodded that I was happy to go ahead and do the run, and it wasn't discussed again.

Early the next morning, we went to Harwich for the ferry to the Hook of Holland. Tony left his car at the port and we got on the ferry. This time, he said that we could talk to each other. Once again, I made a beeline for the restaurant, and Tony raised his eyebrows as I piled more and more fish onto my plate. After I'd finished one helping, I sat for fifteen or twenty minutes, until I had some more room in my stomach, and then went up again and took more food.

We got off the boat at the Hook and jumped onto a train to Amsterdam – there was no sign of Hamid. I'd never been to the city before and couldn't believe it when I saw half-naked girls on rollerblades trying to entice men into restaurants and brothels.

We went into a few low-key hotels to see if they had any vacancies. Eventually, we found a place that Tony was happy with and, after we'd checked in, we took a taxi to a travel agent, where Tony was greeted like an old friend. He knew that there was a flight to Margarita leaving the next day and bought tickets for Nikita and me. I assumed that the tickets were bought at the last minute so that our names wouldn't be sitting around on a list for too long, although I thought it best not to ask any questions.

We went back to the hotel, and after I'd stuffed myself with more food in the restaurant, Tony said that he wasn't going to do anything that evening, so if I wanted to go out, he'd look after Nikita. I agreed, because Nikita liked him, and he seemed like a nice guy.

As I walked down the main street, dealers were approaching me asking if I wanted 'Es, coke, pills?'

Before I'd had a chance to think about what I was saying, the words, 'No thanks, but I'll have some crack if you've got it,' slipped out of my mouth. The dealer had a crack pipe and we smoked some together in a shop doorway. I was amazed that drugs, especially crack, could be used so openly in Amsterdam.

'This is what happens here,' he said with a shrug.

I bought myself a crack pipe, then went back to the hotel to smoke. Once I started, I couldn't stop. I kept going back out to buy more. I was paranoid that Tony would be able to smell the crack on me, and I wasn't enjoying it, but something was driving me, so I carried on scurrying in and out of the hotel and smoking the whole night long.

I was disappointed with myself for having no willpower. Tony said nothing when we met up the following morning, but I'm sure he knew what I'd been doing. We were late, having overslept slightly, so we just got our stuff together and jumped into a taxi. I felt so wrecked from my crack binge that I couldn't think straight and couldn't work out whether I still wanted to go to Venezuela.

When we got to the airport, the woman at the check-in desk told me that I was too late and wouldn't be able to board the flight. 'If the plane is still here, why can't I get on it?' I kept pleading.

Tony seemed calm about the whole thing. I'd only ever seen him being even and placid. We left the airport and headed straight back to the Hook to take the next ferry back to England. 'Don't worry,' he said. 'We'll reschedule.'

This time, Tony told me that we should separate on the boat and meet up after we'd disembarked. I waited and waited for him at Harwich, but he never got off the ferry. Luckily, I had Angie's number, and I phoned her. Feeling panicked, I explained what had happened.

'I'm standing by his car. Where is he?' I cried.

'Stay calm, Natalie, I'll make some calls and find out what's going on.' She called me back ten minutes later and told me that he'd been arrested.

'As far as I know, he didn't have anything on him,' I said, shocked. 'I can't believe he's been arrested. I thought he was far too smart to get caught.'

'I called the port and they told me he's been arrested for a driving offence,' she said. Then, 'Get on a train to London and come and stay at my house.'

I fell asleep on the train and somebody had to wake me up when we reached London. Angie picked Nikita and me up and took us back to her stunning flat that was filled with gorgeous furniture.

All this bought with drugs money, I said to myself, admiringly. Angie tried to persuade me to stay with her for a while but it was Nikita's birthday the following day and I wanted to get home so that she could celebrate it with people she knew.

As soon as I got back, I organised a quick birthday party for her round at Eve's house. Nikita spent a lot of time there and she knew Eve so well that she was almost like her second mum, as well as being an old friend of mine.

Within hours of getting back home, I was smoking crack again, and in even greater quantities, as if I was making up for lost time. Sabrina homed in on the fact that I had lots of cash and helped me smoke my way through it.

Angie called and told me that I was going to get another flight to Venezuela. I'd heard nothing from Tony and now everything seemed to be going through Angie. I asked her what had happened to Tony and she repeated the story about an old outstanding driving offence that had come up on the computer when they had run his name through it. With hindsight, I'm sure it wasn't true, but, perhaps naively, at the time I thought it was plausible.

I called my mum and told her that I'd got a job as a corporate buyer for a clothing chain, which meant that I'd be travelling a lot. I needed a cover story to explain how I'd suddenly got a lot more money and was going abroad regularly. We still didn't speak much, and she didn't help me out often with Nikita. I suppose I called her because I wanted approval from her.

My mum can be quite naive but even she knew I was talking rubbish. I'm not usually a liar, but the drugs were messing with my head so much that I didn't know what I was saying or doing.

As a kid, I was always well behaved, so good things had been expected of me. I still wasn't entirely sure why things had gone so wrong at home, but I realised that once one bad thing happens, it is easy for things to snowball. Controlling the events in my life was clearly not my strong point.

The second flight to Margarita was booked for just a couple of days after Nikita's birthday. Angie arranged that Nikita and I would stay with her this time. Tony picked us up to drive us to Harwich and I joked with him, 'Don't get arrested this time.' He smiled and shrugged, then hurriedly changed the subject.

We got on the boat and went back to Holland, returning to the same hotel. Yet again, I spent most of the night smoking crack.

The next morning, we left plenty of time to get the plane. In the taxi, Tony quietly explained that I wouldn't be expected to take my delivery back to England, just to Holland.

As we sat sipping coffee, waiting for my flight to be called, my instincts told me to get up and walk away while I still could. But foolishly, I ignored these feelings, because I thought I was invincible.

Nikita was running around, excited to be going on holiday, but as I waited, my anxiety increased. I rarely worried about anything – even when I had drugs strapped to me, I could chat with the customs officials – but now I was seriously concerned. I turned to Tony and said, 'I've got a really funny feeling about all this.'

He said, quick as a flash, 'You don't have to do it. You know that.'

'But you've paid for the flight and hotel,' I replied.

'That money is nothing. You don't have to do it if you don't want to.'

No one was putting a gun to my head and I had plenty of opportunities not to do it, but the same voice inside my head that drove me on to smoke more and more crack, even when I didn't want it, was driving me to get on that plane. I seemed to have some sort of self-destruct mechanism ticking away inside me, a bomb that had been primed to go off at a certain time. I had no idea how to deprogram it and I felt that the only option was to let the tide of events carry me along.

'No, don't worry, I'll do it,' I said, and smiled at him.

Tony explained how to bring the suitcase back. 'Don't check in too early or too late. Check in when the staff will be busy.' He was reluctant to say much more about my mission in case we were overheard.

The flight was called, and I said goodbye to Tony. I was still feeling anxious but told myself to stop being silly. I smiled as I thought of a way to describe my new work to my mum and Alan: a high-powered job in a globalised industry, for which I would receive a substantial wage. Lots of foreign travel was involved and generous expenses were paid.

'See you soon,' I called out to Tony. Then I walked briskly through to the departure gate, holding my ever-trusting daughter firmly by the hand.

5 THE WRONG DECISION

Once I got on the plane, I stopped worrying and started to look forward to the holiday. I knew absolutely nothing about Venezuela, just that it would be hot and that we'd be staying in a nice hotel with a swimming pool. The flight took ten hours and both of us slept most of the way. The moment we stepped off the plane, the heat hit me, and I was almost deafened by a noise that I later discovered was the chirping of hundreds of crickets.

Nikita and I walked into the long, low airport building. It was thronging with tourists, all chattering excitedly at the prospect of a holiday in the sun. I felt odd knowing that while I seemed just like them, I was there for a different purpose.

I scanned the people waiting with placards, but most of them seemed to be package tour reps waiting to direct holidaymakers onto coaches that would take them to their hotels. Tony had assured me that Al would be there to meet us, but no one there fitted his description and I felt confused. I felt a jittery sense of alarm in the pit of my stomach, but I took a deep breath and called Tony. He sounded genuinely confused by Al's failure to show up.

'I'll call you back,' he said. A few minutes later, my phone rang.

'I can't get hold of Al, but don't worry. Find the tour operator you're booked in with and jump on a coach to the hotel.'

I felt disappointed, because I had expected the attentive treatment I'd received in Amsterdam. I found out that all the coaches and hotels were owned by the same tour company, and so everybody just got onto the first available coach and would be dropped off at one of the hotels.

We boarded the bus with lots of Dutch tourists and were taken to the Margarita Village Hotel, while a tour guide gave us a potted history of Venezuela. The hotel, as its name suggested, was like a village. Both sides of the huge complex had their own swimming pool and food court. I was delighted to see the pool and had an urge to jump in immediately: I wasn't used to this sort of intense heat and my clothes were sticking to my body. Nikita was also uncomfortable, but she didn't complain.

My spirits lifted a bit when I saw our room, which was a self-contained chalet, with a pretty thatched roof, located at the end of a path. I phoned Tony to let him know where I was and soon afterwards, I got a call from Al. 'Hello, Natalie, sorry my English not good,' he said. Although he spoke with a heavy accent, I thought his English sounded fine. 'Don't go out tomorrow because I am coming see you,' he continued.

'OK, that's fine,' I replied.

I was quite happy to spend a day or two relaxing by the pool, but it was unbearably hot and humid. There was no air conditioning in our room: I was sweating and couldn't stop, and so was Nikita. And we were getting bored: everybody in the hotel seemed to be Dutch, so I had nobody to talk to. I found myself watching the ants scurrying across the concrete path and thinking that time had never passed so slowly.

The next day, the hours ticked away, but there was no sign of Al. I was getting increasingly anxious. By four o'clock in the afternoon, I was still waiting, and was just about to ring Tony to ask him what was going on when a call came through from reception, saying I had some visitors. 'Tell them to come to my chalet,' I said.

A couple of minutes later, there was a knock on the door and a man who reminded me of Bernie Ecclestone was standing in the doorway. Al certainly didn't look Venezuelan. His partner in crime was much more the kind of person I was expecting: a big, dark-skinned guy with a bushy moustache, like an archetypal gangster. Al didn't introduce him.

We exchanged a few pleasantries and then Al told me he'd take Nikita and me out to show us the island. *That's more like it*, I thought. *If I'm prepared to take the risk of smuggling drugs that will earn a fortune for other people, the least they can do is treat me nicely.*

Al and his friend led us out to the car park and gestured to a big white jeep with blacked-out windows.

'Jump in,' he said. 'What would you like to do?'

'I'd like to go shopping,' I said. Nikita and I had few holiday clothes and I presumed that, as in Amsterdam, I'd have carte blanche to buy whatever we needed.

Al nodded. 'That's fine. Let's go.'

I felt relieved and my irritation with Tony and Al evaporated.

Al and his friend were going to take me wherever I wanted to go and spend money on me.

'What do you need?' asked Al.

'A camera, and a bikini for Nikita. I didn't bring much stuff for us.'

I thought that once I got back home, I could show my friends pictures of Nikita and me lounging by the pool.

Al took us to a shopping mall, but I came down to earth with a bump when he said, 'You pay, Natalie.'

I was appalled and shook my head.

'I don't have any money, Al. I don't get paid until I get back to England.'

'OK, we go to cheaper place.'

He took me to a market, but once again refused to pay for me.

I asked him if he'd be picking us up the following day to show us around a bit more.

'Not tomorrow. Very busy,' he replied. 'Next time day before you leave here.'

I had no idea how we were going to get through the next two weeks. I couldn't speak a word of Spanish and didn't have much money to go on outings. Even worse, Al refused to give me his phone number, so I had no way of getting hold of him.

After that, all I wanted was for the time to whizz by so that Nikita and I could go home.

Breakfast was fruit and pancakes, and the rest of the time the food was vile, tasteless slop – various mushy rice and bean dishes.

We were warned not to drink the water, and even though we tried to avoid it, both of us ended up getting the runs.

There was nothing much to do apart from spend a lot of time at the pool. Nikita was enjoying herself, but I was bored with splashing around and it was too hot to be outside all day. I longed to get back to windy, rainy England because the heat in Margarita was so oppressive.

I started noticing a dark-haired man who was always with a woman. Both looked as if they were in their mid-thirties or forties. I was sure that the man was watching me and wondered if Al had sent him.

On our third night in Margarita, I went to the pool in the evening, when the relentless sun was finally setting. Few people were there but suddenly the man and woman appeared. We all swam up to the bar in the middle of the swimming pool and started chatting.

The man, whose name was AJ, explained that he lived in Rotterdam, he had an influential job in an oil company, and that his father was an Arab living in the Middle East.

When his friend, Mary, left the pool to get something from her room, he confided that she was a forty-five-year-old Catholic virgin, a lovely lady but not someone there was any prospect of romance with. I wondered how such an unlikely pair had ended up in Venezuela together, but thought it would be rude to ask. I told AJ the same story I'd told my mum – that I worked for a department store and was here as a buyer.

We talked for a while and I got drunk on piña coladas. Suddenly, I felt awfully ill and just wanted to leave. I ran to my room and was violently sick.

The next morning, I felt much better. I looked up at the dazzling blue sky and the tall palm trees swaying in the breeze, and vowed that I was going to make the best of the trip. I would enjoy myself while I was waiting for my packages. AJ and Mary invited Nikita and me to go to the beach with them. I jumped at the chance of having an alternative to sitting by the swimming pool.

The sea and sand were pristine, although the tide was washing up dead fish the size of trout. I never did find out why, but Nikita thought there was something fairy tale-like about all these fish appearing at her feet. We wrote her name in fish and she clapped her hands with delight.

Over the next few days, we went to various beaches and I got to know the island quite well. I also worked out what the best food was. Once, we bought some chicken covered in green sauce from a street stall. I thought it looked disgusting, but when I tentatively took a mouthful, it turned out to be the nicest thing I ate all holiday.

A week after we met, AJ shyly told me that it was his birthday the following day. Nikita and I went off to the local supermarket and I bought him a bottle of champagne. We sat round the pool and I gave him his present.

'You're so kind. Nobody has ever bought me a bottle of champagne on my birthday before,' he said, beaming and seeming touched by the gesture.

'It's nothing,' I said with a shrug.

One night, AJ invited me to a casino at the Hilton Hotel. Mary offered to babysit Nikita. It was the first time I'd ever been to a casino and I felt a bit in awe of it, but after an hour or so there, I decided I liked being taken to a casino at the Hilton by a rich man involved in an oil company. I got drunk quickly, and when we got back to the hotel, AJ and I had sex. To me, this was just a holiday romance, but by the end of the holiday, AJ would be claiming his undying love for me.

As the holiday drew on, I began to think more and more about the cocaine that was going to be stuffed into my luggage. I felt uneasy but told myself everything would be fine. Al called me and confirmed he'd come to the hotel the day before I was due to fly home. AJ then invited me to go out with him as it was the last day of our holiday, but I said no because I knew I had to wait for Al.

I spent the day drumming my fingers on one of the tables by the pool. Yet again, Al didn't turn up until mid-afternoon, and again he had the same minder with him as the first time we had met.

I felt fed up to be kept waiting. He took my suitcase and we drove to a café on a street corner.

'Everything arranged. Don't worry, all officials know. I've paid them off. So, check your stuff in and say nothing to anyone.'

I hadn't been apprehensive when I'd done – or almost done – the drug runs in Holland and Jamaica. I had been confident that things would turn out fine and I had been right. So why did I have such a queasy feeling while Al was explaining things to me? I couldn't put my finger on it, but things just didn't feel right.

We climbed back into Al's jeep and drove to a ghetto area. The building Al took me into looked like a run-down hotel. My battered old suitcase was exchanged for a brand new, dark green, rigid plastic one. Few words were exchanged between Al and the man who handed over the green suitcase.

We returned to the hotel. Once we were safely inside my room, he put the suitcase on the bed and opened it. I noticed the smell of glue straight away and realised that it might give me away. Whoever had put a false bottom into the suitcase had done a good job. I didn't see the drugs, but I was told I was going to bring back five kilos.

Later that evening, AJ appeared at my door. I'd sprayed perfume around the suitcase and opened all the windows to try to get rid of the smell.

'We're going to the mainland, to Caracas. Come with me, Natalie,' he begged.

'I can't, I've run out of money,' I replied.

'Don't worry, I'll pay for your ticket.'

I started to get quite upset and to begin to think seriously about going with him. He was pleading with me in a sweet and innocent way. I looked at him helplessly and wanted to tell him what was really going on.

'Are you taking something you shouldn't be?' he asked softly.

'No, of course not,' I said, shaking my head, the smell of glue filling my nostrils.

I was worried that my suitcase would weigh too much. When the cleaner came in the morning, I emptied out most of my clothes and gave them to her.

AJ and I exchanged addresses, then he waved us off as we clambered onto the coach. 'There's still time to change your mind and come with me to the mainland,' he said. 'You know I can pay for everything.'

I looked into his eyes and felt extremely tempted to run off the coach, throw my suitcase into the bushes at the side of the road and fall into AJ's arms. Once again, everything was screaming *Don't do it!* I had had so many opportunities to back out, but my stupid pride wouldn't allow me to. It was as if some perverted code of honour compelled me to carry out the task that I'd agreed to undertake. For me, AJ was just a holiday romance, even though our fling seemed to be something much more serious for him. I wasn't too upset to part from him but felt torn about whether to take him up on his enticing offer to go to Caracas.

As I sat on the coach, I started to think for the first time about what would happen when I got back to England. I toyed with the idea of asking Tony for some more work. As usual, though, I wasn't really planning too far ahead. Nikita and I were sitting at the back of the bus, and I noticed a blond-haired English man sitting a few rows in front of us. I guessed he was about twenty-six, and he was talking to the people in the surrounding seats, who were listening to what he was saying with rapt expressions.

I had thought that everyone else staying at the hotel was Dutch and was sure that if this English man had been there, I would have run into him at some point. I wondered where he'd come from and why he was on our bus. He was telling everybody how his bag had been stolen and that the embassy had had to issue him with a new passport.

He was carrying a black holdall and said that his suitcase had been stolen too. He seemed to be revelling in all the attention he was getting and started boasting about all the Porsches and Ferraris he had back in London.

When we got to the airport he vanished. Later, when I was sitting on the bare concrete floor in the filthy police cell, oozing sweat and starting to suspect I'd been set up, I wondered if I had been the fall guy so that the blond-haired English man could get on to the plane with a holdall full of cocaine, no questions asked.

6 HELL HAS THE BIGGEST COCKROACHES

'I must joke and laugh, otherwise I'll break down. I know that when I do it's going to fuck me up, so I won't. I hope that by the time you get this letter Nikita is back in England safe and sound. You know how much I love her so I can't talk about her. The embassy has told me there'll probably be a lot of news coverage about me. I'd rather Nikita doesn't see my face in the news or in the papers if possible. I just can't believe she's going to be fourteen before I see her again.'

Letter from Natalie to Eve, August 2001

'What's going on?' Nikita asked me again.

The police had brought a grubby, striped mattress with a sheet sewn onto it for Nikita and me to lie down on. Because I had a child with me, they didn't put us in a cell, and that, at least, was a small shred of comfort. I felt scared and bewildered, and couldn't really believe that I'd been caught and arrested.

I was expected to sleep handcuffed to a railing. As the handcuffs were clicked on to me, I started to panic. 'I'm so thirsty, please can I have something to drink,' I croaked. My throat felt as dry as sandpaper. The last time I'd had a drink was at breakfast in the hotel. A place that suddenly seemed a world away.

'If you've got any money, we'll get you a can of Coke,' said one of the police officers unsympathetically.

I gave him the equivalent of twenty pounds. He went away and returned with the drink and some food, but no change. Nikita and I fell into a broken sleep. I woke up in the early hours, thirsty again, and took a swig from the can of now warm drink. I tasted something bitter and lumpy, and spat out a mouthful of ants.

I prayed and prayed for God to rewind time by one day, just long enough for me to walk away from the suitcase that had landed me there. I hoped that when I woke up, I'd be back home in England, but of course that wasn't going to happen. I was still in shock and hadn't been able to fully absorb what had happened to me. *How could you be such a stupid idiot, Natalie?* I kept asking myself repeatedly.

The next time I woke up, it was morning. And I was still in the reception area of the police station, my arm aching from having been handcuffed to the rail. Someone brought us some milky coffee, then we were bundled into another police van. The police said nothing to me, and I had no idea what was going on or where we were going.

After a couple of hours, we arrived at what seemed to be some sort of police headquarters. I was taken into a huge room and there was my suitcase, wide open with all the packages of drugs next to it. Lots of police were taking photos of the drugs and discussing their find animatedly. I supposed that this was a good result for them.

Seeing the suitcase laid out with the drugs brought home that there was going to be no let-off for me. The British Embassy was not going to get me out of Venezuela. I had insanely agreed to smuggle drugs and now, for the first time in my life, I had to face the consequences of my actions. Until now, I had always managed to turn situations to my advantage. I now knew, as I gazed at my slashed case, that my luck had run out.

'Why's our suitcase on the floor and why are all those men taking photos of it?' asked Nikita. I couldn't think of a way of giving a simple explanation to a four-year-old, so I tried to change the subject.

One of the police officers walked up to me with an official-looking piece of paper. 'Sign, sign,' he said. At first, I refused, because I had no idea what the Spanish words on the piece of paper meant. In the end, though, I gave in and signed it. Even though the true extent of my predicament had dawned on me, I desperately tried to keep my spirits up by telling myself that I'd be returning to England soon, and that all this bureaucracy was simply a case of going through the motions.

It was obviously a routine set of procedures for the police and I felt as if I didn't exist as far as they were concerned. I had become an inanimate object – an extension of the packages of cocaine I'd been carrying. Bizarrely, I almost felt as if I was getting in the way of this process.

After being escorted out of the suitcase room, Nikita and I were put back into the van. It was boiling hot. I hadn't been able to wash, and I could smell the sweat on me. My stomach started rolling and cramping menacingly, but I didn't know how to tell them that I felt unwell. I'd been drinking the tap water and presumed that that was the cause of my discomfort.

Eventually, I got across to them that I needed the toilet urgently. Reluctantly, they agreed to stop. I raced into the bathroom they led me to and had a bad bout of diarrhoea. It brought me momentary relief but by the time I got back to the van, I needed to go to the toilet again and felt extremely ill. Eventually, when I felt that I'd emptied out the entire contents of my insides, we got back into the van. I felt wretched. Bouts of diarrhoea are no fun at the best of times, but in those circumstances, it was just unbearable. I felt I'd lost all dignity having to beg the police to let me use the toilet.

I leaned back against the sticky plastic seat and shut my eyes. I would have given absolutely anything to have been airlifted back home at that moment. Mercifully, Nikita sat calmly and quietly by my side, and didn't seem to be having any stomach problems. I cuddled her, overwhelmed with guilt about what I was putting her through and once again cursing myself for my stupidity.

Our next stop was a police forensics centre. There were lots of officers everywhere, in various uniforms. All of them seemed to be hanging around doing nothing. I was led down a path that had pretty gardens blooming with flowers on either side. A woman in a white coat explained to me in reasonable English that she was going to do some tests.

'Have you taken any drugs?' I shook my head. She dipped my fingers into a solution and took lots of samples.

Nikita had stopped asking questions by that point. She was such a good and quiet little girl, who had just accepted the situation. I was blessed to have a child like her and at that moment I felt I didn't deserve her.

Then, once again, we were on the move. This time, we stopped at a building I worked out was a court. There was a massive courtyard at the back leading to a big room without doors. I saw two big rooms with bars behind the courtyard, one full of men and the other containing women. The rooms looked dark and dirty, and reminded me of dungeons, but thankfully I wasn't put in there because I had Nikita with me.

Instead, I was taken up to the offices where the lawyers and judges worked. I later learned that many of them worked there not because they wanted to tackle crime and fight for justice, but because they could earn a fortune by demanding bribes and backhanders. I was introduced to a translator. He was a nice, friendly man with grey hair and a round, cheerful face. Then a woman, whom I was told was a judge, said, 'Nikita will be taken from you. She'll be going to a children's home.'

I gasped. I hadn't thought about being separated from Nikita, as I had assumed that we would soon be on a plane back to England. The idea of her being whisked away to a strange children's home where she knew no one and couldn't speak the language was more unbearable to me than anything that had happened so far. But it was clear I had no choice about it.

'Oh my God, what have I done?' I said to myself, putting my head in my hands. The full, horrible reality of my situation was finally dawning on me.

'You're going to get ten years,' the translator said matter-of-factly. Then he took Nikita. I don't know how I managed it, but somehow, I stayed calm and explained everything to her in the simplest way I could. Neither of us cried, but I felt as if my insides were being ripped to ribbons.

'I'll see you soon, darling; this is just for a day or two until Mummy's sorted everything out,' I said. She walked off with the translator quite happily as he explained to her that she was going to a nice place with lots of toys and many other children to play with. If she'd left screaming, I think I would have collapsed.

The translator handed Nikita over to a social worker, then he came back and asked me to give my version of events to the judge. The judge was pleasant enough and, through the translator, she asked me if the drugs were mine. 'Yes, they are. They're my drugs and it's my suitcase.'

'Did someone buy them for you? Did someone take you to the airport?'

'No, they're my drugs,' I repeated.

'Where did you buy them?'

'I'm not saying.' I was determined not to implicate anyone else in this mess.

And that was that. The interview was over. I was overwhelmed with exhaustion and longed for something to eat, some cold, clean water to drink, a shower and a nice bed to curl up in for a long sleep.

I kept thinking about Tony. *Does he know what's happened or does he think I've done a runner?* I wondered. Naively, I hoped he'd get me a good solicitor.

The translator explained that I was going to be spending the night at a police station and that a man called Douglas from the British Embassy would be coming to see me. 'You'll probably be at the police station for a couple of days and then you'll be taken to San Antonio Prison. There will be men there as well as women, and they have guns.' I couldn't believe I'd heard right.

I'm sure he's just saying that to scare me, I said to myself. I could only imagine an English prison with its strict routines and stern officers. *How can prisoners possibly carry guns?*

I was taken back out to the hot, smelly van. This time, the

journey was less than half an hour. I was relieved that Nikita did not have to endure yet another uncomfortable journey in this van, and prayed that she had been taken somewhere nice where people would be kind to her. I thought that I'd probably done a tour of the entire island in the course of the day. Now it looked like a different place to the one I'd seen as a tourist on a package holiday.

We pulled up outside a police station. The reception was an open area set back from the road. The only doors in the police station were those of the cells. Everyone stared at me. I sensed that as I walked in, they were throwing off some sort of heat-induced stupor, and that my arrival was the most interesting thing to have happened for a while. I supposed they didn't have many blonde-haired, blue-eyed English prisoners passing through.

I was met by a male and a female police officer who did their best to be nice to me. They went through all my things that the police I'd been with earlier had allowed me to transfer out of my suitcase into a bag. In broken English, the female officer told me to take off my jewellery because otherwise the girls would steal it from me.

While I was sitting in the reception area, the man from the British Embassy turned up. Douglas was tall and skinny, with a manner that was both laid-back and direct. He had brought a bag of biscuits and some magazines and books for me. He sat down, looked at me sadly and explained what was going to happen. I sensed that he was delivering a speech that he had made several times before. 'You'll be staying at the police station. I don't know for how long. I've given them some money to go out and buy you food, because nothing is provided here. I hope they do buy you food with the money. If they keep the cash, there's nothing I can do about it.

'When you get to the main prison, people will steal your things. There are a few other English people in that prison. You won't be able to make any phone calls from there. You'll get a ten-year sentence. I'm afraid there's nothing I can do to help you.'

He gave me a pitying look and explained that Holland and Venezuela had an extradition treaty that permitted Dutch people to go home to serve their sentence. He said that an equivalent treaty between Venezuela and Britain was under discussion, but nothing had been finalised, so I'd be serving my sentence in Venezuela. I couldn't take in what he was saying. Up until that moment, I had only managed to keep myself going because I kept telling myself I would be getting on a plane sooner rather than later. Douglas's words extinguished my final embers of hope.

He saw the shock in my face and hurriedly changed the subject. 'Everyone takes bribes over here. That's how things work. You need to get used to it.' I felt numb.

'Arrangements will be made to send Nikita back to England,' he said. I had never imagined that Nikita and I would be separated. The thought of not having my adorable little girl by my side was too much to bear. I was racked with guilt because I knew that I had no one to blame but myself, and that my innocent daughter was suffering because of my stupidity. I broke down and started sobbing.

'Good luck,' said Douglas. He shook my hand firmly, then got up and left. I felt upset when he disappeared down the road, and terribly envious of his freedom to walk away from the police station, no doubt to sit in his garden and watch the sun go down with a nice cool drink in his hand.

Douglas was the first English person I'd met in the country. He understood English culture and knew that the way things worked in Venezuela wasn't what I was used to. It was a relief to know what was going on for the first time, although, given the terrible news he'd delivered, I wondered if I might have been better off not knowing. I tried my hardest not to think about Nikita and to focus instead on what was happening in the jail. I prayed that she was safe.

You know that a police cell isn't the right environment for a child. It's for the best, I kept saying to myself repeatedly, to try to make the whole thing bearable.

The female police officer told me that she was going to show me to where I would be living and sleeping. I knew that the conditions would be basic, but the room I was led to was somewhere that, even in my worst nightmares, I could not have imagined.

7 HOT BODIES AND NO TOILETS

'There is a hole the size of a bath plug that we piss down. We sleep and eat on the stone floor. Everybody smells and we never get let out. I woke up and found a cockroach in my hair. The bastards wait until I'm asleep and then attack me.'

Letter from Natalie to Eve, September 2001

The policewoman led me down a corridor past a room crammed with men. I was horrified to see so many human beings squashed into such a small place. The stench of sweat was overwhelming, and it was hard to work out which arms and legs belonged to which bodies because everyone was packed so closely together.

The appalling conditions made the prisoners look as if they were no longer human. They reminded me of monkeys, or battery chickens crammed into a cage. I thought it was a scene from a horror movie, not real life.

Various words were shouted out to me in Spanish but, of course, I didn't have a clue what they were saying. The prisoners were only wearing shorts or pants, and as I walked past, I could feel the heat of their bodies radiating towards me.

I comforted myself with the thought that the women's quarters were bound to be better. I was led around the corner and immediately my hopes were dashed. One wall of the women's cell had bars from floor to ceiling, and another had bars in the top quarter of the wall to let some air in.

The heat was more intense than anything I'd ever experienced before. How could I have complained about the heat by the pool of our hotel now that I'd been thrown into an environment that resembled the furnaces of hell. My chest felt tight.

This is unbelievable. I can't be expected to stay in here, I thought weakly. But there was nobody to appeal to. *Even if I tried to make a fuss, who would understand me? Absolutely nobody.* The gate clanged shut and suddenly I was surrounded by a flock of women, all staring at my fair skin and blonde hair as if I was a creature from another planet.

Like the men, they too were dressed in minimal clothing, mostly crop tops and shorts. The brick walls were soaking wet. At first, I thought there was a leak in the ceiling, but after a couple of minutes, I realised that the wetness came from everyone's bodily fluids dripping down the walls into fetid little puddles on the concrete floor.

From what I could see, the women's quarters consisted of two large rooms of the same size. An important-looking woman bustled up to me. She looked half-Venezuelan and half-Chinese.

She had long, black hair but the front bit was short and almost shaved, making her look hard. She seemed to oversee the other women. I found out later that her name was LaChine, and that she was a drug dealer who had a lot of respect from the other women. Whenever she had visits, lots of food was brought into her. She had a girlfriend in the cell and shared her food with her.

'Hello, my friend,' she said, beaming. She seemed pleased with herself for speaking English to me. I was overjoyed to find someone I'd be able to communicate with. *Thank goodness, someone who can speak some English at last*, I thought. I soon discovered that those were her only words of English.

'Hi, I'm so pleased to meet you,' I said.

She gabbled back at me in Spanish, and the hopelessness of having no one to explain this hell to me descended once more.

Most of the women in the prison had never been to school but everyone tried to practise any odds and ends of English they'd picked up, even though they often didn't know the meaning of the words.

One girl said, 'Could I have a beer please?' She grinned, proud of being able to say so many English words. When the women realised that I understood absolutely no Spanish, they started speaking slowly in the hope that that would help me understand, but of course it didn't. At first, they all seemed excited to have a diversion from the gruelling boredom of their daily lives in the holding cell. But they quickly got bored with me because I couldn't communicate with them and provide the entertainment they wanted.

I slumped onto the only available square of floor, in the corner of one of the rooms, and thought about Nikita. I was overwhelmed with wretchedness and despair about everything that had happened. More than anything, I was extremely disappointed in myself. I'd been carried along by the whirlwind of events, but now I had some time to reflect I knew, just as I'd known when I sat smoking pipe after pipe of crack, that this behaviour wasn't the real Natalie. I was sure that I could do better for myself in life.

People had said that to me before, but I'd dismissed their remarks, thinking that I knew best. Now, squatting in the stinking cell and facing ten years behind bars, I knew that they had been right.

The police station was just a few yards from the main road, and it was torture to hear motorists, all free to come and go as they pleased, driving along the road all day long. Every street corner in Venezuela has a food stall, and the delicious smell of frying chicken wafted through the bars, but of course there was none for us. Most of the women ate reasonably well because their friends and relatives brought in freshly cooked food at least once a day.

There were only three of us who didn't have food. The other two were Venezuelan and they bartered for food by offering to clean the cell or do some other menial task.

I started off by surviving on the Club Social biscuits Douglas had given me. There were three wafer-thin biscuits in a packet, and they looked and tasted like cream crackers. Then some of the women took pity on me and started giving me scraps of their meals. I found myself nibbling on a hard crust of bread, a stringy piece of meat or a few spicy beans with gratitude.

How have things come to this? I kept asking myself repeatedly. I longed to get hold of Tony and demand that he got me out, but even if I'd had access to a phone, I didn't have a number for him on me. I wished my mum could come and rescue me, but that wasn't on the cards, either. I thought constantly about Nikita, alternately longing to hold her in my arms and grateful that she didn't have to endure what I was going through.

Gradually, I began to adjust to my living conditions and understood more about the way things worked as I observed what the other women were doing and picked up the rhythms of cell life.

The arrival of cigarettes caused epic battles among the women. Anyone who was given a packet found that the rest of the women descended like a frenzied flock of buzzards. While they were reluctant to give any of their cigarettes to me, when Douglas brought me some, everyone wanted them.

We were like sardines in a tin. I had to sleep sitting up on the dank floor, which smelt of old and new sweat, because there wasn't enough space to lie down in the sticky mass of bodies. Some people had thin bedrolls that they'd either inherited from prisoners who had left, or that their families had brought in for them. I didn't have one and had no way of getting one.

The women plugged electric fans into the sockets that were hanging off the walls. There weren't enough sockets for all the fans, so some women had pulled the plugs off their fans and had linked them up to the bare wires in the wall. It was a miracle that nobody got electrocuted.

I still couldn't quite take in the fact that I'd been sent to a place where you weren't given any food and had no place to sleep. There was an indolent acceptance of the status quo amongst the women, and although I was screaming inside, I gritted my teeth and tried my best to survive. I had no choice.

Twice a day, the police officers brought in buckets of brown water for us to wash in. We stood, trying to get clean and to cool down. When we needed to urinate, it had to be done in the same room. The space in the corner that I crawled into when I first arrived turned out to be right next to the pee hole, a tiny space the size of a plughole. We were expected to hover above it and aim at the hole. Defecating could never be a private matter. The tops were cut off big plastic bottles and a plastic bag was put inside.

Nothing could be more degrading than squatting over a plastic bottle in full view of everyone. When we'd finished, we scooped the bag out of the bottle, tied it up and flung it into a big black rubbish sack in the corner of the room. At the end of the day, that bag was taken out, but in the intense heat, the smell became unbearable.

Strangely, although it had seemed that my entire life back home was focused on smoking crack, I didn't give the drug a second thought there and never longed to smoke it. My craving for crack had got me into this mess, but now it belonged to a different life far away. Since I had been arrested and put in prison, I had not thought about crack once.

There was little conversation between me and the other women, due to my inability to speak their language, and so every boiled minute dragged. I had no idea what was going to happen to me, how long I'd be staying there or how Nikita was getting on. There was a big black void where all this information should have been, and I had no alternative but to watch and wait.

The men's and women's quarters were within shouting distance of each other, and one of the few diversions during the long, stifling days was the disjointed conversations between the men and the women. The girls took it in turns to sit by the bars and talk to their boyfriends.

After a week in the police cell, I developed huge infected abscesses on my arms. I needed medication but couldn't get hold of any antibiotics, so instead some of the other girls offered to squeeze the pus out of them for me. The process left me in agony, and it took about three days of regular squeezing to get enough pus out to bring me some relief. I had to hold onto the wall and bite down on a rag while they pressed, to stop myself from screaming or passing out. One time I got an abscess in my armpit that was so painful that I couldn't bear to put my arm down.

Every morning when I woke up, I wondered if that would be the day that I'd be taken to San Antonio Prison. One of the other prisoners, Gina, had told me, 'San Antonio … fucky fucky, very good, many men.'

I longed to be taken there but for different reasons: I was sure that it couldn't be as hellish as the police cell and I thought that maybe I would be able to find myself a lawyer, who could get me out or, at the very least, phone home and summon help.

Gradually, I began to pick up a few words of Spanish. The first word I learnt was *agua* – water. I kept hearing this word all the time, and one young woman who was kind to me finally explained. I kept saying to her, 'What's *agua*?' She picked up a bottle of water and pointed to it. The next word I learnt was *ventilador*, which means fan; the third was *Yo*, 'I'.

Soon, one day rolled into another and then one week rolled into the next. Although I found the conditions no less intolerable as the weeks went by, the shock subsided. It made me realise how infinitely adaptable human beings are to the situations they find themselves in, however extreme they may be.

The police officers had as little as possible to do with us, leaving us to rot. Most foreigners didn't spend more than a day or two in a police cell and I never found out why I was there for so long. The police in Venezuela aren't accountable to their prisoners and there was no obligation for them to explain anything to me. Perhaps I just got lost in the paperwork.

One night, to my horror, I was woken up by one of the girls to find one of the police officers standing at the gate of our room with his trousers unbuttoned, demanding a sexual favour from me. I turned away in disgust and told him to get lost. The conditions were degrading enough, without having to endure sexual exploitation as well.

Douglas came to visit me a second time. I was wary of him at first because I hadn't been expecting him and wondered if he came bearing bad news. He brought me more magazines and Club Social biscuits. There was also a packet of cigarettes, which the other girls fell upon when I went back to the cell.

He seemed impressed that I was still in one piece, but once again he didn't mince his words: 'I've told your mother.'

'Oh God. How did she take it?'

'She seemed upset.'

I shuddered when I thought of how horrified my mum would be. I was racked with guilt about all the anxiety and disappointment I'd caused her. I knew there couldn't be many worse things for a mother to go through than having her daughter holed up in a squalid cell on the other side of the world for trying to smuggle large quantities of illegal drugs into Europe.

I longed to make things up to her and hoped that, somehow, I'd find a way to get out of jail, get back to England and turn over a new leaf. I tried desperately to push the image of my mum's tear-stained face out of my mind. It was too painful to contemplate, as I needed every ounce of strength I possessed to survive this ordeal.

'And what about Nikita? What's happening to her?'

'She'll be taken back to England.'

'Oh, that's good. She can stay with my friend Eve. I'm sure she'll look after her.' I was enormously relieved to hear that Nikita, at least, would be able to resume a normal life. She loved Eve and I knew she'd be happy and well cared for.

Every day, a few more women were moved out of the police station. I prayed I'd be one of them, because I was sure that whatever else the Venezuelan authorities had in store for me couldn't be as bad as this.

One day, the police officers came for LaChine. I was sad to see her go, because she had treated me kindly and her handful of English words had been like manna from heaven to me when I first arrived. 'I'm going to San Antonio, see you there,' she called out cheerily to me.

I was called to go to court in September 2001. I felt happy

to be leaving the police cell but was apprehensive about what lay ahead. I was put into a van and taken to the court building, where I was put in a cell. The bars reached from the floor to the ceiling and the room stank of urine. I sat on the bare floor and waited for almost two hours. It was a luxury to have a cell to myself after having been crammed in with so many women for the past few weeks. Once again, nobody told me what was happening.

A guard came and took me upstairs to the offices, then my judge and translator arrived. The judge spoke to me in a soft tone, and even though I didn't know what she was saying, she seemed sympathetic. 'Nikita will be leaving tonight. Someone from the embassy will be taking her back. You're here purely to say goodbye to your daughter.'

Tears sprang into my eyes, but I was determined to compose myself. I didn't want to break down in front of the judge. Nikita had been in the forefront of my thoughts during every moment that I had sat in the sweltering, airless cell, and I was beside myself with excitement at the prospect of seeing her again, although I couldn't bear the thought of having to say goodbye to her.

An administrator brought her into the judge's office. I was shocked by how much she'd changed in such a short space of time. I felt as if I'd been away from her for three years, not three weeks, because she'd aged so much. She had somehow lost her innocence and had an old and weary expression on her face, as if she'd seen too much. I saw her before she saw me and clapped my hand over my mouth to stop myself from crying out.

The moment she saw me, her mouth turned down and she started crying. But even before she did that, I could see how incredibly sad she was. Before she reached me, I was sobbing. She ran up to me and hugged me tight, then she blurted out, 'I wet myself, Mummy, because I kept asking to go to the toilet and they didn't understand what I was saying.'

We were left alone. I thought I saw a tear in the office worker's eye as she turned to leave the room. Nikita clung to me and cried and cried. She buried her head into my neck, and I did the same to her without her realising. Holding my precious daughter close to me after being in the cell full of strangers was particularly poignant, but the thought of not seeing her again for years and years was too much to bear.

I was trying to cry in as silent and controlled a way as I could for her sake. She was wearing her own clothes and her hair was still in braids. I knew that I'd put her through things a child of her age should never have gone through when we were at home in England, but she'd never looked as unhappy as this.

I was terrified that someone might have abused her while she was in the children's home, so when her sobs subsided, I questioned her as gently as I could. 'Are you OK?'

'Yes, Mummy, but I hated wetting myself because I always go to the toilet.' Hearing her so distraught about that broke my heart. She was such a good little girl and she didn't deserve any of this.

She told me about the place she'd been taken to, and said it had a garden with a swing. She insisted that nobody had touched her. I was sure she was telling the truth and was relieved that at least she hadn't had to endure anything like that.

If, before I had agreed to take the drugs from Venezuela, someone had said to me, 'There's a good chance that you'll end up in prison for ten years,' that may not have stopped me, but if someone had said, 'Your daughter will stand in a garden in a children's home and ask to go to the toilet, but because no one will understand what she's saying she will wet herself and be filled with shame for something that is not her fault,' that would have stopped me in my tracks. I couldn't bear that Nikita's suffering was because of my stupid actions.

I opened the door of the room we were in and asked one of the police officers sitting outside for some paper and colouring pens. I wanted Nikita to do some drawing for me, so that she would be occupied and to calm her down, but also so that I would have something to remind me of her. Much later, when I finally returned to England, I threw all the drawings away, because I couldn't bear to remember those painful times that I had been apart from her, something that I bitterly regret now.

As I sat watching Nikita scribbling, I was desperately trying to photograph her into my memory. I kept looking and looking at her to try to make sure that the image of her sitting innocently in that room would be bolted down in my memory for as long as I was apart from her. I wanted to take as much of her as I could with me into the jail that I'd been told I was going to spend the next ten years in.

'Nikita, you're going to live with Eve,' I said to her softly. 'I'll be back to look after you, although it might not be for a long time. But I'll always love you and I'll never forget you. Don't forget me.' I tried to make it not sound like such a big deal.

She couldn't understand why I wasn't going back with her, but because I had explained everything in such a calm and matter-of-fact way – even though it nearly killed me not to break down into loud, racking sobs – she accepted it.

I'm sure she didn't properly understand what I was saying to her, which was a blessing. A four-year-old barely has a concept of ten minutes, let alone ten years. She gazed up at me with her big brown eyes. 'Will you be back soon, Mummy?'

'I promise you I'll do everything I can to get back to you as soon as I can,' I said. I'd always been truthful to her, even about bad things, and I didn't want to make a promise I couldn't keep.

I gave her a long, tight hug and then the office worker came back to take her away. As soon as she'd left the room, the tears flowed. My sobs were so deep and hard that they hurt my ribcage.

Like Nikita, I couldn't really take in what ten years of separation meant. The pain of being apart from her for three weeks had gnawed into my bones as if a rat was chewing on me: how would I be able to bear ten years? I couldn't really comprehend that I'd be away from her for such a long time and decided that, whatever it took, I'd find a way to get back to her sooner rather than later.

I remembered what Douglas had said about trying to sort out

the extradition treaty, and clung on to the hope that in a few months' time, the treaty would be sorted out and I would at least be able to serve my sentence in Britain.

I was taken back to the police cell and sobbed all the way. I had been sure that now that Nikita had gone, I'd be moved to San Antonio, and couldn't believe that I was being returned to the same hellhole. I tried to convey to the women in the cell, with clumsy sign language, that I'd just seen my daughter and that she was now on her way back to England, but none of them seemed interested. All of them had lived hard lives and they were fatalistic about the consequences on family and personal life of smuggling drugs for money.

I went back to the days of doing absolutely nothing for hours on end, convinced that I was going to melt or starve to death. I listened as hard as I could to the Spanish being spoken to understand a little of it, and tried to sleep as much as possible.

Sometimes, I woke up in the night to find cockroaches the size of small birds crawling on my head and neck. Nobody else was bothered by them, but I wanted to scream out every time I felt them running up and down me. I'd seen small scuttling cockroaches in England, but they were nothing like these monsters.

A few days after Nikita had gone, I was called to court again. It was 18 September 2001. This time, I was put in front of a panel of people, without a translator. I had absolutely no idea what was being said to me, but once again, they indicated that I was to sign a piece of paper. Again, I tried to resist, and again, I was bullied into signing my name on the dotted line. Later, one of the guards who spoke a few words of English said, 'You've been sentenced to ten years in jail for trying to smuggle five kilos of cocaine out of the country.'

I had been warned that it would happen, but when I heard it confirmed, I felt physically sick. I started to shake. This was real and there was no rewinding of time. Somehow, I was going to have to get through ten years of hell. It was too hard to imagine, and I tried my best to block it all out.

I was taken back to the police station and was informed by the prisoners that I'd soon be taken to San Antonio. I was relieved that I was finally going to get out of the police cell and felt that the sooner I started my sentence proper, the sooner I could get home. Every time I heard footsteps, I thought, *Is this someone coming to take me to prison?* I had absolutely no idea what was going on and no control over my life.

A few days after my appearance in court, I was finally collected to be transported to San Antonio. My bag of possessions was returned to me intact – which is apparently quite unusual – then I was handcuffed to a male prisoner and put in a van with about eight or nine others. It sounds strange, but I felt excited to be leaving the stinking holding cell with my boils, boredom and hunger. Surely no prison could be as bad as that place.

In the van, I was the centre of attention because of my light skin and hair, but I couldn't understand the comments the other prisoners were making. One of them had clearly committed some major and important crime, as we had a convoy of cars all around us and roads were blocked off for us. When I looked out of the window, I assumed this was normal, but later discovered that this was in fact exceptional because of the special prisoner. Amid a fanfare of police sirens circling the van, I arrived at San Antonio.

8 A DIFFERENT KIND OF PRISON

'Is Nikita all right? I'll never forgive myself for putting her through this; I punish myself every day. My only memory is of the last time I saw her and all the bad things I put her through. Why can't I find any good memories? Are there any?

'I pray I haven't messed Nikita's head up. Does she know I'm in prison? If not, where does she think I am? Does she know when I'm coming home? Eve, I really think I'm going to be in here for a long time. I miss everyone from England loads, and I wonder how much everyone will have changed by the time I get home. I know I'm a different person.'

Letter from Natalie to Eve, September 2001

I was led out of the van, still handcuffed to the male prisoner. The first thing I saw was dogs everywhere, all scraggy strays with bland, sandy-coloured fur, scavenging for food. I soon discovered that the dogs wandered in and out of the prison at will. Most of those who wandered in chose to stay there, because, unlike the humans, they had a better life inside San Antonio than on the outside.

There was a small door into the prison, which was surrounded by a wall. Over the top of the wall, I could see a complex of nondescript buildings, with lots of bare-chested men on the roof. They were carrying guns and so I assumed that they were guards. I later discovered, to my horror and amazement, that they were prisoners.

I looked at the buildings and told myself that I wouldn't be there for too long. I still couldn't accept that I would be serving my sentence on this island, and the only way I could comfort myself was by saying, repeatedly like a mantra, that I'd soon be on a plane back to England.

The guards let the prisoners in a few at a time, and I caught a glimpse of the courtyard while I was standing on the hot sandy road outside the prison. There were lots of brilliantly coloured flowers and trees, a fountain, a stone bench and a public phone.

After the hell of the police cell, I thought I'd arrived in paradise, or at the very least the Hilton. The phone box particularly excited me, because at last I had a link with the outside world. Suddenly, I heard a familiar voice calling to me through the front door. 'Hello, my friend.' It was LaChine, waving cheerily.

I waved back and smiled. I was overjoyed to see her round jolly face.

Douglas from the embassy had warned me that San Antonio was a dreadful place but in those first few moments I saw no evidence of that. I was just bowled over by the banana, coconut and palm trees, all heavy with fruit, in the courtyard.

I was expecting to be strip-searched but wasn't. We were let in two at a time, handcuffed together. The guards went through my bag of things. I still had all my clothes, my nice toiletries and a disposable camera that they let me keep. I also had a bottle of poppers that I'd bought in Amsterdam. Nobody had confiscated them because they didn't know what they were.

'Inhale and you'll see,' I said to the guard checking my things, who had looked puzzled when he picked them up. He inhaled, then handed them back, screwing up his face to indicate that he didn't like the sensation the drugs gave him.

Everyone was being nice to me and for some reason they kept pointing at my eyes. I didn't realise what they were doing: if I'd been smarter, I could have used my novelty value to my advantage.

I was taken to a building called the *anexo*, which was the women's quarters. LaChine had already told all the other women that I was coming, and Douglas had visited the jail and told the English girls that I'd be joining them, so nobody was particularly surprised to see me.

A new girl called Cindy arrived later in the day, and one of the girls grabbed her suitcase and ran off with it. I was lucky that I didn't get that sort of greeting.

Both English girls had been there for a long time, Dawn for six years and Kate for six and a half. My heart sank when I heard that. It was the first time I really began to understand that I was unlikely to be able to wriggle out of my long sentence.

'The embassy here is shit. It's all a real waste of time,' said Dawn bitterly.

'You can't count on anyone here. We've been hearing about the extradition for years, but nothing ever seems to happen,' added Kate.

This wasn't what I wanted to hear, but Dawn and Kate obviously had no intention of breaking me in gently.

'You'll see the men tomorrow,' said Kate. I had no idea what sort of contact there would be between the male and female prisoners.

'Get yourself a boyfriend, it'll help pass the time,' advised Dawn.

There was also an English woman of sixty-one called Irene, who had been on holiday with some friends and had been asked to carry a bag onto the plane, which turned out to have drugs in it. She seemed nice and normal, not tainted by the bitterness that Dawn and Kate harboured.

Kate said, 'Just look out for yourself, because no one else will do anything for you here.'

'No, you should share with other people,' said Irene quietly.

People were crowding round and asking me a hundred questions, which Dawn and Kate translated. They also told me how corrupt the system was, something I would find out soon enough.

The other Europeans were a Dutch girl called Ellen, who had an eating disorder, and a German girl called Mary, who seemed serious. She had been a model and was beautiful, with an elegant bone structure and piercing blue eyes.

One of the other girls told me that Mary really knew how

to budget, and that she had a boyfriend who was one of the important prisoners on the men's side. I could see straight away that Mary knew how to handle herself, though I wondered how a woman who seemed to be so cosmopolitan had got caught up in drug smuggling.

It was up to the girls to decide who slept in which room and, as with many other aspects of prison life, the guards didn't interfere. The room I was shown to was large and clean, and to my delight, was split into sections with flimsy curtains held up by wires. Each room had a shower in it and this luxury amazed me after the police cell. In fact, all the surroundings seemed entirely palatial after the subhuman conditions at the police station.

'I'm desperate to have a proper shower,' I said. I felt like I had been trudging for days through a desert and had finally reached the oasis. It was bliss to scrub off the dirt that had accumulated since my arrest. Everyone offered me soap and deodorant, and I was touched by their kindness. I had never enjoyed a shower so much. I watched with satisfaction as the rivulets of grime spiralled down the plughole.

After I'd showered and changed, I walked around touching everything in amazement. I couldn't believe it, but the rooms had beautiful wooden beds that male prisoners had made in the workshops. In San Antonio, you could buy a bed, along with a fridge and a cooker.

I was given a rubbishy mattress on the floor. Like in the police station, prisoners start at the bottom and work their way up. But I didn't care how low I was in the pecking order. I was exhausted and was grateful, because I had the luxury of stretching out to sleep in a way that I hadn't been able to in the sardine tin conditions of the police cell. There were a few fans in the room and feeling their breeze on my face added to the sense of pleasure I felt, but as soon as I lay down, I started to think about Nikita. I couldn't bear to imagine that she'd be fourteen the next time I saw her, so once again I told myself that I'd be seeing her much sooner than that. I fell asleep clutching her drawings and slept more soundly than on any other night since my arrest.

9 ADJUSTING TO AN ABNORMAL WORLD

'Prisons in Venezuela are probably the harshest and among the poorest in the world. It is difficult enough for adults to cope in such circumstances, where there is inadequate food, poor sanitation and the constant threat of violence. To subject a young child to these conditions is appalling and must have been extremely distressing for both the child and her mother.'

A spokeswoman for Prisoners Abroad, talking about Natalie's case in an article in the Independent, *September 2001*

I was awakened the next morning to the sound of gunshots. The sound wasn't a familiar one to me and I didn't realise what it was at first.

'The guys are shooting again,' said Kate, as I sat up and rubbed my sleep-crusted eyes. Nobody made much of it, but I just couldn't believe that prisoners had guns and were firing them, apparently without any sort of intervention from the guards. It was explained to me that it was the men sleeping on the other side of the wall, next to the *anexo*, who were doing the shooting. What wasn't explained was why they were shooting.

The night before, I had thought that I was going to have a relatively easy time of it in San Antonio; ducking in terror in case the shooting came inside our room, I quickly changed my mind. I covered my ears with my hands to try to deaden the harsh, staccato sound, but then I heard another loud, aggressive noise that seemed to be getting closer. I looked fearfully at Kate.

'Don't worry, it's the guards banging on the doors to let us know it's time to rise and shine,' she said drily when she saw my expression.

The guards appeared armed with big blunt swords. I was terrified and almost jumped out of my skin.

'Get up quickly,' hissed Kate. 'They hit people with the swords if they don't get out of bed.' She explained that the prison had two groups of guards: the national guards, who were based outside the prison and came in for their shifts, and the resident guards, who were based inside the prison. The resident guards unlocked the doors of our rooms before everyone woke up, and an hour or so later, the national guards came in, ran their swords across the wall and woke us up.

I copied the other women lining up against the wall and calling out numbers. This process, which happened religiously every morning and evening, was known as *numero*. Nobody was given a number, but the first woman called out 'one', the second one 'two' and so on. If the number that was reached by the end of the roll call tallied with the number of prisoners on their list, the guards were happy. Kate explained to me that there was an unwritten law that you did not mess around at *numero*. I later discovered that it was one of the few rules that couldn't be bent in San Antonio.

The morning *numero* usually took place at seven o'clock. Most of us were still three-quarters asleep and we fell back into bed for a couple of hours after the guards had gone.

The days stretched ahead of us with few organised activities to fill them. We all wanted to make the nothingness pass as fast as possible, and sleeping seemed to be the most painless way of passing time.

When we did finally get up, I noticed that a lot of women who had husbands or boyfriends in jail met up for breakfast with their partners. The breakfast consisted of *arepas* – a round, thick bread that tastes best fried and eaten with cheese, ham, eggs or just butter. On that first morning, I thought it tasted vile, and only just managed not to spit it out, but after a while I began to really like it. When I eventually came back to England, I searched all over for the special flour used to make *arepas*, but I never managed to track it down.

A lot of the Venezuelan women sat by the side of the prison wall with their husbands. They kept moving around so that they could always be in the shade, and their position depended on where the sun was in the sky. Everyone seemed to have their own designated spot. Every now and again, the guards half-heartedly fired warning shots into the air to encourage the men to go back to their quarters.

On my first day, I sat with Mary, the German woman, and in her perfect English she explained how things worked in San Antonio. On the left-hand side of the *anexo* wall were holes bigger than doorways and the men and women walked through to see each other freely. 'Occasionally, the guards fill up the holes with concrete, but even before it dries, the holes are back. Generally, the guards are relaxed about the men and the women being together.'

Money was apparently passed from one side of the wall to the other via a series of Chinese whispers. I couldn't imagine such a laid-back system operating in England, where male and female prisoners are strictly segregated. It was clear that few things in the Venezuelan prison system resembled the arrangements back home.

The following day, Mary said that she'd take me over to the men's side and show me how things worked there. She explained that the right-hand side of the jail was the more 'upper class' male area, with the 'lower-class' men living on the other side of the wall from us. To my amazement, I saw a small swimming pool and a kitchen, both built by prisoners.

'They don't mind if prisoners want to make improvements to their surroundings,' said Mary with a shrug, seeing me open-mouthed at the luxury that was permitted.

Behind the courtyard, however, things looked more sinister. This was an area known as no-man's-land. Trenches had been dug on both sides, with an igloo-shaped brick structure built on top.

There were slots in the wall for the lookouts to spy on the enemy. These were manned twenty-four hours a day. All the male prisoners were assigned a shift, but they could pay someone else to do their lookout duty for them. At first, I didn't understand why there would be trenches in a prison, but later discovered that battles between rival gangs of prisoners were fought there.

There were a series of small, tiled-roof dormitory buildings. On the left of the courtyard was the director's office and the administrative section. Mary explained that this was the safest area to walk for people who were in fear of their lives. Further left of the entrance were our quarters, the *anexo*.

'How many prisoners are there here? The place looks huge.'

'About fifteen hundred men and around a hundred women. A few of the men are inside for gun and stabbing crimes, although most of both the men and women are here for drug offences.'

As we walked through the area where Mary said the rich male prisoners lived, I was aware of more affluence. The right-hand-side guys wore nice clean clothes and their gardens were well tended. They paid the poorer male prisoners, often those addicted to crack, to do their washing and gardening for them.

I couldn't reconcile the image of the hardened gangsters patrolling the roof of the prison with guns to them living in these genteel surroundings. The contrasts I'd encountered so far in San Antonio were too much for me to take in. I felt as if my head was spinning. I wasn't used to seeing swimming pools and flowerbeds in war zones.

On the left side, nothing had been done to improve the land allotted to the prisoners – the grass had been left to grow tall and wild. Meanwhile, some of the guys on the rich side were converting wasteland into allotments and growing vegetables there. They tended their crops carefully and discussed the prospects for the various vegetables and the trees hanging heavy with coconuts. I smiled to myself. It was surreal to hear these gangsters talking proudly about what they'd planted, like a bunch of farmers.

Each gang was led by a *comandante* or *prang*. Mary explained that the *prangs* controlled everything. They had an enormous amount of power but generally used it wisely. The *prang* issued orders for new building work and those selling drugs inside the jail had to pay a proportion of their earnings to fund this 'regeneration' work. On the rich men's side, we walked past simple restaurants selling hamburgers and other meals. Each time I was told a new fact about the way the jail was run, I found myself letting out a gasp.

The prisoners on the rich side had built themselves a metal gate and the guards had allowed it: I was never sure why, because the guards then depended on the goodwill of the prisoners to unlock the gate and allow them in to do *numero*. Maybe a *prang* paid a rent to the guards to allow the gate to remain. If there was a search going on – *raqueta* – the men wouldn't open the gate immediately to allow prisoners enough time to hide items like drugs and guns that were officially forbidden. In practice, the guards often turned a blind eye to both drugs and guns, unless they were on the warpath for one reason or another.

There were five English men on the rich side and one on the poor side. I decided that I wanted to spend as much time as possible on the rich side. There was music playing, the men sat outdoors, drinking in the shade of the lovely trees, and I felt as if I could have been on holiday. The men also provided me with much more useful information than Dawn and Kate had, and were much less negative about everything.

The two men I started chatting to, Mike and Paul, had been caught with a boatful of drugs, the biggest consignment ever found on Margarita. Everyone had a story to tell about how they'd ended up in San Antonio and this was always the first topic of discussion when a new person arrived.

Paul wasn't a drug user but a transporter. He had started off doing runs between England and Holland in a rubber dinghy with an outboard motor. Then he bought a boat to get to Margarita. En route, he needed a bigger boat and so bought one, along with a book on how to steer it, because he had no idea how to sail such a big boat. He soon realised that the book wasn't going to help him, so he found Mike, who was also English and who knew how to handle the boat. Paul didn't tell him he would be bringing drugs back until the boat was loaded up. Mike agreed to take the drugs, but they were caught before they even got out of the port.

Mike was in his late forties. He'd worked hard all his life and had never done anything like this before. Paul was a nice guy from Lancashire with rosy cheeks. Neither of them fitted the hard-faced stereotype of a drug trafficker. Paul explained Douglas's role in a more neutral way than Dawn and Kate.

'If you need anything, let me know,' Paul said kindly.

There was also a guy from London, called Tom. He, Paul and Mike all had enough money to pay someone else to do their lookout duty for them.

'I can't believe there are prisoners on the roof with guns,' I said.

They tried to play the whole thing down. 'You get used to it,' said Paul. 'It's the way things are here.'

The male foreigners congregated in their own little group, but it didn't work like that with the women, who blended in with the Venezuelan inmates. I felt reasonably happy on my first day in San Antonio, especially after all the horrors I'd been led to believe I would encounter there.

In some ways, it looked as though the prisoners had a great deal of control, but ultimately, the guards had the upper hand. The politics of the prison were strictly a men-only affair and I never really got to know the inner workings of the place.

In my early weeks in San Antonio, I learnt the rhythm of the women's days and found it easy to fall in with it. Outside the women's quarters, on the patio, there was a big tank, some blue soap, washing powder and a rough brush. There were certainly no washing machines – we were expected to wash our clothes the old-fashioned way. The hardest things to wash were bed sheets and towels, because they were so bulky. By the time I'd finished hanging out the last item, the first thing I'd hung up was dry, because it was so hot.

Most of the time we had running water, although it couldn't be drunk. Occasionally, the water was switched off and we had to make do with washing in buckets. Buckets of water were always used to flush the toilet.

Because of the heat and the lack of things to do, everything was done at a leisurely pace. In this prison, like in the other prisons I went to and in fact all over Venezuela, the air was always filled with music, usually salsa and merengue and reggaeton, as well as Colombian vallenato music. It made life much more bearable, because everything pulsed to a joyful beat.

Venezuelan TV was different from what I'd been used to in England. We had to put up with seven-hour monologues by President Chávez, which were broadcast at least once a week. Sometimes, a soap would be on and it would suddenly be interrupted by something from Chávez.

'How many hours is he going to be on for this time? He's a shit talker, diarrhoea mouth. How many hours is he going to be talking for?' the prisoners moaned. He was generally well liked among the prisoners because he was regarded as a man of the people who, I was told, had served time in jail himself. But the monologues tried the patience of even his most loyal followers behind bars.

Almost everyone was serving the 'flat rate' ten-year sentence for drugs offences and so we had new people coming in but few leaving. In fact, I didn't see a single woman leave while I was there. They didn't complain much, though; they just accepted their jail terms and concentrated on getting through it as best they could.

Over the next few weeks, I tried to spend as much time as I could on the men's side. Sometimes we played volleyball and sometimes football matches were organised between the rich side and the poor side, which the women watched. The national guard were called in on these occasions, to make sure they were held in controlled conditions and that no one tried to sneak across no-man's-land to shoot somebody from the other side!

Although I tried to make the best of daily life in San Antonio, deep down I still couldn't believe that I was really going to be there for a decade. For the whole of the first year, I harboured foolish hopes that the embassy was going to come in and tell me the whole thing had been a terrible mistake. I spent a lot of the time lying in my bed and trying to force myself to sleep, because there was absolutely nothing to do. There were no books to read and no education available.

Visitors came in on Saturdays and Sundays, and brought food in for the prisoners. In the women's quarters, we cooked on one electric ring. There were no plugs, so we had to hook the hotplate up to the wires in the walls. Chicken and rice were our staple diet. Sometimes we were brought disgusting stewed chicken by the guards, which we tried to rejuvenate with soy sauce and various spices.

We had a cleaning rota for the rooms and the areas outside. Every morning and every evening, the communal areas would be cleaned, and washing powder was often used to clean the floors.

The women were fastidious about keeping their living quarters clean, and I was relieved to no longer be living in the disgusting conditions of the police cell. This order and routine made prison life more bearable for me.

Mary seemed to be the only female prisoner I could communicate with properly, and over the months, she became an absolute rock for me. She was reserved, and never told me why she'd smuggled drugs or said much about anything else.

Her boyfriend was fourth highest in the prisoners' hierarchy. Sometimes she went to see him and came back crying. I wondered if she was upset about the violence he was involved in. Because Mary said so little about important things, when she did pass comment, I took her words seriously. Soon, I moved into her room and we had our own little section.

One of the female prison guards doubled up as an Avon lady – another bizarre aspect of prison life – and Mary bought lots of products from her.

I was desperate to speak to my mum. I knew she must be going through hell wondering what was happening to me. I owed her a big apology for the mess I'd got myself into and all the trouble

I'd caused. I had no idea if I'd ever be able to make it up to her. The last time I'd spoken to her was when I was in Amsterdam. I had managed to make a reverse-charge call to her from the phone box near the front gate. I was dreading speaking to her but knew it had to be done.

'Hi, Mum,' I said nervously; my voice was shaking.

She was distraught and I could hear her trying to hold back sobs. 'Your gran's died,' was one of the first things she said.

I loved my gran dearly and was devastated to hear the news. I hated the thought that she might have ended her days with the knowledge of the terrible situation I'd got myself into.

'Did Gran know what had happened to me before she died?' I asked.

'No,' Mum said, no longer trying to hold back her tears. 'Oh, Natalie, what on earth have you got yourself into?' she cried. I could almost hear her wringing her hands down the phone.

'I'm sorry, Mum, it's just one of those things that happened. I know I'm an idiot, but I'm paying for my mistake and will have to serve my sentence in the same way as everybody else. How's Nikita? Have you seen her?'

'Yes, I've seen her. Eve's doing a great job; she loves her like her own daughter. How could you do a thing like that when you had Nikita with you?'

'I'm so sorry; I never intended for this to happen, but now that it's done, I've just got to try and make the best of it and take my punishment.'

There was a pause on the other end of the phone. I knew I might get cut off at any moment, so took a deep breath and said, 'Mum, do you think you could send some money out to me? Without money you can't eat here. I've got absolutely nothing and I'm really starving.'

My mum agreed that she'd find a way to send funds out to me and she put the phone down, still crying.

Then I phoned Eve. As soon as I'd said hello, she hurled a

torrent of abuse down the phone at me. 'You stupid cow! What the hell did you think you were doing?' She was certainly not sympathetic to me being in jail. Eve was sensible and had her head screwed on the right way. It was no wonder that she was furious with me for my stupidity.

'I'm sorry, Eve,' I said. 'Thank you so much for taking Nikita. It means the world to me that you're looking after her and I know she's in safe hands. I know I'll never be able to repay you.'

I knew and she knew that she could have refused to look after Nikita, but she'd never have let her be taken into care. Eve was a young single parent with a daughter of a similar age to Nikita. She was on benefits and I wasn't making things any easier for her by giving her another mouth to feed. But she loved Nikita and I comforted myself with the thought that my daughter was better off there than she would have been either stuck in Venezuela with me or hanging onto me back home while I smoked more and more crack.

Eve didn't ask me any questions about my conditions and, to my relief, didn't ask me for money for Nikita. I knew there was no justification for what I'd done. What could I say? That I'd needed the cash so that I could burn it all on crack? Or to launch my new career as an international drugs smuggler? I remained silent while Eve told me off.

Then I spoke to Nikita, who had been back in England for a few weeks by this time. I prayed that she had settled in with Eve. To my enormous relief, she sounded almost completely normal. She didn't even really want to speak to me, because she was absorbed in a game.

I cried when I heard her innocent little voice on the other end of the phone. It meant so much to me that at least I could hear her, find out what she was doing and reassure myself that she was happy.

I felt devastated when I put down the phone, but I soon got caught up with trying to work out what was going on in my new surroundings and how I was going to survive in that place. It was less painful to do that than to dwell on what was going on at home.

I was dying to tell some of the other girls that I'd spoken to my mum and my daughter, but as in the police cell, nobody was particularly interested in my news. Everyone at San Antonio was caught up in their own lives.

The honeymoon period at San Antonio lasted for about two weeks. After that, I began to learn about the brutal underbelly of daily life, the guts of which sometimes spilled out into all areas of the prison.

Soon after I arrived, one man fell afoul of the system. People were smuggling in weapons all the time and the rich prisoners were hiding a machine gun. Now and again, they tested it, along with some of their other weapons. At one point, they had too much ammunition to hide, so they asked the guards to keep the women locked in because they wanted to get rid of some of the ammunition for the machine gun by firing it off. Money must have been exchanged for this to have gone on. I couldn't believe this: it was astonishing what was and wasn't permitted in the prison.

The national guards brought in weapons for the prisoners in exchange for money, but once the guards handed the weapons over and were paid for their delivery, they weren't party to where the hiding places were. There was a tree we all used to sit under on the men's side. I was told that it had been hollowed out and a lot of guns were concealed inside it. The coconuts on the trees never had a chance to ripen because some of the male prisoners picked them and stored ammunition inside them. When the guards were doing a search, they hit everything with their huge swords to check for hollow areas.

All the male prisoners knew where the guns were hidden but it was a matter of honour never to reveal the hiding places to the guards. But one day a prisoner told the guards, presumably in exchange for a large sum of money or the promise of release. I can't believe the prisoner did that. He must have been extremely desperate to get out. To nobody's surprise, the prisoner was killed – the other prisoners made an example of him. They killed him by hanging, but first they cut his tongue out. None of the women were allowed to see such a barbaric act, but the execution was apparently performed in front of many of the male prisoners.

I was horrified at the brutality and scared. I knew that there was an undercurrent of violence there but wasn't aware of just how bad things could get. Some of the prisoners stood watch to make sure the guards didn't interrupt the killing.

Although we didn't witness this horrific killing, we saw the man after the men had finished with him. His ripped-out tongue was sewn to the outside of his lips, which had been stitched together as a warning to others not to talk. He was hanged on the main pavilion for everyone to see. We didn't want to look too closely but we stole glances at him out of the corner of our eyes. I made sure I never got too close to the corpse, but I imagine the smell was unbearable in the burning heat.

10 SUNBATHING, SWIMMING AND SHOOTING

'What a day. Both factions on the men's side have got a comandante. If a prisoner wants to kill another one, they must get the OK from the commandant. One of the prisoners left today and then there was war between the prisoners and the guards. I can't believe the guards. Sometimes they shoot someone and leave him to crawl to the hospital, it's sick. But do you know what? I always thought the pain of being shot would make you scream. It does something to you, but it doesn't look as if it hurts as much as you'd think. I'm sorry to write about this but I can't hold it in. I need to talk about these things otherwise I'll go mad.'
Letter from Natalie to Eve, December 2001

San Antonio was famous for its parties. Sometimes the prison director would ask the men to organise one if there had been lots of tension and killings. The incident where the prisoner had his tongue ripped out was a perfect occasion.

'Have a party, try to get the atmosphere back to normal,' he said to the *prangs*. I could not believe that the guards were sanctioning it, but Mary told me that there were sometimes two parties a month. Almost anything seemed to be an excuse to throw a party: when it was carnival in Venezuela, or whenever there was a national festival.

Before I attended my first party, I tried to copy what all the other girls were doing. They started getting ready the night before, and all dressed up in their best outfits or borrowed each other's clothes, put on make-up and did each other's hair. I had no idea what to expect and was amazed to discover that the party was going to start at ten o'clock in the morning.

One of the *prangs* organised it and the rich men were expected to donate money, as a sort of entertainment tax. If you didn't have money, you had to work in exchange for alcohol. Even if you were a crackhead, you could be respected in the prisoners' hierarchy if you worked.

Gigantic speakers were hired from outside the prison. They were so big they had to be brought in on two pick-up trucks. Although I didn't know it at the time, weapons and alcohol were often concealed in the speakers – killing two birds with one stone! The sound system was set up on the patio on the rich men's side.

A dancing competition was arranged, and there were games of volleyball going on. People sat down drinking, smoking and sniffing drugs. A lot of people were using crack and it was openly being sold. Probably about 75 per cent of prisoners were addicted to the stuff and it wasn't cut with rubbish the way the crack I'd smoked at home had been. But even though I saw so much crack smoking going on, it didn't really interest me. Not yet, anyway.

The national guard stayed outside the prison walls while the resident guards joined in the party. A vile-tasting home brew made from apples and bread was on offer. It took a lot of it to get you drunk, and was an off-putting sludgy colour littered with lots of bits. A cup of the stuff was passed around, so I sat back and waited for it to come my way.

As my first party got under way, I thought I was in heaven. I sat in the small swimming pool on the rich men's side drinking and surrounded by admiring men. I enjoyed the hypnotic beat of the salsa music and the cooling shade of the trees, while the sun burned down on us. Salsa is a passionate type of music, well suited to the fiery Venezuelan temperament. I kept pinching myself to make sure I wasn't dreaming, especially after the hell of life in the police cell.

I had finally started to pick up a little Spanish and I found I could have simple conversations, particularly with the men, who I felt more comfortable with than with the girls. The guys kept telling me how beautiful I was. They all seemed much more passionate and romantic than English men. Their comments were not exactly original, but I loved hearing them nonetheless. 'Your eyes are the colour of the sea,' said one, gazing at me adoringly.

'My love for you is as deep as the ocean,' said another, who had only just met me. The well-rehearsed lines were corny, but somehow the passion and sincerity with which they were delivered made them sound appealing.

At that moment, I was loving every moment of the party, the music and the sunshine. For the first time in years, I felt blissfully happy. Crack had made me miserable and I was keen to avoid being sucked back into its vortex. As I lounged in the pool, I felt I had some status there. Back home, I was nothing, just a common-or-garden crackhead. There at San Antonio, I didn't have that label. I was pretty, and I was building up a character for myself that I liked.

I'm not going to be a crackhead. I'm going to be somebody, somebody who's respected. I'm going to get a mobile phone and a bit of status, I said to myself. *This prison business really isn't too bad at all.* But my thoughts were shot through with reminders of Nikita. Her absence gnawed at me constantly.

The novelty of having parties and lots of freedom within the jail soon wore off. I realised what a long and ugly shadow the frequent prisoner shootings cast over everything. These were never spoken about openly and we rarely saw the action, just heard the gunshots, but in a private conversation, a husband might say to his wife, 'This is why so and so got killed.'

There was a siren at San Antonio that sounded similar to those I'd heard in Second World War films. It was sounded after a shooting and sometimes I didn't even hear the gunshots, just the siren. The Venezuelan women prisoners hated that siren, because they had no way of knowing if it was their husband who had been shot when they heard it. It chilled me to the bone every time it went off, because it reminded me of just how cheap life was at San Antonio, and how ruthless the men who smiled at me, paid me compliments and danced exuberantly to the salsa music really were.

Life in prison quickly became monotonous, and to relieve the tedium I started having boyfriends. Everyone else had boyfriends and so I felt I needed to have one, too. I also felt I needed one for protection, after I found out that one girl who didn't have a boyfriend was raped in the kitchen. She was threatened that if she told anyone about it, they'd kill her brother, who was also in the jail. If she'd had a boyfriend, she would have been 'owned' and as a result shielded from that sort of violence. No one dared rape a woman with a boyfriend.

The guys on the rich side kept sending freshly cooked food over in a bid to seduce me. Mary also shared her food with me, so thankfully I never went hungry. Those who had money would write a shopping list, just as if they were going to the supermarket themselves, and then give it to someone they trusted on the outside, who would get the food for them. Many of the prisoners also had delicious home-cooked food sent in at the weekends. I longed to have someone sending food into me and my taste buds went into overdrive when the aroma of the still-warm food hit my nostrils. Now that I wasn't smoking crack, I had the same insatiable appetite as I'd had in Amsterdam, and I never managed to fill myself up.

Sadly, my good intentions to stay away from crack didn't last long. When my first lot of money came through from my mum, I bought what I needed and had some left over. At a time when we were locked up and I was bored and miserable, I decided to get just one rock. Once I'd got the taste for it, that was it: it gripped me all over again. I sold all my stuff, my nice clothes and my toiletries, to buy more and more. Back home, crack was a block-like substance, but here it was soft and grainy like sand. It was different, and you only needed a small amount to get a hit, compared with the amount needed at home, because it wasn't adulterated with anything.

Once I started smoking crack again, I wondered how I'd managed to resist it during my first few weeks in San Antonio. It was so cheap and plentiful. I'd smelt it when I was walking past certain rooms, and when I decided to smoke some, I didn't need to go out and look for it. After my initial pleasure at being reunited with the drug, I felt damned again because it took such a firm hold of me so quickly – any dealer who could evade capture by the police was sitting on a goldmine of a business, because it was the kind of product that was guaranteed to have customers running back for more and more and more.

I hated myself for smoking crack. I never liked to think of myself as a crack smoker and had been proud of myself for kicking the habit, but now I was imprisoned not only by the four walls but also by the drug. And the more crack I used, the more miserable I became. But still, while I knew exactly what I was getting myself into, during the long, hot days with so little to do, smoking crack made life a little more bearable, and helped me forget that I'd served less than a tenth of my sentence.

While I was in San Antonio, there were several prisoners' strikes. I asked one of the Venezuelan women to explain to me how these actions worked, and she told me that the male prisoners went on strike from time to time. The women were never expected to go on strike, but it was compulsory for the men, and when a strike was agreed, every single prison in the country would participate.

It always started with a hunger strike, which isn't as drastic as it sounds. It meant not accepting canteen food, though people continued to cook for themselves. No one would eat during the day, but at night, when everyone was locked in, they would cook. Poor men and crackheads had difficulty surviving without prison food, but the gang leaders paid for food for them.

If the hunger strike wasn't successful, it was followed by a blood strike: volunteers and senior gang members had to cut themselves. The cut had to be fifty stitches long and it had to be on the forearm. At any one time, fifty or sixty guys would be cutting themselves in a prison at the same time, and again that would happen right across the country. If the blood strike didn't work, the next step was a death strike, where prisoners would volunteer to die for the cause. It happened once while I was in San Antonio, but thankfully nobody there died, though we heard that someone in another prison had.

I really didn't understand what was going on, nor what the strikes were for – when the men were striking, they wouldn't speak to us, because there were serious political matters to be dealt with. The only information I could glean about the motivation for the strikes was that they were generally connected with what was happening on the national political scene rather than about prison conditions.

The violence in San Antonio didn't only affect the human inmates. As well as the dogs, the place was overrun with cats. There were at least thirty of them and they weren't treated well by either the guards or the prisoners. Whenever the prison provided food for us, it usually ended up thrown away because it was inedible. Then the cats moved in to eat it.

One day, the guards decided they'd had enough of the infestation of cats and announced that it was time to get rid of them. They recruited a few of the male prisoners and started clubbing the cats to death using rocks and swords. It was a massacre: the dead cats were casually piled up in a heap in the *anexo*. Their heads had been smashed open and some of them were still jerking. I couldn't stop sobbing. The cats had done nothing wrong, but they were suffering such horrible deaths.

One of the female prisoners had a pet cat who she had tamed. She managed to hide him and so kept him out of the clutches of the rampaging cat killers. I tried to not look at the sickening pile of dead and dying cats, but I remembered what someone had once said to me about how people who behaved in a sadistic way towards animals often treated humans the same way. I shuddered and ran out of the *anexo*.

The gang set-up had briefly been explained to me on my first day in San Antonio, and although I never got to grips with the detailed politics of the gang rivalries, I got used to seeing bare-chested men brandishing guns patrolling the roof.

After I'd been there for a few months, a long-running battle between the guys on the rich side and those on the poor side intensified. It felt as if the whole place had turned into a war zone. We women were locked in for our own safety.

From our *anexo*, we could hear gunshots, but saw nothing until the second day of the 'war', when a wounded man was half-dragged, half-carried through one of the holes in the wall. One of the English prisoners ran through the wall into the women's quarters, carrying a guy with a serious gunshot wound to his stomach. He was trying to get this man to the office, where medical help could be summoned – there was what was called a hospital at the prison, but it was more like a school sickbay, with just a couple of beds.

There was blood everywhere. I hadn't realised that a human body contained that much blood, and was sure that most of his now lay in a trail between the battlefield on the men's side and our quarters. The whole thing was horrific: it looked more like a scene from a Quentin Tarantino movie than real life.

I hadn't experienced a war of any description in my twenty-one years, and had no experience of the terrible reality of gun violence. Although crack smoking and dealing circles have a reputation for mad and ruthless behaviour, I had never witnessed anything like this. It was hard to comprehend that this brutal anarchy was going on inside a prison, under the noses of the guards, who seemed powerless to stop it.

In fact, while the 'war' was going on, the internal guards hid, cowering in their offices. It was simply too dangerous for them to venture out. The acrid smell of fired bullets hung in the air and all of us felt trapped and helpless.

The shootings continued over the next couple of days and a constant stream of wounded men were brought through the wall. Some had sustained only minor injuries, but it was clear from looking at others that they were taking their final breaths. The dead were left outside for everyone to see, because I don't think there was anywhere else to put them until the mortuary people came to collect them.

I had no idea why this conflict had started or what it was about. The culture in Venezuela is a macho one and women aren't allowed to get involved with 'men's business'.

After three days, and with more than ten prisoners dead, an uneasy peace was declared. Then the guards took control of the prison and in re-establishing their authority sought bitter revenge by torturing the warring prisoners. After the shooting had stopped, the women were unlocked, but what we saw was almost as bad as the gang warfare that had been raging until recently.

We got as far as the men's gate and then stopped, gasping. I guessed that the guards had had to climb over the men's gate, because the prisoners who had erected the gate refused to unlock it for them in circumstances like these. We watched in horror as the guards tortured the men. All of them had been stripped naked and forced to lie face down on the burning hot concrete.

The concrete was too hot to walk across barefoot, so I couldn't imagine the pain the men must have felt as their skin contacted the ground. They had been forced to lie there since ten o'clock that morning. It was now two in the afternoon, the hottest part of the day. There was heat above them and heat below them, roasting them like a furnace. If any of the men dared to move, they were whacked across their backs with the swords the guards carried. There were more than a thousand men laid out like that.

It was an extraordinary and horrific sight. All the men suffered from horrendous burns and blisters that ended up as ugly scabs. I wanted to cry, and I felt so sorry for the English guys because it wasn't their war. The *prangs* would have got an extra punishment on top of the one meted out to their foot soldiers. I wished I could have taken photos of the treatment the men endured and smuggled them out to a human rights organisation or a newspaper. I'm sure people would have been shocked and appalled to see such things going on.

Throughout my time in prison, I never worked out what the

gang feuds and rivalries were about. After a while, I switched off from the violence because I knew that to dwell on it for too long would quite literally drive me crazy. There were more battles and more wars during my time in San Antonio, but I tried my best to filter them out and get on with the difficult business of surviving. It is remarkable how adaptable human beings are to even the most extreme circumstances.

There was an area of the prison called the *maxima*. This was inhabited by men who led the life of lepers. They had been rejected by both groups of men in the prison – those on the rich side and those on the poor side. If they ventured into the territory of either group, they'd be killed. They usually became outcasts after starting their sentence on the rich side, getting kicked out because they violated part of the code of behaviour and fleeing to the poor side, but then getting involved in some form of antisocial behaviour such as stealing someone's stash of drugs.

If it was decided by one of the *prangs* that their crime or misdemeanour warranted being gunned down, it had to be authorised first. The rules drawn up by the prisoners for the prisoners were strict and detailed. If a man from the *maxima* killed someone without authorisation, they would be sentenced to death because they had shown a lack of respect for the prisoners' rules. Although all the male prisoners were severely punished by the guards after a war, few sanctions seemed to operate against one prisoner who shot another. It was considered by the guards to be prisoners' business and they generally kept out of it.

One afternoon, four guys from the *maxima* raced, white-faced, into our section. The guards rushed in, in hot pursuit. We didn't know what the prisoners had done, but instinctively tried to protect them from the wrath of the guards, forming a protective cordon around them. The guards broke up the circle of women and shot one of the guys, wounding him in his side, and then grabbed the other men. They took them back to the *maxima* and punished them there, abandoning the guy they'd shot to his fate, as he lay groaning and bleeding on the floor.

This poor man had to propel himself along the floor using his arm. He left a trail of blood in his wake. We tried our best to scrub it off the next day using an industrial cleaning brush, but some of it remained like a big scar, reminding the guards of their brutality. At times like this, I didn't manage to block out the horror around me. There was no escaping the fact that, although the sun shone, crack was plentiful and there were lots of parties, I was living in what could only be described as hell.

It was during these moments, when I faced my circumstances head on, that I felt I couldn't go on. *How can I survive another nine and a half years of this?* I phoned my mum regularly and always tried to sound as upbeat as possible, because I didn't want her to worry. It was wonderful to hear a voice from home, one that had nothing to do with the orgy of killing and violence that I constantly witnessed.

I called her soon after the guards shot one of the men from the *maxima* in our quarters, and suddenly burst into tears. I felt as if I couldn't cope with any more prison wars. I longed to cuddle Nikita and to be back home with my friends. Even just walking down a law-abiding English street where most of the male population wasn't brandishing a gun seemed extremely appealing.

'I've had enough of it here,' I sobbed. She hadn't heard me cry for years. 'I want to come home; I don't think I can take much more.'

My mum sounded upset at hearing me in such distress. She phoned me on one of the girls' mobile phones the next day to say she'd booked a trip to Venezuela with her children. I was overjoyed at the prospect of seeing my mum and my half-brother and sister again. And I harboured a secret hope that my mum would bring Nikita, too.

I gave her a long list of clothes that I needed, without, of course, explaining that the reason why I had nothing to wear was because I'd sold everything to buy crack. I also missed music from home, so my mum agreed to bring some CDs out, and I gave her a list of toiletries that I needed.

The languid days of heat and boredom and crickets singing at the tops of their voices seemed to go on forever. Eventually, the day arrived. I had butterflies in my stomach. I was excited and nervous about seeing everyone again. I had tried to warn my mum about what San Antonio was like, but I knew she didn't believe me. I suppose that to any English person, the set-up at the jail sounded too incredible to be true.

The day my family were due to come, I climbed a tree near the prison wall so that I would be able to see them as soon as their taxi pulled into the car park. Douglas had been to visit me about once every six weeks since I arrived, and today he brought my mum, along with my brother, sister and Alan.

I was overjoyed to see Mum and flung my arms around her neck. Although we hadn't always seen eye to eye, she was my mum and at that moment there was nobody in the world I wanted to see more than her. She brought me everything I wanted, as well as an excellent Discman.

My mum hadn't changed much from when I'd last seen her. She was still a slim, attractive woman, although I noticed some new worry lines etched around her eyes and mouth. My brother and sister had grown up a lot and I barely recognised them. The whole family seemed horrified by the prison.

'You stupid girl. Look what a mess you've got yourself into,' said Alan crossly, as he glanced around the prison yard. I felt I was a bit old for yet another telling off and said nothing.

My mum commented on the lack of uniform of the bare-chested guards patrolling the roof. Gently, I told her that they were prisoners, not guards. She looked shocked but said nothing.

Some of the prisoners came and showed her their guns. I didn't want to upset her, but I was determined to prove to her that I wasn't exaggerating when I described the prison. I showed her parts of the prison but a *prang* on the men's side said she couldn't go there because he didn't want to be responsible for anything happening to her.

After I'd shown my mum around, we could sit together at a

table outside the prison walls with no supervision, though I knew that if I tried to run, I'd be recaptured immediately. It felt strange to be back in the outside world. I looked enviously at my family, who were free to walk away at the end of the visit, while I had to go back inside the prison gates, holed up with crazy people who settled feuds by putting a bullet through someone's head.

My mum came to see me nearly every day, but after the first day, she didn't bring Alan or my siblings. I was relieved that she came by herself, as I didn't want to expose my brother and sister to any of the harsh realities of prison life.

Although I was happy to see my mum, nothing had really changed between us. She tried to lecture me, even though she knew it was pointless. 'I'm not a child – look where I am, Mum,' I said quietly. She gave up after that.

After my mum's initial tour of the prison, all the rest of our meetings took place just outside the gates at her request. I think she was too scared to come back into the prison. I asked her lots and lots of questions about Nikita. She tried to answer as best she could, but it was no substitute for holding my daughter in my arms and chatting to her.

On the last day that my mum visited, we said tearful goodbyes, then I watched her walk off. I looked hard at her disappearing back. A little voice inside me whispered, 'Take a mental photograph of her, because this is the last time you're going to see her.' I tried to push the thought to the back of my mind. I told myself that my mum was still young, and I was determined that I'd find a way of getting out of jail before I'd spent ten years festering behind bars. My intuition proved to be right, though: I never did see her again.

As well as crack, the prescription drug Ritalin, given to children with attention deficit disorders, was available at the prison for recreational use. You could always tell when a batch of Ritalin had arrived, because men started to get shot left, right and centre – people became agitated when they took the drug.

I was eager to try the drug. The tablets had the effect of making me feel almost comatose, which helped the long days pass a little more easily. But afterwards, when I came down from them, I felt extremely depressed. I'd never had suicidal tendencies before, but now I began to feel that I'd just had enough. I'd been in San Antonio for a year and I couldn't imagine surviving another nine there. I'd tried so hard to block it out, but now the enormity of my sentence hit me. A massive chunk of what should have been the best years of my life had been snatched away because of my stupidity. How could I ever have thought that I'd get away with something as insane as smuggling shedloads of cocaine?

A quiet certainty washed over me. I knew that there was simply no way I could endure another nine years eking out this utterly abnormal existence. I decided I'd rather be dead. I felt sad to be abandoning Nikita, but hadn't I done that already? At least I knew she was safe, happy and loved being brought up by Eve.

Now that I'd made my decision to die, I felt much calmer, even happy. At last, I'd found a way out. I collected as many tablets as I could and lots of cocaine, which I decided to take in one huge line. 'Goodbye world,' I mumbled, and then everything went black.

I woke up what I thought was a couple of hours later, furious that my suicide plan hadn't worked. My heart sank as I looked around the room and saw the same dirty walls and crowded conditions that I had hoped I was seeing for the last time when I drifted into unconsciousness.

'Welcome back. You've been out of it for two days; you must have taken some pretty strong stuff,' Mary told me. I couldn't believe it. I was bitterly disappointed that I was still there.

The following day, there was a party, and for the first time I decided not to go. The failed overdose had brought about a profound change in me. I wasn't religious but I started thinking, *With all the things I've done, I should be dead by now, but I'm not. That must be because God doesn't want me dead.*

The room was deserted, because everyone was at the party, and suddenly – uncharacteristically – I got down on my hands and knees. I was bathed in a strange, spiritual sensation. It was as if I'd been possessed. I shifted into the foetal position and prayed like I'd never prayed before.

'Please God, just get me off the drugs. I know that taking drugs isn't the real me.' I was sick and tired of the hold the drugs had on me.

I was covered in a film of sweat. I remained in this trance-like state for hours: I had no idea what I was doing, yet at the same time there was a thread of logic running through my brain. It sounds silly, but I wanted to give God the opportunity to help me. Curled up on the bare floor of my room in the San Antonio jail, I made a pact with God: get me out of here and I'll never use drugs again. I uncurled myself and felt calm and peaceful. My desire to smoke crack or to take any other drug had quite literally vanished.

In the year I'd been there, I hadn't realised how much I hated life in San Antonio. The crack had deadened my responses to the true awfulness of what was going on around me. There was never any chance of getting out of this prison on benefits, such as parole or day release, but I'd heard that prisoners in Caracas were eligible for these perks. One of the girls in San Antonio who'd asked for a transfer to Caracas hadn't got it. I told Mary that I was going to apply for a transfer because I wanted a fresh start, even though it was unlikely to be granted.

I could see that she was tempted to apply, too, but she wavered because she really loved Carlos, her boyfriend in San Antonio, and was reluctant to leave him. But he was due to be released soon and they worked out a plan that he would visit her regularly in Caracas if she was granted a transfer there. Their idea was that she would be granted day release and that they'd meet in the street like normal lovers. So, we both applied and didn't expect to hear anything more.

At night, Mary and I lay outside on the patio and looked up at the sky. To me, it looked like the clearest, most beautiful sky in the world, always full of shooting stars. Now that I'd stopped smoking crack, I talked to her about how I was going to change my life. I hoped that transferring to a prison in Caracas and getting day release to do an ordinary job outside the prison would be the first step on that road.

I'd never really wanted to work before, but now it had become the most important thing to me. I wanted to earn an honest living to support Nikita. Before, my dreams had been to live in a huge house with a swimming pool and fancy cars in the driveway, but suddenly, I didn't want that anymore. My dream became to get married, and to have a mortgage and some kids, the trappings of 'normal' life that I'd been dismissive of before. I wasn't aware of it at the time, but I was starting to grow up.

I talked to Mary about Nikita. 'I can't describe how much I miss her,' I said repeatedly. 'All I want to do is get back home so I can be a better parent to her. I'm terrified she will have forgotten me by the time I get back home.'

'I'm sure she won't have. I think you'll be a great mum with her once you're back home.' Sometimes, she talked to me about her boyfriend Carlos.

'He's so different from the guys I used to date in Germany and the type of guys I used to be attracted to. I really love him, Natalie.'

'Everyone knows he's head over heels in love with you.'

A week later, to our amazement, one of the girls said casually, 'You're going on a transfer and you're going right now.'

11 NO MEN ALLOWED

'So now I've moved. I'm working. Sewing! I make slippers and cush-ions. And I play volleyball, table tennis, basketball and chess. And there are computers here as well, so I'm on the Net. How is Nikita? Please send me a photo of her in her school uniform. I love you, Eve, and I'll never forget what you've done for me. I know I'll never be able to repay you, but I know how much you have sacrificed for Nikita. Every night I pray for you and thank the Lord that I've got a friend like you.'
Letter from Natalie to Eve, October 2002

'What?' we both gasped. We couldn't believe that we were leaving San Antonio just like that. I was overjoyed. Mary smiled but looked uncertain. Not expecting the transfer to be granted, she hadn't emotionally prepared herself for leaving her boyfriend.

Still in shock, we went to the office and they confirmed that the transfer was indeed going ahead. We rushed back to our room and hurriedly packed our few belongings. It didn't take me long, as I had sold so much of my stuff. I threw my remaining clothes into a bag.

We had four male guards and no female guards escorting us. Generally, the male guards were less strict than the female ones, so we thought it would probably be a relaxed journey. I was rejoicing to be leaving San Antonio and didn't even cast a backwards glance at the place as we were taken out of the front gates.

It was a place I wanted to blot out of my memory as quickly as possible. Witnessing the levels of extreme violence in there was what I imagined living in hell would be like. I was convinced that no other jail in Venezuela could be as bad as San Antonio.

We climbed into the police van that was going to take us to

a boat that would ferry us to the mainland. I took a deep breath of the air outside in the street before stepping into the van. Although we had spent a lot of the time outdoors, the air outside the prison felt different from the air inside its walls. For just a few moments, I was breathing in the air of freedom. I felt more excited and positive about the move to Caracas than I had done about anything since my arrest at Margarita Airport.

We were driven to the port, a journey of an hour or so. To my delight, we weren't handcuffed once we stepped onto the boat, and the guards let us go wherever we wanted. It was a dark, starry night, and as the wind on the deck blew softly into my face, I briefly felt that I was free. I tried to savour the moment and store it, because I knew I still had another nine years to go. I longed to stuff the moment in a jar and pickle it, so that I could at least gaze at the memory during bleak moments.

I was now aware, in a way I'd never been before my arrest, to make the most of any good thing that happened. I no longer took anything for granted – a new departure for me. I had always lived entirely for the moment but now, for the first time in my life, I was starting to think about the consequences of my actions.

For the duration of the boat journey we were free people, not prisoners. I loved not being branded as a criminal and hoped that the other passengers on the boat would simply regard Mary and me as a couple of tourists. If we'd been taken by female guards, I'm sure we would have been handcuffed all the way.

I sat on deck racking my brains to try to think of a way to escape, but I couldn't think of any plan that would work. Jumping into the water would be stupid, and if I tried to run off when the boat docked, I knew I wouldn't get far.

When the boat arrived in Caracas, we were handcuffed and led on to an ordinary coach. Once we were seated, the handcuffs were removed. I smiled to myself, imagining prisoners being transferred from one jail to another by bus in England.

After an hour, there was a truck stop. 'We're hungry and thirsty,' we said to the guards.

'OK, what do you want?' one of them asked.

'A bottle of Jack Daniels,' I said jokingly.

To my amazement, the guard bought a bottle for us. We all sat down, drank some, then took it onto the coach. I started to get drunk and one of the guards tried to push me into having sex with him on the back seat of the coach. I wasn't too drunk to fend him off.

'I can't do that with all these people here,' I said.

'But I bought you Jack Daniels,' he said, as if I'd reneged on an unspoken deal. The whole thing was so far removed from anything that would happen in England that I thought if I ever got back home and told my friends about experiences like this, they simply wouldn't believe me.

The guard grumpily stopped pawing me and the rest of the journey went by without incident. Eventually, we got off the coach in an area called Los Teques and the guards hailed a taxi. They explained that we were going to a women's prison called INOF, which used to be a convent before it became the 'National Institute for Feminine Orientation'.

I shivered when I first set eyes on the prison. It was perched on the top of the hill and looked scarily remote, nothing like San Antonio. Our male guards handed us over and, once inside, we were strip-searched. This was the first time it had happened to me. I was on my period and had been on a coach for hours. The whole thing made me feel embarrassed and humiliated.

A guard showed us to our sleeping quarters. I could see right away that this place was nothing like San Antonio. We were led down an open corridor with a low wall on one side. I caught sight of the biggest rat I'd ever seen, scurrying purposefully along the wall. It was almost the size of a well-fed cat. I cringed and wondered if the place was overrun with them. Fortunately, there weren't too many in the main prison building.

There were also huge snakes in INOF. I had no idea whether they were poisonous, but one of the women once caught and skinned one. I couldn't believe how huge it was when she showed it to me. I prayed that one would never slither into my bed.

I could see women standing outside pouring boiling water over their furniture. 'What are they doing?' I asked the guard.

'Driving out the cockroaches.'

As I looked more closely, I could see hundreds of them scurrying out of the bed frames. The sight of them made my stomach churn. I soon discovered that they were everywhere, and we just had to coexist with them as best we could. Whenever they crawled out of a hiding place, the women calmly picked up a flip-flop and bashed them until they crunched.

Mary was put into a different room from me, with a girl who'd arrived from San Antonio a couple of days earlier. I was put into a room with lots of other women. Once again, I was a novelty with my blonde hair and blue eyes. There were bunk beds in the room and some women slept on the floor. It reminded me a bit of the horrible conditions at the police station, with lots of bodies everywhere. My heart sank.

'Oh no, I wish I'd stayed in San Antonio,' I said under my breath.

It was morning when we arrived, so we had the whole day to explore the place. I started scratching my leg and saw a line of distinctive blotches. It was strange that whenever I went to a new place, I was attacked by mosquitoes, but after a day or two of feasting on me, they seemed to lose interest.

There was a main block in INOF with lots of storeys. I could see that there were girls on different landings communicating with each other using sign language. They were using all their upper bodies to speak in this silent language so that it could be seen from far away. I discovered later that sometimes when people who had been in prison met each other on the street after their release, they would speak to each other in this secret, private sign language.

I looked down into the courtyard area and saw some people were playing volleyball. I asked one of the girls from my room if anyone could play. She explained that the jail had teams and a coach from outside came in to train the women. Teams from different prisons played against each other and sometimes teams from outside came to play prison teams.

Mary and I strolled around together. There was a church in the centre of the prison and a big community hall. We found a small factory managed and staffed by prisoners, and I realised that you could work there. This wasn't an option that was available in San Antonio, and being able to earn money in this way was a new concept to me. There was free and edible food, too – rice, plantain, eggs, chicken, stews, bananas, oranges – all prepared in a big industrial kitchen. There was a shop that stocked a similar range of goods to an English corner shop – everything prisoners were likely to need while they were incarcerated.

I began to think that maybe INOF wouldn't be so bad after all. It was obvious from our walk around the prison that it was a different world from San Antonio. I couldn't imagine outbreaks of violence in this women-only institution and I felt reassured that some sort of rule of law operated there.

Mary went off because she wanted to be by herself for a while. I guessed that she was missing her boyfriend back in San Antonio. I suddenly felt lonely.

The prison was in the mountains and there were seats where you could sit quietly and gaze at the beautiful, tranquil view. As I looked out at the peaceful mountains, I thought about the laid-back chaos of San Antonio and was convinced I'd done the right thing.

There were five public phones, and phone cards for sale that worked. I was back in civilisation. To my delight, there was also access to the Internet and we could book an hour's use every two days, though you could also go to the Internet room on the off chance that there would be a spare computer.

Now I could be in regular contact with my mum, my brother and sister. I was overjoyed to be back in touch with my beloved mum.

Thanks to email, we stayed in close contact, and she kept me up to date with news from home, especially information about what Nikita was doing, which I devoured hungrily. I was able to paint a reasonably cheerful picture for her about the orderly life in INOF, and to reassure her that I was no longer living in the war zone that San Antonio had been. I began to feel closer to my mum, despite the physical distance between us, and our relationship through cyberspace was better than it had been for years.

At first, because I hardly knew anyone, I found myself walking around aimlessly in circles, even more bored than I had been at San Antonio. But I soon enrolled at the prison school and started learning Spanish – I had picked up lots of street slang and was keen to learn Spanish proper. I also found myself some work at the cushion factory and started earning money.

The woman who ran the factory, a prisoner herself, gave other prisoners materials to embroider cushions which were then sold outside the prison. There was also a factory in INOF that made Venezuelan flags and a lot of the country's flags were made there. This, too, was run by a prisoner. When a prisoner factory boss was about to be released, she sold the business on to somebody else.

The boss lady gave us a pattern and material, and we could work as fast or as slow as we wanted, embroidering cushions and towels with simple cross stitch. We went in the *taller* to sew; it felt just like going to work outside the prison.

There was a big plastic table in the middle of the room with metal legs. While we sat with our threads, our material and our needles, we chatted about visits we'd just had and those we were looking forward to. People talked about their families, about kicking-ball games (a variation on rounders, with a football and no bat) and forthcoming events.

The women were protective of their loved ones and there was a strong sense of family identity. While my only visits were from British Embassy staff, many of the women were from Caracas and had lots of family members and friends coming to visit them regularly. The conversations followed the peaceful rhythm of the thread weaving in and out of the fabric.

I kept to my deal with God. I was terrified not to, because I was sure it was down to Him that I'd got out of San Antonio so swiftly and unexpectedly. Only a minority of women smoked drugs in this prison and crack use was much more covert in INOF than it had been at San Antonio. I was no longer interested in drugs and so never sought out the people who used them.

Unlike in English prisons, visiting time was a relaxed and sociable affair. Sometimes people from local churches came and brought nice food and toiletries. Prisoners chattered excitedly to their families about when they were getting out on benefit. I was thrilled when I received my first pay packet for sewing: it was the equivalent of £1.50 and I celebrated by buying myself a packet of Oreo cookies, which are popular in Venezuela.

Once a year, someone came in to help the girls prepare for a big fashion show. It was a famous event and lots of people from all over the country came to watch it. It was on occasions like these, when there was an influx of outsiders into the prison, that mobile phones and drugs were smuggled in. The scale of crime in INOF, however, was nothing like it had been at San Antonio. Prisoners disciplined themselves and each other, and behaviour like muggings was deemed unacceptable. Guns and shootings were becoming a distant memory, and my nerves improved enormously as a result.

I discovered that San Antonio had a bad reputation in the Venezuelan prison system. When I told prisoners that I'd come from there they said, 'Oh my God, that's a terrible place.' In the early weeks at INOF, I disagreed. I missed the vibe and vitality of San Antonio at first, and I missed the presence of men. It sounds bizarre, given what went on, but I pined for the excitement of the place.

Soon, though, I got caught up in the routine of life in the prison and started to feel much happier. I was enjoying learning Spanish and applied myself in a way that I never had at school. This time, I was choosing to learn rather than being told I had to do it, and there seemed much more point to this than learning about what had happened in 1066.

There were different corridors and landings in the prison and Mary and I were eventually given rooms opposite each other. Some girls had made their rooms homely: they had brightly coloured textiles hanging on the walls, nice beds and TVs. The rooms were nothing like those in San Antonio. Sometimes, it felt like normal life rather than prison.

British Embassy officials had visited me once in San Antonio and came to see me twice in INOF. Everybody got excited when embassy officials from any country came because they brought gifts for the prisoners they were visiting. The Venezuelans quickly recognised who was attached to which embassy. American, English and Dutch embassies were top of the pecking order because they brought the most stuff. A lot of the embassies didn't give money from their own coffers but passed on money that had been sent by families, but the Venezuelans often thought that the embassies were showering us with money and gifts. The officials did bring us magazines and toiletries though. It must have looked like we were having an extra Christmas.

Sometimes we would know when they were coming and sometimes we wouldn't. On one of my visits, the embassy sent a Venezuelan member of staff, although I'd been yearning to see an English person. She was business-like and didn't seem to care about what was happening to me. One of the main topics of conversation was the extradition treaty. Every time I spoke to an embassy or consulate official, I was told the same story: they were waiting for Venezuela to sign the crucial document and it wasn't going to happen anytime soon. During all my years of incarceration in Venezuelan jails, that treaty was never signed.

There was a lot of routine and structure at INOF, which was nothing like the lax regime at San Antonio. There we were called to the courtyard every day, lining up on our landings and trooping outside. Then prison notices and events were read out to us while we stood in neat lines. It reminded me of going to assembly at junior school.

If any of us were caught talking, we were sent to our room.

This was the one time the whole prison was together, and messages could be passed between girls. We were expected to sing the national anthem – the words were something to do with 'glory is the country'. These were not sentiments I endorsed about the place that had given me a ten-year prison sentence.

Once I'd learnt the words of the anthem and knew it properly, I sang it at the top of my voice, tongue firmly in my cheek. *If you're going to force me to sing it, I'll really sing it,* I said to myself.

There was no brutality from the guards. It was as if people felt sorry for us and were trying to help us make things better. They took bribes and wielded a lot of power, but they didn't lord it over us.

There were lots of foreigners there – probably about fifty out of five or six hundred prisoners. I met a girl whom everybody thought was Swedish, called Vivi. She had come to Venezuela on a Swedish passport, although she was from Romania. I didn't know her well there, but I was to come across her again later.

Mary had been trying to phone her boyfriend Carlos since we'd arrived, but couldn't get hold of him. She had a friend who was a guard at San Antonio and eventually she phoned him in desperation. 'Oh, you know, Carlos got killed,' he said casually.

She didn't know whether to believe him or not, because he'd never liked Carlos, but tears sprang into her eyes. It was the first time I'd seen Mary reveal her emotions. She called one of Carlos's friends, hoping and praying that the guard had told her a malicious lie, but he confirmed his death. She was absolutely devastated.

We couldn't believe it. When Mary was there, Carlos behaved himself, and she was absolutely convinced that if she'd remained in San Antonio, he would have stayed away from whatever argument he got into that had cost him his life. Mary's grief was acute, but to the guards and inmates of San Antonio his death was unremarkable. Life was cheap there and death from gunshot wounds routine. After her initial tears, Mary never referred to Carlos again. She was a dignified woman and kept her grief to herself.

While I was in INOF, a state of emergency was declared in Venezuela. I understood little about Venezuelan politics or the attitudes of prisoners to President Chávez, but it seemed that a decision was going to be made about what position prisoners throughout the country would adopt in response to the state of emergency. Prisoners had apparently been told that they could take their chances and walk out of the prison during the state of emergency, but that they would risk one of the guards putting a bullet in their back. A collective decision was made, I've no idea how, and word went around the prison that we were all going to stay put during the state of emergency.

I witnessed many incredible things at INOF, but the Venezuelan prisoners didn't bat an eyelid about them. Incidents that shocked me were routine to them. One day, a woman called Faith arrived at the prison. She'd been caught at the airport with drugs in her suitcase. If they'd bothered to X-ray her, they would have found that she'd also swallowed large quantities of cocaine.

A few hours after she arrived, she calmly went to the toilet, excreted the condoms stuffed with cocaine, smoked her fill and sold the rest. I don't know whether the drugs were smuggled out of the prison to be sold on the street or whether Faith sold them all to her fellow inmates.

It wasn't as hot in INOF as it had been in San Antonio because it was in the mountains, and that made life a bit easier. I wasn't exactly happy, and I still tried my best not to think about the yawning expanse of time behind bars that stretched ahead of me, but life was certainly bearable. It wasn't long, though, before my relative peace of mind was shattered by some bad news.

My mum had been telling me for a while that she wasn't feeling well. She explained that she'd been feeling tired and lethargic, and that the doctor had told her she was suffering from depression. She was adamant that the doctor was wrong. A few weeks later, she had passed out and was rushed to hospital. Someone phoned the embassy and they informed the prison. The doctors had done lots of tests but had found nothing. This went on for a couple of months and eventually she got signed off from her job as a secretary in the local council's social services. It was odd that she now worked with the people she used to have arguments with when I was in care, but she was popular and well liked there.

My mum seemed to be deteriorating, but still no diagnosis had been made. One day, when I couldn't book time on the Internet, but Mary was about to log on for her hour, I asked if she could check my email to see if there was any news. She returned looking pale and solemn. Mary was a straight-talking woman and I'd never known her to beat around the bush. 'I'm really sorry, Natalie, your mum's got lung cancer.'

I stood there with my mouth open. I knew that my mum had had lots of tests and nothing had been discovered, and I'd convinced myself that the doctor had been right, and she was suffering from some sort of depression. Cancer was the last thing I'd been expecting. I raced to the phone and made a reverse-charge call to her.

I fought back tears as I spoke to her. I wanted to be strong for her sake, but I was absolutely devastated. I expected my mum to always be there on the end of the phone or to be pinging back cheerful emails to me.

'Yes, I've got cancer. It isn't going to get any better. I'm going to have some chemotherapy,' she said. She seemed calm about the whole thing and made no fuss at all. *It really must be bad*, I thought. But I told myself that she'd have the chemotherapy and then she'd be OK. In the same way that I'd been in denial for so long about spending ten years behind bars in Venezuela, I wasn't prepared to accept that my mum was seriously ill.

Soon afterwards, I spoke to her on the phone and she said wearily, 'I'm going to stop the chemotherapy. It's making me feel so awful. I'd rather have a shorter life of better quality and spend whatever time I've got left with the kids.'

'Don't talk like that, Mum, I'm sure there's something the doctors can do for you,' I cried. When I'd put down the phone, I tried to block out what my mum had just said. It didn't sound as if she had long left to live but I just couldn't accept that, especially not when I was so far away and couldn't even see her. I prayed that a miracle would keep her alive. A shiver ran down my spine as I remembered seeing her walk away from San Antonio and getting an overwhelming sense that that would be the last time I'd ever see her.

In a bid to forget what was happening to her, I threw myself into various activities, like kicking-ball. I played a lot, but I didn't get selected for the team. I'd always been good at sport at school and was quite upset.

The prison was surrounded by a fence, and even though it had various guard points they weren't always manned. I looked at weak points in the fence and thought that if I had a pair of wire cutters, I could just cut through and go.

I dreamed of finding a way to get back to England so that I could be with my mum once again. I knew that even if I did manage to escape, I'd have nowhere to go and would be recaptured almost immediately, but fantasising about freedom helped to pass the time.

I got into trouble only once at INOF. There was a Hungarian girl called Dalma there and people used to say, 'The wires in her head are jumbled together.' She kept on repeating that she was going to die in prison. She had no friends and no interest in learning Spanish.

I got annoyed with foreign prisoners who made no effort to learn Spanish, and thought it was ignorant to be in someone else's country but not to make any effort to fit in. Being unable to communicate and understand what was going on made life far more difficult than it was already.

Once Dalma went on a bender – I wondered if she'd got hold of some Ritalin – and spent days painting her room black. She had some money and ordered the paint and the paintbrush from outside the prison. It was the talk of INOF and lots of the women came to gawp at her. She painted herself black when she'd finished doing her room – she was obviously seriously disturbed.

She started trying to talk to me about something that made no sense. I was preoccupied with my mum's health and wasn't interested in listening to her jabbering. When I went downstairs to collect my food in the canteen, she followed me. I wanted to brush her off like an irritating, buzzing fly, but I gritted my teeth and said nothing.

She came up to me and said nastily, 'In the same way you're not interested in me, no one's interested in your mum. I hope she dies.'

Something inside me snapped and before I'd even had time to think about what I was doing, I punched her in the face. Although I knew she was mentally ill, I couldn't help myself. She was a small, skinny girl and I put a lot of weight and force into the blow.

She was taken off to the hospital suffering from a bad black eye. Unfortunately, I had struck her right in front of the prison guards. The following day, both of us were called into the office about the incident.

Suddenly, I felt terrified and was sure I'd be punished by being sent to the hole. Just the mention of the place made all the girls shiver: 'It's a disgusting place right up in the mountains that is used for punishments.' The other women had explained to me that a guard would escort prisoners who are being punished to a filthy room with no lights, no water, no windows and no toilet facilities. They could be sent there for as long as four days.

Oh my God, I don't want to be sent to the hole, I said to myself. I explained to the guards why I'd struck Dalma. Then someone came to translate for Dalma, and her story matched up with mine, so in the end neither of us were punished. I breathed a huge sigh of relief as I left the office. I hoped that I'd never get to see the terrifying hole. The incident made me more desperate than ever to find a way of getting home to see my mum.

A few weeks later, I got called to the office. Some Venezuelan officials dressed in suits were waiting for me there. They explained that they wanted to take my photo and my fingerprints. 'What's all this about?' I asked. 'I've never seen any other prisoners having to do this.'

'Oh, it won't be long before you're going home,' one of the men said, raising his eyebrow at me.

I rushed back to my room and excitedly told Mary. I started thinking seriously about going home and planned all the things I'd do with my mum and Nikita. I wondered if the men had come from Interpol. To my enormous disappointment, though, I never heard anything more about it.

I'd just got used to the daily routine at INOF when suddenly it was announced that the place was going to become a remand prison and would no longer be used for sentenced prisoners. The next day, a hundred women were shipped out. In Venezuela, major changes such as this one seemed to happen with little or no warning.

Mary and I were absolutely mortified that after all our efforts to get there, we were being moved. We had been there for three months, just long enough for me to recover from my crack smoking, and I was getting used to not being with the guys. We felt like hopeless pawns that could be picked up and dropped depending on the whim of the powers that be in the prison system.

I realised that INOF was the place in which I had finally started to grow up. My thoughts now were of living my life as a responsible adult, going back to England and getting a job. I fixed all my hopes on getting employment and convinced myself that everything in my life would fall into place if I could just do an honest day's work.

'We may as well go back to San Antonio,' we said to each other despairingly. 'All the other places sound awful. At least we know what to expect there.'

We went to the office and asked if we could do this.

'Yes, you can go back if you can pay for it,' said one of the guards.

But it never happened. The next day, Mary and I were told that we were being transferred to two places in different parts of the country. '*Translado*' was the abrupt way the news was delivered to us.

Mary and I hugged each other and promised that we'd stay in touch.

I was told that I was going to a place a long way away, a prison called San Juan, close to San Juan de Lagunillas village in Mérida, and not too far from the border with Colombia.

12 THE MOST BEAUTIFUL MOUNTAIN

'Hello, Nikita. I want you to know that I love you very much and that because I can't see you, I am sad. I hope you are being a good girl for Eve, and I hope you're happy. I'm sorry I've made you sad. Please don't stop loving me. I think of you every day and will do until I see you again.'

Letter from Natalie to Nikita, October 2002

Fifteen of us were led out onto the prison coach. When I'd first arrived at INOF, I had hated it, but now that I'd got used to it, I didn't want to leave to be hauled across the country like a parcel. I assumed that San Juan Mérida would be like San Antonio and panicked that I wouldn't be able to communicate with my mum as easily as I'd been able to at INOF. Since her cancer had been diagnosed, we'd become even closer. Every day, I told myself what an idiot I'd been to end up where I was, as I now knew what the important things in life were – to be with my mum while she was sick, and to bring up Nikita. Prison strips away all the trappings and leaves the true essentials exposed.

The journey took all day and most of the night. When we arrived in the early hours of the morning and peered, bleary-eyed, out of the coach window, the sight that greeted us was extraordinary. There was a milky mist hanging over everything, the kind you sometimes see just before the sun comes up. It made everything look magical.

The prison was on top of a mountain, and I couldn't see it properly because of the dim light. For just a few moments before it came into view, I pretended that we were approaching an enchanted castle. As the rising sun began to burn away the mist, the view took my breath away. The mountains were vast and calm, and their darkness was illuminated by the pink dawn light. The bus chugged up the steep, winding road sounding as if the engine was on its last legs. At first, all I could see was the entrance to the prison and a big field. The layout looked like that of San Antonio.

Although we'd been cooped up on the coach for so many hours, we were left sitting in our seats for another hour and a half at the entrance to the prison because *numero* was under way and we weren't allowed in until it was completed. I could see various guard posts towering over the fence, which was topped with a menacing lace of razor wire.

We watched as the internal gates were opened for the prisoners to come out of their rooms. Then I saw a bizarre sight: six or seven girls climbed onto a big wall close to the perimeter fence. More and more women joined them, hoisting themselves onto this high wall in one agile movement. They started waving their arms around in the same expansive gestures I'd seen at INOF.

From our position in the coach, I couldn't see that they were communicating with the men on the opposite side of the prison and thought the girls were involved in some strange cult. Later, I realised that what they were doing was saying good morning to their boyfriends and asking them to send over some breakfast.

We walked in and I got a better view of the huge wall that everyone referred to as *el muro*. Because I'd spent so many months entirely in the company of female guards and prisoners, I'd almost forgotten what men looked like. The first ones I set eyes on didn't particularly endear me to the species. They looked poor and rough, and I guessed that they were the crack users who had to work for the other prisoners to get money for their drugs.

One of the guards explained that we weren't allowed to mix freely with the men – that was why the women chatted to their boyfriends in sign language.

When we were led towards the *anexo*, I began to get a sense of just how big the prison was. The place looked like a self-contained town, with tarmac roads complete with cars driving up and down them.

To my relief, we weren't searched, although I was told later that it depended on the whim of the guards whether we had to remove our clothes and empty our bags.

The *anexo* looked tiny and boring after all the facilities I'd enjoyed at INOF. It wasn't even a hundred metres square.

Inside, the facilities were pretty much the same as at San Antonio. Our rooms ran along the perimeter of a courtyard. There were two single rooms that were often used by the guards to punish people. The others were much larger and about twenty women shared a bunk-bedded room with a shower and toilet attached. Some of the women had hung makeshift curtains over their beds to provide them with some privacy. Others had two-ringed cookers next to their beds, with a small area to prepare food. One of the prisoners explained that the women had the freedom to make what they wanted of the living space without interference from the guards.

Some of the women I'd arrived with had friends there and had moved into their rooms. But I knew no one. I felt lonely as I looked at the other women chattering to each other. I couldn't think of anything to say to anyone, so tried to find myself a place to sleep.

I thought about my comfortable room in INOF and longed to go back there. One of the women led me to a room that was sparsely decorated and gestured to a mattress on the floor. 'Sleep there for now,' she said.

Here we go again, I said to myself. *Back to the bottom of the food chain.* This room was nowhere near as nice as the other ones I'd seen with all their homely touches. I sat down on the bare mattress and hugged my legs to my chest.

'There are two public phones outside the *anexo*. They work most of the time and we can use them whenever we want,' said the woman to cheer me up a bit. I sighed with relief and thought, *At least I can phone home.*

I cheered up a bit more when I stepped out of the *anexo*. The courtyard around which the women's quarters were grouped had an ordinary-looking door in one corner. When I opened the door, I couldn't believe it: I saw a huge green space stretching out in front of me. This was the only way you could get to *el muro*, and from there you could see the outside of the prison and put your hands through the fence.

The top level was just grass. Down a flight of concrete steps there was more grass and a plant that, I later discovered, some of the women made into a tea to bring down the temperature of people who had a fever. And there was a netball court, too. I christened the place the secret garden, because it was such an unexpected thing to find. Most people spent a lot of their time out there even though there was no shelter or shade. I breathed a sigh of relief to be out in a large open space, but because I hardly knew anyone, I felt like an outsider. I found myself walking around in circles not knowing what to do with myself.

I was desperate to speak to my mum and find out if her treatment was working, but I had absolutely no money and no means of earning any. She had asked me not to make so many reverse-charge calls, because now that she wasn't working, money was tight. There was no Internet access at San Juan, so I was stuck. We always spoke on Christmas Day, which was several weeks away, and I told myself I'd just have to wait until then to talk to her. I prayed that a miracle had happened, and that she was in remission. I simply couldn't cope with the idea of her not being OK.

There were great big tanks in the courtyard area where women showered and did their washing. One of the women told me glumly that the water got cut off every single day. I soon discovered that whatever time of day I chose to have a shower would be the time at which the water would suddenly go off, usually when my hair was full of shampoo. As a result, there was always a clamour to have a shower and fill buckets when the water did come back on.

It was possible to manage a day or two without water, but by the third day we all got desperate. The men found ways of getting water and sometimes they sent some over to us. I never found out why the water kept going off. I don't know if it was because we were on a mountain or because the guards turned it off deliberately and were in no hurry to turn it back on.

On my first night in San Juan, the room I was locked in was full of girls who were all smoking crack. I could hear the drug's distinctive cracking sound through the darkness. I desperately missed Mary and felt miserable. The smell of the drug was so strong that I was tempted to break my pact with God and ask one of the girls if I could share her pipe. It was extremely hard to resist the stuff, but I'd made my deal and I was determined to stick to it. I cried myself to sleep, feeling more desolate than I'd felt for a long time.

For weeks, I hated everything about San Juan. I tried to pass the first couple of weeks by sleeping for as many hours as I could manage. I was depressed. I had no money, no friends and was reduced to eating scraps the other women had left, as I had done in the police cell.

It was a case of eating whatever I could get in order to survive. To keep me going, I chewed on spoonfuls of powdered milk. It stuck together in a lump in my mouth, yet at the same time was slightly crunchy. It didn't taste too bad and it staved off a few hunger pangs. I longed for something substantial to munch on, like a burger, and couldn't see how I was going to get through another eight and a half years of this miserable half-life.

All the guards on the women's side were female, but the male guards came over all the time. Some of the male guards were going out with the female guards, and the women's quarters were a good place for a rendezvous. Unlike at INOF, there was little discipline amongst the guards, and the laid-back attitude had much more in common with that of San Antonio.

In those early weeks when I was at a loss at San Juan, I tried to pick up as much information as I could about how the prison worked. The fact that I could now speak fluent Spanish helped enormously. If there was something I wanted to know more about, I asked one of the Venezuelan girls or one of the guards.

We weren't allowed to go over to the men's side whenever we wanted to, although I heard that sometimes the women were escorted over there by the guards for joint activities such as basketball games. Occasionally, the men came over to our side, but when I finally did get over to the men's side, I realised it was much more fun there than having the men come over to us, because they had so many more facilities.

The prison was divided into four pavilions – long huts with their own grounds. Each pavilion had basketball courts and workshops. Guards would be told which pavilion they were assigned to on the day and would work there for the duration of their shift. All the prisoners sat around drinking, listening to music and smoking weed.

A kind of class system operated. It was sexist, and a woman's status was determined by how young and attractive she was. The men sent their washing over to the *anexo* for the women to do, and the women also cooked for them.

One girl had come from a poor family, but she was pretty and had a powerful boyfriend. Her destiny was neither to cook nor wash for a man. Her boyfriend gave her money to pay someone in the *anexo* to do her washing, or she sent her washing to him and he paid someone on his side to do it.

While youth and beauty were the most valuable currency a woman could have, for the men money and power held the greatest sway. However, the men with money and power also seemed to be the most attractive ones.

The poor men were those with drug problems. Many people using crack for any significant length of time develop a distinctive sunken, ugly look, with damaged or missing teeth. The drug addicts, both male and female, were the ones who worked for the other prisoners. There were more prisoners addicted to crack than those free of the drug's vice-like grip – perhaps 70 per cent of the men and about 10 per cent of the women. There were no treatment or rehabilitation programmes, and the prison guards showed no interest in helping people get off drugs.

I discovered that some of the guys had wives outside, but that the girls in the *anexo* who were having relationships with them didn't know that. There was an understanding amongst the prisoners that those who knew about the marital status of some of the men kept the information to themselves. The female guards could say what they wanted about prison relationships, but if a male guard said to a female prisoner that her boyfriend had another girlfriend, he would be shot. It was simply against the unspoken rules to make that sort of comment. Sometimes, it was just too complicated to have a boyfriend if you weren't prepared to be totally and utterly devoted to him.

The women occasionally talked about the crimes they'd committed, but for the men this was a taboo subject. It was considered bad manners to broach indelicate subjects like how many kilos of cocaine you'd stashed away in a container or orifice.

The male prisoners who had been powerful on the street were the same ones who were powerful on the inside. Sometimes there were power struggles between different male prisoners, or different groups of male prisoners. But these matters were kept from the women even more than they had been in San Antonio.

People got killed on the men's side regularly, but we never saw it. And thankfully, unlike in San Antonio, we were never caught in the crossfire. Sometimes husbands and wives came to prison together. There were a few incidents where the husbands got shot in prison, leaving their wives distraught and alone.

Often, the shootings were over unpaid drug debts. The targets had a warning before they were killed. The first would be a shot in a non-life-threatening part of the body, such as a kneecap. If that warning was ignored, a fatal shot would be fired.

Rapists and paedophiles received no such warnings. They were unlikely to survive for more than a couple of days once they'd been sentenced and dispatched to jail. They were told to say their final goodbye to their families at the court, because everyone knew they wouldn't survive in prison. There is no formal death penalty in Venezuela, but this is how it worked informally.

The guards went to every *prang* on every pavilion and alerted them to the fact that a paedophile was on his way. As soon as he arrived, the prisoners would get to work persuading him to kill himself. They'd torture the guy first and then they would often make him hang himself. They'd help him to take his life by tying a noose round his neck and would make him jump off a chair. We never witnessed these enforced suicides but heard many shocked and reverential whispers about the fate of such men.

One paedophile arrived and was gunned down as soon as he walked into the men's area. I was shocked to find out that this was how justice was done in San Juan. In INOF, all the prisoners were women and in San Antonio I had never heard of a convicted paedophile being sent there. This form of justice meted out by the prisoners was new to me.

The judges who sentence sex offenders know what will happen, the police know, and the guards know. This alternative death sentence appears to be acceptable to all of them. The Venezuelan logic is simple: rapists and paedophiles come in, they're tortured and then they die. That's it. It's not a matter that is ever discussed. When someone got killed in a drugs row, everyone talked about it, yet when it came to sex offenders, nobody said a word. Swift and silent justice was delivered and then the prison moved on with its daily routine, as if the man had never existed.

For the couples who managed to survive the prison regime, there was something called *camera*, which allowed husbands and wives to be together to have sex. It was given once a week, on Mondays, in two shifts – one in the morning and one in the afternoon. There was even a special building for these amorous meetings. During the rest of the week, prisoners could book sessions with partners who lived outside the prison.

Women weren't allowed to have visitors in their rooms on visiting day, but the male prisoners could have female visitors in their rooms. The women went down there to meet their husbands with a bag containing food and music. But not just anybody could get *camera*. It depended on what the prison director at the time was like. For a long time, the rule was that you had to have been with your partner on the outside and there had to be proof that you had previously been cohabiting or you had to be married. If couples met in prison and got married, then they could have *camera*.

Whenever there was any trouble in the prison, we'd be locked in, although we would have no idea what was going on. Sometimes, the male prisoners phoned the women and told them who'd been shot.

The national guard did big searches over the whole prison. These would go on for the whole day and they ransacked the places where we stored all our belongings. The internal guards did three day-on, three day-off shifts and slept in the prison. They did the smaller searches. To my enormous relief, there were no prisoners on the roof with guns, and no big wars going on like there had been in San Antonio.

There was conflict sometimes, though. At those times, the *prangs* would get called down to the office and asked what was going on. They were quite wise and sensible, and they would negotiate with the aggrieved parties and come up with a solution that was acceptable to all. The *prangs* were generally well liked and respected by the prisoners. When I looked back at San Antonio, it seemed like a zoo in comparison.

One day, the *prang* from number one pavilion had a hospital appointment to go to. His enemies on the outside must have been tipped off about it because they were waiting for him. He was shot and killed while handcuffed to the guard.

I'd never seen this before, but the collective grief among the prisoners was so great that he was carried around the prison in an open casket so that everyone could pay their respects. The *prang* from number two pavilion organised this and paid the director to allow it to happen. I wondered what he had done to land him in jail, because he struck me as a decent person from the little I knew of him.

The *prangs* at San Juan seemed to be correct and they tried to find pragmatic solutions to problems. They had a clearly defined code of conduct: right was right and wrong was wrong. And they seemed fair about most things. Prisoners didn't get killed without reason; they were given ample warning. There were no written rules, but everybody knew the correct way to behave. At San Juan, I realised that I was gaining a lot more understanding of what was going on than I'd had at San Antonio. It was almost as if San Antonio was preparing me for San Juan.

After a couple of weeks, we were told that we could go over to the men's side. It had been explained to me that the best pavilions were one and two – nobody was interested in three or four.

One and two were the best pavilions because of the way the *prangs* maintained them. They had money and spent it on making conditions better for everyone. Two was the favoured pavilion, then one, followed by three. Four was the worst and it was always messy and filthy. Two was tidy and clean, and the men there held the best events and treated the women well, making sure there were seats for us to sit on and food to eat. The director had to be paid by the *prang* to let us go over there and take part in organised games.

As we walked over to the men's side, I realised it was the first time I'd get to see the rest of the prison. In the last few days, I'd started to take more interest in what was going on around me.

We passed the main kitchen; it wasn't a place where I could ever imagine cooking a meal. There was a concrete block of a table, which reminded me of the slab on which carcasses are chopped up in an abattoir. It seemed more like an outdoor fruit and vegetable market than a prison kitchen. There were hundreds of flies buzzing around the food, but no cats or dogs.

Perhaps the place was too remote for them to reach. The kitchen had its own yard and you could see into the kitchen as you walked past the yard. I got a different view of the prison now that we were on walkabout and saw just how big it really was. I'd been up on the wall a couple of times and had seen the men talking in sign language, but now for the first time I was seeing everything close-up and from a different angle.

I was surprised at how long the road was. There were the four pavilions, the *anexo* and the offices. Then there was a small hospital that had its own fence around it with a gate, and there was an *educativa*. It contained a school where you could enrol for various classes and a large hall where activities like aerobics and singing took place. One of the women explained to me that various kinds of presentations were also held there. It was in the *educativa* that female prisoners sometimes tried to have sex with their boyfriends, although apparently nobody ever got away with it.

There was also a Catholic church and women sometimes tried to have sex with their boyfriends in one of the back rooms there. If the female guards caught a woman trying to have sex, they told everyone what she'd been doing to try to shame her. I started to get to know the two shifts of guards in the *anexo*; one shift was popular with the women and the other one wasn't.

When we reached the men's side, I was amazed by how many men there were – at least a thousand. I went over to the men's side with Vivi, the girl I knew from INOF. We hadn't been particularly friendly there, but now we had become close. She introduced me to a *paisano* – a person from my own country.

The man was black, and I don't think he was English, although he said he was. He hung around with the black Dutch guys and seemed to be a serious person. I imagined he had played a role a bit like Tony's in the drug-smuggling hierarchy. Later, he helped me out with money if I needed it and never expected anything in return.

Most of the prisoners seemed to be drug users or gang members. There were also hijackers in there, especially lorry jackers. They watched the main routes and knew which lorries to target.

I was introduced to a lot of Americans and I attracted a lot of attention from the Venezuelan guys. By now, I knew how I could use the appeal of my blonde hair and blue eyes to my advantage. Various men ordered drinks and burgers to be brought over to me. The burgers were the first decent food I'd eaten since I'd arrived, and I wolfed them down greedily. They tasted fantastic.

That evening, when we returned to the *anexo*, I had lots of notes sent over to me saying, 'Oh, you have such beautiful eyes, I can help you if you need anything.' A lot of them were love letters, some from people who hadn't even spoken to me. If a real boyfriend had written something so romantic, I would have been choked up, but coming from total strangers, one after another, they were meaningless. However, the attention I received was a great ego boost. I no longer wanted to sleep the days away, and from that moment on things changed for me in San Juan.

13 TWO DEATHS AND A SHOP

'I'm writing to you because my mum is ill. She has been diagnosed with cancer. I wanted to find out if there is any way I can be sent home on compassionate grounds. I know that England is close to signing a repatriation agreement with Venezuela. I wondered if you could tell me how far into the process they are. I hope that you can do something to help me. I really want to see my mum.'
Letter from Natalie to Prisoners Abroad, November 2002

The love letters kept on coming. A *moto* – a courier who could go wherever he wanted – ferried them across the prison to me.

Reading the declarations of undying love made me smile and took my mind off the tedium of prison life.

After a few weeks, I'd managed to move up the food chain and had got myself into a crack-free room with a bed in it. I met the British consul and he gave me some money my mum had sent. I went back to bed after *numero* the day after we'd visited the men's quarters for the first time, but was shaken awake by one of the girls, who told me I was being called to *el muro*.

'One of the guys says he wants to say, "Good morning" to you and to know if you have received the breakfast he sent over with the *moto*,' she said.

Sleepily, I climbed out of bed and hurried to the wall. One of the girls on *el muro* gesticulating wildly spoke back in sign language for me. It was fun and clever. At various points through the day, I kept on getting called to *el muro*. If you didn't get called there, it meant you weren't popular.

Monica, a girl I knew from INOF, was an aerobics instructor, and so were a couple of the guys. 'Why don't you come along and give my class a try?' she said a few weeks after I arrived.

Feeling generally more positive towards the place, I agreed to go. It was better than lying aimlessly on my bed, counting down the years and months and weeks and days and hours of the remainder of my sentence. She led me through a door in a fence to get into the big hall where the class was taking place.

If a woman's husband was living outside the prison there was an unwritten rule that she wouldn't get involved in the prison activities in case she fell for another guy, even in something as innocent as an aerobics class. This purdah was a sign of respect for her husband. I thought this was unfair on the married women and that it condemned them to an extremely dull life. Of course, no such restriction applied to the men who had wives waiting outside. Even when they had affairs, no sanctions were applied to them.

Some of the male prisoners brought a powerful stereo down to the aerobics session. It had been donated by Che, the *prang* of number two pavilion. We knew it had to be looked after and that Che was doing us a favour by loaning it for the exercise session. The routine was simple, but it was also tough. I found the whole thing exhilarating, and although I was worn out when we'd finished, I also felt energised.

Monica said that after the aerobics session, if the shift of female guards we liked were on duty, we would be allowed to stay in the hall for a little while. But the other shift of guards would usher us back to the *anexo* at top speed. It was almost as if they enjoyed making us miserable. It was uncalled for to deny us a few minutes of social contact with the male prisoners, but as far as these guards were concerned, their policy of removing us quickly was non-negotiable.

I settled into the swing of things quickly after my first aerobics class. I enrolled in the school – the set-up seemed like a high school – and studied Spanish, English and General Studies.

It was as much to get out of the *anexo* as to get myself lots of qualifications. I was keen to visit the men's side whenever we could because there were so many things to do there: playing chess or dining in the amazing restaurant that served great burgers, fried chicken and rice. Fresh food was brought in on the bus that came to the prison to collect the prisoners who were on day release. The prison was the end of the line for the bus as well as for us.

There were big workshops on the men's side where wooden furniture was made. They carved beds with beautiful, intricate designs on them and visitors could order a range of furniture.

I was envious of the amount of freedom the men had compared with us. The important men like the *prangs* walked around surrounded by their people – armed bodyguards. A *prang* would never leave his pavilion with fewer than ten bodyguards. The bodyguards hid their guns, but everyone knew they were armed.

Sometimes, if a *prang* was leaving his pavilion to talk about something important, there would be a crowd of more than sixty people around him. It was an extraordinary sight to see this huge convoy of men who could walk wherever they wanted to within the prison. If there was an organised event on the women's side, anyone could come over, but sometimes Che also came over to discuss things that needed to be done. For example, if any repairs were required, he would assess the problem and then send his men over to fix it.

Che had a girlfriend who he had met in prison. She carried on seeing him when she got out, then she ended up back in prison. On her return to prison, she was treated like a princess. Che sent her over a great bed, a new TV and the best food. She only stayed in prison for a couple of weeks because he got her one of the best lawyers in Mérida.

Che was heartbroken because quite soon after her release, she went off with another man. She had to leave the state because otherwise she and her new man would have been killed on Che's orders.

On Sundays, couples were granted *entrevista*, which literally means interview, but in prison meant kissing and cuddling time. It took place in the main offices and lasted for an hour. Girlfriends and boyfriends tried to get away with going further than just kissing and cuddling, behaviour that became a battleground between us and the female guards. The question always was, would we or the guards win the groping wars?

On *el muro*, couples discussed what they'd bring to *entrevista*. Unlike the women, the guys didn't get searched and they brought along a hot, fiery home brew. Even in the bottle, the alcohol was so potent it felt as if it was burning the glass. I don't know what it was, but I was told it had been distilled in a long and painstaking process.

Sometimes, to pass the long, hot days, the women created a makeshift canopy out of sticks and sheets, and spent all day chatting in sign language under the sheets to the men. Like handwriting, this form of communication was personalised. I hadn't learnt sign language in INOF, because there hadn't really been any pressing need to do so, but here the other girls taught me how to do it. You had to be able to write Spanish to use it. I got the odd word wrong, but I picked the secret language up quickly and, to my delight, found that I could make myself understood quite easily. Better still, the guards didn't understand the sign language.

On Christmas Day 2002, we were served traditional Venezuelan food. It was vile: some unidentifiable meat that looked like dog food, mixed with raisins, wrapped in leaves and cooked in the oven. Decorations were put up and there were special programmes on TV, heavily featuring Chávez. I was homesick thinking about Christmas at home. I desperately missed Nikita and tried to get a picture in my head of her excitedly opening her Christmas presents. The previous year, my mum had bought Nikita a teddy bear from me for Christmas, but this year she was far too ill.

I'd gone a couple of months without speaking to my mum, as I didn't have much money to call her, nor Internet access. I was worried about her, but as usual tried to push my anxieties to the back of my mind, hoping for the best.

I always phoned home on birthdays and Christmas – my mum and I shared the same birthday. As I chewed on the inedible lunch, I tried not to think about how ill my mum was. I still hadn't really grasped the fact that she was dying and was deluding myself that doctors had found a miracle cure for her.

I dialled my mum's number nervously, praying that I'd hear her cheerful voice on the other end of the line. This was the first time I'd spoken to her since I'd arrived at San Juan and I was totally unprepared for the voice that greeted me. She had obviously deteriorated dramatically. Her voice was so faint and feeble I could barely hear her. She seemed to lack the energy even to open her mouth.

'I'm going to die soon, Natalie,' she whispered. Tears pricked my eyes, but I tried my best to hold them back. I'd never heard anyone sound so exhausted just from talking. I was too shocked to take in just how bad things obviously were. I tried my best to compose myself, wondering if this would be the last time I'd be able to say some of the things I badly wanted her to know. I took a deep breath and said as calmly as I could, 'I'm going to be OK, Mum. Whatever happens, don't worry about me. I'm going to get through this and when I come out, I'm going to be everything that you want me to be. I'm going to be a different person, a daughter you can be proud of. You can die in peace. I promise that when I come home, I'll sort myself out and get a job and leave all the bad things behind me forever.'

She didn't have the energy to say anything more, but I sensed that my words had somehow soothed her. Then Alan came on the phone.

'She can't talk any more. Her whole day's energy has been used up.' He sounded upset but didn't cry then. I think he was forcing himself to be strong in front of Mum. I felt totally numb. It was hard to accept that she was dying when I hadn't even seen her looking ill. When she came to visit me in San Antonio, she was well and looked the same as she'd always looked.

When I put the phone down, I couldn't stop sobbing. All I wanted at that moment was to be with my mum, to look her in the face and tell her how sorry I was for all the grief and worry I'd caused her. I was sure that if I could just see her, I would be able to prove to her how much I'd changed and how determined I was to make a new start once I got back to England.

The consul wasn't due, but he visited me a couple of weeks after I'd spoken to my mum. It took me about ten seconds to realise why he was there. For the first five, I was delighted to see him and thought he had good news for me about the extradition treaty between the UK and Venezuela finally being signed. Then I realised why he had come.

'I haven't got good news for you, Natalie,' he said quietly. He didn't have to say that Mum had died. I just knew. I sat down in the *anexo* reception and started wailing. He gave me a bag of stuff including some magazines, shook me awkwardly by the hand and left.

Apparently, my mum had died on Boxing Day, the day after I had spoken to her. I like to think that she was waiting for me to call and was relieved that I'd been able to reassure her that I'd turned over a new leaf.

News got around that I was sitting in the reception area crying, so most people left me alone, although a couple of people tried to find out what had happened and to comfort me. I phoned Alan and both of us cried down the phone. I got more information from my brother and sister about the circumstances of her death. My brother was just twelve and my sister was fourteen. My heart reached out to them across the continents. I really cried for them and wondered how they were going to manage without their mum at such a young age.

I spent a long time grieving. People say that the loss of a loved one is sometimes harder if the relationship hasn't been good. I wished that we could have got along better, that we'd understood each other more before it was too late and that I could have reconciled with her face to face before she died.

The second night, after I'd been given the news, the girls I shared a room with said that I'd been crying in my sleep. I had no recollection of it but knew that my grief ran deep. The only shred of comfort I had was that I'd managed to have that final conversation with Mum.

Sometimes, I'm relieved I didn't see my mum suffering, but often I feel I should have been there. I felt a jumble of emotions every time I thought about her. I knew I'd let her down with my wild ways and wished I'd been a bit wiser and less headstrong during my teenage years.

In San Juan, everyone carried on with their daily lives and I didn't talk about Mum's death much. I tried to push my grief to one side just so that I could get through the long, dull days in prison. At that point, we weren't going over to the men's side much. We were stuck in the *anexo*, it was difficult to be distracted and I was bored.

On a practical level, life became difficult for me after my mum's death. She had taken care of money left to me by my gran and sent regular instalments out to me. But after she'd gone, it was difficult to get Alan to pass the cash on. I received no news from home and so I didn't realise that family and friends of Mum and friends of mine were trying to get hold of me to give me their condolences. I could have got so much comfort from their letters, but instead I was left to deal with the loss alone. As the weeks and months passed, I gradually began to adjust. Thinking about her became more of a dull ache than a sharp pain, and I tried to get on with surviving prison life.

I was standing on the wall one day when I 'met' Leo. We began chatting regularly in sign language. He was tall and good-looking, but what appealed to me most was that he seemed different from the other Venezuelan men, more intelligent and less brash. He explained that he had come over from a jail in Panama – his dad had paid a lot of money for him to be repatriated to Venezuela.

And, to my delight, he didn't come out with the usual platitudes about the colour of my eyes.

When the women were finally allowed to go over to the men's side, I began chatting to him face to face. Our friendship developed gradually and one day he said, 'Why don't you come to *gaita*, Venezuelan folk songs practice?'

I can't sing and you must be able to pronounce the words clearly, but I went along anyway. Four girls and four guys formed a group. We had to practise rigorously and were expected to go to other prisons to perform. The rehearsals were building up towards a *gaita* competition with teams from other prisons. There was going to be a presentation to the judges at the competition and a TV station was going to come along and film it all. Other prisoners in San Juan got to hear about us practising and came to watch us. I loved the singing; it lifted my spirits and took my mind off my mum for a while.

'It's the strangest thing we've ever seen, a European taking part in *gaita*,' the Venezuelan prisoners remarked.

There were dance moves as well as the singing to get right and it was complicated. Leo was always by my side, guiding and encouraging me, and without him to navigate, I would have been completely lost.

Things continued to develop at a slow and natural pace between us and after a while I agreed to become Leo's girlfriend. We became a popular couple. I was apparently classed as attractive and he was one of the best-looking guys in the prison. He also had money. When it was time for *camera*, I assumed Leo and I wouldn't be eligible for it because I'd been told it wasn't available to foreigners. However, he told me he was working on a way round the ban and that all I needed to do was keep my mouth shut. I assumed that 'working on a way' meant handing over substantial sums of money to certain prison guards.

'When the other women in the *anexo* get ready to go to *camera*, just follow them. Wait until the gates open and then run out,' he advised.

I waited nervously in my room. Then one of the female prisoners told me that the gates had opened, and I obediently raced out. The female guards tried to stop me, but the male guards said, 'No, she's on the list, she can go.' It made me feel important.

Camera took place in a series of small rooms in the *educativa*. Leo had made everything as romantic as possible and had got hold of nice sheets and flowers. He had paid extra money to the guards, so we had the whole day together.

I liked him but I didn't harbour any burning desire for him. The experience of *camera* made me feel like I was a chicken on a battery farm. While we were making love, all I could think about was that a row of couples in the rooms along the corridor were doing the same thing.

When I got back to the *anexo*, the other girls were furious that I'd received a special privilege and they complained bitterly to the guards about it. After that, everybody who wanted *camera* could have it. Soon, Leo got out of prison. It was obvious he would because his father was rich and well-connected. I felt a bit lost without him.

'Please don't go over to the men's side when I'm gone,' he begged me. 'I promise you, I'm going to stay in contact and come and visit you.' I agreed and didn't go over for a while. But Leo was really asking a lot of me. As in San Antonio, the men's side was a thousand times better than the women's. Leo didn't keep to his side of the bargain. He didn't call me for nine days after he was released.

After three or four weeks of not having a phone call and not having a visit, I got fed up of playing the obedient girlfriend role and went back to visiting the men's side.

My career as a *gaita* singer also ended abruptly after Leo had been released from jail. I was way out of my depth doing *gaita*. Previously, Leo had always been by my side whispering words of encouragement and guiding me. Without him there, I panicked before performances. Stupidly, I decided to get drunk to calm my nerves before one performance and as a result completely messed things up. This, of course, went down badly and I was unceremoniously booted out of the group.

Almost a year after I arrived at San Juan, two of the foreign prisoners escaped. We had all been locked in for the night. A guard somewhere had obviously been paid and suddenly the electricity went off. The girls started screaming, 'Put the lights on! Put the lights on!'

Then we heard gunshots and shouting. We knew it was the national guard shouting from outside the perimeter fence. After about half an hour, the lights came back on again. We heard in the morning that two prisoners – one French and one South African – had escaped. I felt proud that it was foreigners who'd made a run for it. But they were found in the village the next day and were brought back.

They were beaten by the guards once they were back inside the prison. They knew the risk they were running by escaping, but I felt sorry that they were punished so severely. Their faces had been pummelled so badly that they were unrecognisable, and they spent weeks in the prison hospital recovering. My heart went out to them when I saw their injuries.

There were a few shoot-outs at San Juan but no wars that went on for days the way they had in San Antonio. I was pretty much in the dark about what was going on in terms of gang allegiances and grievances on the men's side, and I was quite happy not to know all the ins and outs.

About a year after I arrived in San Juan, a great-aunt of mine died and the executor, a woman called Shona who was a distant cousin, got in touch with me via the British Embassy. I used to see my great-aunt regularly as a child and was sad that she had died. Shona asked me what I wanted to do with my inheritance. We communicated by phone, letter and messages passed to and fro by embassy officials. I wasn't sure what to do with the money, but eventually decided that I wanted to invest it and see a return on my investment.

In the *anexo* was a disused Portakabin and I suddenly got the idea to turn it into a shop. All the male pavilions had shops but there had never been one in the *anexo*. It wasn't something that interested the female prisoners. If they had money, they spent it on getting a good solicitor to get them out on benefit. It was easier for a solicitor to get a prisoner released before sentence. After a prisoner was sentenced, it was almost impossible to get released by paying off officials, however good the prisoner's solicitor was.

I went to the main offices in the hope of seeing the director of the prison and persuading him to let me open a shop. Standing in the secret garden on the higher level, I shouted to the *moto* to ask if the director was there. Fortunately, the director seemed to like me, and I hoped that he'd agree to have a meeting with me.

'Yes,' replied the *moto*.

'Can you ask him to send for me please?'

The *moto* nodded and a letter was duly brought up to me, asking me to go down and see him.

He was a harsh and abrupt man but there seemed to be a few chinks in his tough exterior. He was broad, around six feet tall, with a voice so deep and strong you could almost hear the floor vibrating when he spoke. With his thick and bristly moustache, he oozed authority, and everyone feared him. I always felt nervous around him.

'Ah, Natalie, my blue-eyed doll,' he said, when I walked into his office. 'What can I do for you?'

I took a deep breath and decided to get straight to the point. 'I'd like to open a shop in the *anexo* in the old Portakabin.'

'I know you're going to apply for day release soon. As a foreigner, why do you want to get so involved with the life of the prison?'

'The *anexo* needs it. I want to do something where I've got regular money coming in. I also want to do something for the women.'

He rocked backwards on his chair, scratched his chin and couldn't seem to think of any reason not to allow me to open a shop.

'OK, what do you need? Is there a fridge in there?'

I beamed. I couldn't believe he'd agreed so easily, and had thought that I might have to spend a long time convincing him. 'No, I'll have to buy one.'

'No need. I'm going to donate a fridge to the *anexo*,' he said. 'It will be good for the women.'

I was overjoyed. It would have been impossible to have the shop without the fridge. People wanted to buy cold drinks more than anything else. 'Could you let the staff know so they'll cooperate?' I asked.

He agreed to do this and my first enterprise behind bars was under way. I felt a thrill of excitement. I'd got the green light to set up my first-ever legitimate business. It would be good for me, but I also genuinely wanted to provide something useful for the women. There was a man who ran a cash and carry-type shop just outside the prison and the director said he would give the man permission to come in to bring me supplies.

I bought some strips of metal and had them welded across the hatch I planned to serve behind so there was plenty of room to pass goods through, but not enough space for someone to jump over the counter and steal things. The director had the fridge delivered the next day: I suddenly heard my name being shouted and saw some delivery men wheeling a fridge over to me. I was amazed by how quickly the whole thing was taking shape.

One of the first things I did was send out to buy a padlock and keys for the fridge. I didn't broadcast what I was doing because some of the prisoners were envious about this kind of thing. My embassy brought me the first five hundred pounds of the money that had been left to me by my great-aunt and I bought my first lot of stock: sugar, coffee, powdered milk, different flours and tuna. I also ordered lots of sweets, the equivalent of penny sweets, and chocolates. A few of the women had children living with them in San Juan and I knew they'd love them.

Visiting day was the most profitable day of the week. Relatives bought things to give to the prisoners and I allowed some people credit, depending on how trustworthy they were. Relatives brought in money for the prisoners and often this was when the women paid off their debts.

The director saw how well the business was going and sometimes came over for a drink. 'Well done, Natalie, you've really worked hard and made a go at this,' he said. I swelled with pride. It was ironic that my first proper business venture was inside a prison. When some of the prisoners and guards told me I had a good eye for business, I was delighted.

I often used to give the handful of small children who were imprisoned with their mums some of the sweets or chocolates I stocked. I felt sorry for them being stuck in prison and wanted to cheer them up as much as I could.

After a couple of months of successful trading, I asked the director if I could have a landline phone to sell minutes to prisoners. Once again, he agreed. It was unheard of for someone to be allowed to have their own personal landline and having it made me feel important. This addition to the shop was popular. It was rare that I had to go out and pay the full price for phone cards because people sold me their phone cards and I used them to top up my phone.

The next thing I bought was a big stereo for the benefit of all the women in the *anexo*. I loved hearing music. All the male pavilions had stereos, but music wasn't often heard in the *anexo*. I spent the equivalent of £350 on a decent one.

People gave me a lot more respect once I had the shop. It changed my status quite considerably. Most of the time, the stereo was in the shop, but sometimes we took it out into the courtyard and Monica held an aerobics class there. I loved the Venezuelan music but sometimes I played UK chart music like Shaggy's 'It Wasn't Me', which the other girls loved.

Even though everyone was benefiting from the shop and the stereo, I knew that some of the women resented what I was doing.

When it was my birthday, I had lots of the home brew called *miche* sent over from the men's side and a few of us went down on the netball court. Lots of the other women joined us to play an impromptu game of volleyball. It was nice to be doing our own thing, and for once the activity hadn't been organised by the men.

Even though the guards could see we were getting drunk, they left us alone. I felt happy that day.

14 BAD GIRLS

'I have just spoken to the Cross-Border Transfer Section of the Prison Service here in the UK to find out what the latest situation is with the transfer agreement between the UK and Venezuela. The ratification has been put on hold. The UK authorities are not able to say when the transfer treaty is likely to be ratified by the Venezuelans. However, you could start the process by applying for a transfer. It is our understanding that there is no official clemency scheme in the Venezuelan penal system. There is a system of presidential pardon but no one in our experience has applied for this so we do not have details of the process.'
    Letter from Prisoners Abroad official to Natalie

There were prisons in Venezuela for *mala conductas*, inmates who behaved badly. A few months after I arrived at San Juan, a group of girls came to the prison who fitted the definition of *mala conductas*. All of them behaved unpleasantly. One of the chief mischief-makers was a small, scrawny woman called Ingrid. She robbed and snarled and carried out random acts of cruelty. The girls' leader, Becky, decided she was going to appoint herself as female *prang*. This had never happened before because the women organised themselves in a less hierarchical way than the men.

All of us were dismayed to see the arrival of these girls, who destroyed what had previously been a harmonious atmosphere in the *anexo*. Becky had tight, curly hair; she was big-boned and looked hard. Until these girls came, there had been little fighting in the women's quarters. Some of the other female prisoners whispered to me that this group had a reputation throughout the country's prison system. They started terrorising us and stealing stuff discreetly at first, then became more brazen about what they were doing.

They robbed people at knifepoint early in the mornings, targeting anyone who had something they wanted. The attacks were particularly bad after women had visits and had been brought things by their families and friends. They often appeared in a room brandishing a knife, saying menacingly, 'If you don't give me your stuff, I'll stab you. Have you got any money? If we find out later that you've got some and you haven't handed it over, we'll stab you, so either way you lose.'

I was waiting for my turn to be robbed and vowed that I wasn't going to give them any of the things that I'd worked hard for. One morning, I went over to the community centre, and when I got back, they'd broken into my padlocked box and stolen my toiletries. I knew straight away that it was them who had stolen my stuff.

I wasn't in the mood for their bad behaviour and ran into one of their rooms swearing at them in Spanish. I felt low and decided I had nothing to lose. One of the girls was like a monkey, leaping over all the beds to get away from me. In anger, I broke a wooden plank off the bed and started chasing her, brandishing it. She was swinging across the electrical wires and running from bed to bed.

Much to my annoyance, I didn't catch her in the end. My anger was spent, and I threw the plank of wood away. 'Stab me if you want to, I really don't care,' I goaded her. But she never did. The girls continued to steal from us, and the atmosphere became worse and worse.

We were all trying to split the girls up but Becky, the wannabe *prang*, shrugged and said, 'Leave them to fight.' One girl was slashed in the arm and had to be taken to hospital to have it stitched.

'We're going to show you how an *anexo* should be run; it should be the same as on the men's side,' barked Becky.

Becky and China, the woman who was her enforcer, weren't crackheads, but the rest of the girls in their gang were, so their behaviour was quite unpredictable. The girls were split into two different rooms and the rest of us didn't want to go into either of them.

China looked Chinese; she was small with long black hair, athletic and sporty and quite popular, even though she came from the 'bad' crowd.

I received a tip-off from one of the women that the bad crowd were planning to rob my shop. We weren't far away from the shop at the time. I was with Monica and she suddenly went mad at Ingrid.

'I've heard you were planning on robbing the shop. Well, think again. Natalie hasn't done anything to anybody. The shop benefits everyone. She leaves the stereo out so that everyone can use it.

'Natalie doesn't pick on anyone. And she doesn't have family here like the other girls.'

Monica was articulate and was so angry that she burst into tears while she was shouting at them. They got upset because they respected Monica. They looked shamefaced and stood there with their heads bowed.

'Sorry,' they said. Monica commanded a lot of respect in the *anexo*.

One afternoon, all the women went over to an event in pavilion two. When we got back, we didn't notice that a girl called Millie, who wasn't particularly popular but didn't cause any trouble and kept herself to herself, was missing. She hadn't come with us and it wasn't until the next day that one of the girls noticed she'd gone and asked one of the friendly guards what had happened.

The guard looked shocked and distressed, and whispered that she had been raped with a broomstick and ripped open from her vagina to her anus by Becky and Ingrid's gang. Not coming along with us to the event at the pavilion was the worst decision she ever made. All of us were totally appalled by what had happened to her and tensions increased between the bad crowd and the rest of us.

It was so shocking that it took me a while to take in the horror of what I'd been told. I couldn't believe that women could do something so brutal to another woman. I felt absolutely disgusted and was determined to give the *mala conductas* an even wider berth than usual. The poor girl was in hospital for at least four months with female guards taking it in turns to sit with her. They told us, wide-eyed, that she could no longer shit or piss.

The gang weren't punished, perhaps because there was no evidence linking the gang to the crime. Millie was a completely lost soul when she returned and couldn't give evidence against them. It was pitiful to see her shuffling sadly from one side of the room to the other. She would stand there and pee herself and had to be bathed and looked after like a baby. Her eyes were chillingly blank. Nothing registered anymore and perhaps that was a blessing. The gang ignored her and showed not a single shred of remorse. Millie hadn't done anything to them, but the gang had punished her simply because they felt like it and because they could.

I tried to talk to her a few times, but she was gone, totally broken. There was no way of getting through to her. Nobody ever knew exactly how the vile attack had happened. My heart went out to her; she shouldn't have had to suffer like that. What future did she have now?

The men hated the bad crowd, and they never went over to the men's side. The gang were keen to get a transfer to a *mala conductas* prison and did everything they could think of to make this happen, including threatening the director. I couldn't believe that they held so much power and that neither the guards nor the director seemed able or willing to rein them in.

'We're behaving as badly as we possibly can so we can get out of here,' they said. They didn't like San Juan because it was too peaceful.

China continued to work as the gang's enforcer. She went around to many of the women saying, 'If you don't pay the money you owe by such and such a date, I'll stab you.'

There was a girl I owed some phone minutes to. I was waiting for my money to come from the embassy and I told her I'd pay her then. 'I know I owe her some money,' I said irritably to China when she came up to me and threatened me for not repaying my debt. 'Everybody knows that my embassy comes and then I get money and pay back what I owe.'

Things came to a head after China repeatedly bullied a crack-head called Rosanna. If Rosanna got money, she spent it on crack. However, if she got a visit, she didn't sell her stuff for drugs and she didn't really bother anybody. Every time she had a visit, China grabbed her stuff off her. She bullied her when there was no one else around to witness it. Rosanna said nothing but, unbeknown to us, China was making her life complete hell.

In the end, Rosanna got so desperate that she spoke to Oriente, one of the senior men in pavilion two. He went to Che, who gave permission for a hand pistol to be sent over the wall so Rosanna could deal with China, although we didn't discover this until much later. Che didn't usually get involved in women's stuff, but he had heard about these girls going around terrorising people and wanted it to stop.

The following afternoon, I was sitting in a courtyard with a Dutch woman called Marsha. We were sitting in the burning sun with our backs against the wall near the door to the secret garden. A lot of women were at school so there weren't many people around. Suddenly, China came running across the courtyard looking horribly pale and panicked. I'd only ever seen her in total control before and wondered what was going on. Rosanna was running after her.

'No, don't do it!' she screamed at Rosanna.

We looked and were horrified to see that Rosanna had a gun in her hand and was pointing it at China. This was unheard of in the women's section and it could never have happened without Che's permission. China was terrified, and she wasn't embarrassed to beg Rosanna for mercy.

'Please, Rosanna, I promise I'll never disturb you again. Just put that gun down,' she cried. But Rosanna looked as if she hadn't heard her. She had a stubborn, resolute but at the same time scarily blank expression on her face and ran past us. She looked simultaneously frenzied and dazed.

Marsha pleaded with Rosanna, 'Don't do it, Rosanna. Don't do it.'

Rosanna either ignored her or didn't hear. She shot China in the back of the knee with a remarkably steady hand. China fell to the floor. Then Rosanna walked up to her and shot her calmly in the back of the head. She died instantly. It's hard to describe the horror of seeing someone perfectly healthy one minute and lying limp and lifeless on the floor the next. She reminded me of a freshly swatted fly.

The shooting had happened in the secret garden, the peaceful place I loved to sit and think in. Now it would never be the same again. I couldn't believe that a fatal shooting had taken place in the women's section and that I'd witnessed it. This was men's business, not a female way of sorting out problems. I found out later that this was the first time there'd ever been a shooting in the women's section of a jail in Venezuela. It was too much for me. Trembling from head to toe, we went back into the courtyard.

People were always letting off firecrackers and the guards at first thought that that was what the noise was, so they didn't come running out. It took a minute or two for them to realise that China had been shot. Not many people knew that it was Rosanna who had shot her. I said nothing about it: it wasn't my war and I didn't want to be involved in it at all. But someone told the guards China had been gunned down and they raced out to her.

When the guards saw what had happened, they locked us in our rooms. At first, not everyone knew what was going on, but the news quickly spread. There was no feeling of adrenalin following the shooting, just silent shockwaves as if part of us had died, too.

None of us spoke. Then the news got to the men and we could hear them cheering. For them, a shooting was a more routine matter than it was for us women, and they saw it as a perfectly reasonable way to settle scores.

China was unpopular with the men, so none of them were crying any tears for her. Rumour had it that China had been having an affair with Che's ex-girlfriend Marisol, and this was probably one of the reasons why Che had allowed the gun to be given to Rosanna.

The men were drinking, cheering and celebrating – the usual way they marked a shooting. Someone told the guards that Rosanna had killed China and so they put her in a small room at the end of a corridor. They locked the gate to protect her from the other women, who were outraged not so much at the loss of China but at the fact that a woman had breached the prison code by gunning down another woman. They did a search, turned the place upside down and found the gun.

Eventually, we were unlocked at the end of that day. For about a week, we were allowed out of our rooms but were locked in the *anexo* and had no contact whatsoever with the men. The women, still furious, started pouring boiling water onto Rosanna through the window of her cell.

Becky positioned herself by the phone and she wouldn't let anyone use it. Someone called for me, but she wouldn't allow me to go to the phone. She was trying to behave like a male *prang*.

After a killing on the male side, it wasn't talked about, and she wanted things to be run in the same macho way on the women's side, imposing the same sort of information blackout.

'How dare you dictate who I can and can't speak to,' I said. It turned out that the caller was someone from the men's section trying to get information about what had happened. Becky grabbed the phone when she realised.

Eventually, Che came over to the *anexo*, negotiated with Becky and communications were restored. We heard that Rosanna was going to be moved to another prison.

Becky started pleading with the national guard to let her fight Rosanna. 'She's killed someone and she's going to go to another prison without a mark on her. This isn't right,' she barked.

All the women started making various implements. Some carved grooves into broom handles and stuck razor blades into them to poke out through the bars of their room doors at Rosanna.

I felt sorry for Rosanna: she'd been in that room for weeks and looked terrible when she was finally released and walked shakily down the corridor. She looked even scrawnier than usual. Her long, wavy brown hair was matted, her clothes were dirty and she had a dull, hopeless look in her eyes.

As she was walking past the women's rooms, they were poking brooms and other improvised weapons out. Nobody managed to touch her as she kept ducking and darting out of the way. She looked terrified, her brown skin turning a sickly shade of grey in fear.

Her face dropped a mile when she saw Becky standing at the end of the corridor with her arms folded. She reminded me of a coiled snake, waiting to pounce. One of the conditions the guards had insisted on was that Becky could not be armed. Rosanna didn't even try to fight back. She sighed and resigned herself to her fate, trying to defend herself as best she could.

Becky was crying her eyes out because she had loved China and missed her enormously. As she was punching Rosanna, tears were pouring down her face and she was saying, 'This is for China.' I wasn't sure if Becky and China had been having a relationship, but during all the violent punching, there was something strangely moving about tough Becky's love for China.

After a few blows, Rosanna fell to the floor. Becky continued punching her. The national guard let her carry on for a couple of minutes. Then, when blood started to flow, they said, 'That's enough.'

Becky looked disappointed. In her opinion, she'd hardly started. Energy pulsed through her body and she looked as if she could have kept going much longer.

As in many other areas of prison life, there were double standards about acceptable behaviour for men and women. When the men killed someone, nobody got prosecuted, but when a woman did it, she would have been killed in a prison, so she was taken to a police station for her own safety. A bloodied, battered, broken Rosanna was bundled into the prison van and taken away. I never got to know what happened to her after that. Nothing was ever quite the same again in the *anexo*. We women had lost our innocence.

15 TRULY, MADLY, DEEPLY

'I'd like to thank your department for all the support they are giving Eve and Nikita. I have one question. Is there any way it could be arranged for her to have a visit? I'd desperately like to see Nikita, to hold her, to kiss her, to be with her a little while. But I also understand she is happy and content and I don't want to unbalance her stability. If your department could investigate this, I'd be grateful.'

Letter from Natalie to her local social services department in England

I had lost interest in Venezuelan men. Now that I had my shop, I was financially secure and no longer reliant on men to send me over food and toiletries. Unlike the other women, who did what their boyfriends told them, I was free and could go wherever I wanted. I loved my independence. For some reason, I'd never built up any sort of friendship with the male guards the way some of the women had.

But one day, all of that changed. A new group of guards arrived at the prison and one of them stood out straight away. A strange sensation came over me when I looked at him, as if some invisible force was screaming, 'Look at me! Look at me!'

Although I couldn't take my eyes off him, he never once looked in my direction. He was wearing a white shirt and tight black trousers. His uniform showed off his strong, toned body. I was mesmerised by him but never imagined that anything would ever happen between us and suggested to a female guard I liked that he might appeal to her.

A lot of the male guards flirted with the girls, but he was always serious and never did that. I started doing little things to try to catch his attention, like swinging my hips, but it was as if I didn't exist. His indifference baffled me. I was used to men in Venezuelan prisons responding to me if I flirted with them. I was desperate to elicit some sort of reaction from him but how could I do that when he seemed totally unaware that I existed? I really wanted him to do the running but there seemed to be no chance of that. I even memorised his shift pattern and every time I caught a glimpse of him, my heart beat faster.

One day, we were in the *educativa* doing aerobics. Suddenly, I saw him and nudged Monica. 'Oh look, there's that hot guard again,' I whispered to her. He was leaning up against the outside of the *educativa* with his arms crossed, looking in.

Monica was sick and tired of me going on about him. 'I'm so fed up with hearing you talking about him. I'm going to go and tell him you fancy him.'

'No, no, don't do that, I'll die of embarrassment,' I said, taking her by the arm to restrain her. Then, impulsively, before Monica could do anything to sabotage my chances, I rushed up to him, without having thought through what I was going to say. 'Hi,' I said, as casually as I could. My mouth felt as dry as sandpaper.

He looked at me with a serious expression on his face and said nothing. My brain must have shut down at that moment, because before I'd realised it, I blurted out, 'I really fancy you.' I couldn't believe that those words had slipped out, and lowered my head to hide my blushes.

'Well, in that case I'll bring you a photo next time,' he said, finally smiling. I was impressed by his quick wit and the coolness of his response. It made a nice change from the usual line I got about my beautiful blue eyes. Then, the guards called us to go back to the *anexo*.

It was the nasty shift of female guards, who we nicknamed *brugas* – which means witches. Black magic is popular in some parts of Venezuelan society, and the term *brugas* is an insulting one.

We went back to the *anexo*. Still reeling from my rash

confession, I said to Monica, 'Can you believe it? I told him straight out that I fancied him!'

'Oh my,' she said, clapping her hand over her mouth in shock.

We went to *el muro* to discuss the implications of this foolish admission. As we sat down, I could see him and Alejandro, another of the new guards, sitting below us near the main offices.

I'd never noticed guards just sitting outside on chairs before, and from where we were sitting, we had a good view of them. I looked down and, deciding I had nothing left to lose, grinned boldly at him. He looked up and waved and said, 'Hola.' Every word he said made my stomach somersault. I was so excited to have any sort of contact with him and felt as if I was thirteen all over again.

One of the male prisoners had a business making ice creams and another walked around selling them for him all day. The ice creams were insulated in polystyrene cups.

I was dying to give the guard my phone number but couldn't think of how to do it. When I caught sight of the ice-cream guy, I decided I'd send ice creams to the two guards.

I scribbled my phone number on one of the cups.

'Make sure you give this to the man in the white shirt,' I said to the ice-cream seller. I paid, then went back outside and watched the ice-cream man hand the little cups over.

'Thanks for the ice creams,' the guard called up.

'It's because you look hot,' I called back cheesily. *What is happening to me?* I asked myself. I decided that I'd completely lost my mind, because all these unplanned words, words that usually I wouldn't dream of uttering, were spilling out of my mouth.

Monica and I sat on the wall and the two guards continued sitting in their chairs. It had been a long time since I'd fancied anyone, and I'd been waiting months to speak to this stunningly attractive man. Now that it had finally happened, I was worried that he might not like me.

To my delight, he phoned me that night. He told me that his name was José Guedez. I kept on asking him to repeat it.

'Burra,' he replied, as I struggled to get my tongue around the words. *Burra* is Spanish for a female donkey and means 'stupid'. Thankfully, there was an indulgent tone in his voice when he said that.

Cheeky bugger, calling me stupid, when he doesn't even know me and when he's got such a difficult name to boot, I said to myself.

The following day, he sent me a lollipop. Monica and I had passed a lot of time in the shop, sitting and eating and talking, but now I had a new diversion. I didn't see him the next day, but I was overjoyed when he called me in the evening. From then on, he rang me every single night. We just couldn't stop talking. I didn't have much in common with most of the prisoners and guards, and rarely exchanged more than small talk with them, but with José it was different. Although I barely knew him, he seemed to understand exactly how I was feeling and thinking. I poured my heart and soul out to him. We talked about England a lot.

'What's it like? We'll go there. I'll help you escape, and we can go to England and get married,' he joked. I felt warm inside when he said that, although apart from our lengthy phone calls, all we'd had together were a few snatched conversations in the prison grounds.

We learnt a lot about each other. He was twenty-three years old, the same as me. He lived with his mother and had a daughter, whose mother he was separated from. He loved riding his motorbike and hanging out with his friends. He was from Caracas and went home as often as he could to see his mother and daughter. We built up a close friendship and I found myself talking to him more than to anyone else in the prison. He seemed genuinely interested in what I had to say. I talked to him about the female guards, especially the mean ones, and kept on wondering whether he fancied me.

On visiting day, he engineered it that he came and stood guard at the shop, and while the other prisoners were engrossed in their families and friends, we talked and talked. 'My two-week shift finishes today and I'm going back to Caracas to see my mother and my daughter,' he said.

I felt crushed. Now that we'd struck up a friendship, I didn't want to let him out of my sight.

'Do you like me?' he asked.

'Are you going to bring my photo back?' I asked by way of a response.

'I really do like you, Natalie. I'm sincere,' he said, suddenly looking serious. I knew straight away that he was speaking from the heart. I teased him about the way he'd ignored me in the beginning, when I had so obviously fallen for him.

'It's because I'm a serious-minded person. I'm new in this job at Mérida and I want to do everything right,' he explained.

One night, he asked me to call him, but I explained that I had no credit. He texted me a pin number to put credit into my phone – a generous thirty pounds' worth. Sometimes, he'd call me at three o'clock in the morning when he was doing night shifts.

Chatting to José had become part of my routine and I was bored without him. I got it into my head that I wasn't going to hear from him for the two weeks he was back home in Caracas, but he started sending me text messages and calling me every night from there. We never, ever ran out of things to talk about.

A lot of the conversation was prison news and gossip. It got to the point where the other girls in the room got really fed up with me for keeping them awake. At first, I'd dismissed his assertions that he didn't have a girlfriend and that he lived with his mother as a case of saying what he thought I wanted to hear, but gradually I started to believe him.

When he got back to San Juan, I wanted to be with him more than ever. We both whispered on the phone how much we wanted to kiss each other, but couldn't think of a way to be alone, even for a few moments.

One evening, there was a party in the *anexo*. José came over to escort the male prisoners. He came with his friend Alejandro, who knew about our feelings for each other.

By the end of the party, we still hadn't kissed, and he didn't seem to have made much effort to grab a few minutes alone with me. 'I'm going now,' he said at the end of the evening.

'Fine, go,' I said. I was upset that he hadn't made any effort to kiss me in a quiet corner somewhere.

Alejandro ran after me and said, 'What's the matter?'

'He's full of shit. He said he wanted to kiss me, but he didn't do anything about it,' I said. José was watching us.

I ran out to the secret garden, crying. José followed me there, pushed me up against the wall and gave me the biggest kiss I'd ever had in my whole life. It completely and utterly took my breath away. Anyone could have caught us – a female guard, one of the girls – but thankfully no one did.

It was a full-on, passionate kiss. I'd never had a kiss with so much emotion crammed into it before. At that moment, I fell in love. I really understood now why the word 'fall' is used in connection with love. I felt that I was falling deeper and deeper into some deliciously dark, velvety hole. After that kiss, I could not stop thinking about him, even for a second. Every single thought I had featured José. After our first kiss, he returned to Caracas for two weeks' leave.

My emotions were in turmoil. I knew I loved José, but I was desperately trying to stop myself from loving him because I knew that I was going to get hurt and that this was a relationship with no future. But these sensible thoughts failed to put out the flames of my passion for him. And he seemed to feel the same way. He was constantly phoning me and texting me – he often sent me at least fifty text messages a day. So even when he wasn't there, part of him was with me.

I was still going to activities on the men's side of the prison but, unlike most of the Venezuelan men there, he wasn't possessive and didn't try to ban me from having a life. So, although the whole thing had to be kept secret, there was no pressure on me to behave in a certain way because I was in a relationship.

José wasn't discreet. When he came back from leave, he sent a

Tasmanian teddy bear to me and blew kisses up to me, so it didn't take the rest of the guards long to work out what was going on.

He often used to phone me on one of the two public phones that were near my shop. One day, he called me and said, 'Go to the secret garden. Don't ask why, just go.'

Obediently, I went, and there were a group of *mariachis* there in their big, black hats. They serenaded me with a well-known Venezuelan love song. José had obviously paid them. I'd taught him the prisoners' sign language and he stood close to them, signing that he loved me.

Now that all the guards knew what was going on between us, some were more helpful than others. Penelope, a female guard on the nice shift, was particularly supportive. One day, José poured his heart out to her. After that, she promised to do everything she could to help us have a few private moments together.

We couldn't kiss and cuddle in front of an *anexo* full of women, but sometimes she came to get me late at night after everyone had been locked in for the night. At the door of the gate she shouted, 'Natalie, we want to get something from the shop.'

Usually, José was in the reception area of the *anexo* where the female guards congregated. We walked just outside the reception area where, although we could still be seen, we had a bit more privacy. When the *brugas* shift was on, however, we had little chance of meeting. There was no way they would help us.

Before long, word filtered back to the director about our relationship. Of course, he wasn't pleased, as relationships between prisoners and guards were frowned upon. One day, he called me into his office. 'What's all this I hear about you going out with one of the guards?' he asked.

I tried to laugh the whole thing off. 'It's just prison gossip. People are being pathetic,' I said, trying to sound convincing. 'I don't usually speak to the guards, but I speak to this guy and people are misinterpreting it.'

He believed me at first, because he allowed José to remain

in his job. If he had decided we were having a relationship, José would have been removed from the prison straight away.

'That's good, I'm glad there's nothing between you and José because you know you're my special girl.'

About six months later, at the beginning of 2004, one of the *motos* betrayed us. I'd given him money to get some *miche* and he'd told me that he'd got caught with it and that's why he could give me neither my money back nor the *miche*. But he was lying: he'd spent the money on crack. When I found out what had happened, I was furious, and I told José. The next thing I knew, the *moto* had been locked up in solitary confinement. He'd broken the prisoners' rule about not shafting another prisoner. To get his revenge, the *moto* went and told the director everything about José. He explained that José tipped us off about *racettas*, and that I had two mobile phones. Once again, a double standard operated where it was fine for a male prisoner to walk around chatting on his mobile phone but not for a female to do so, who would have the phone confiscated.

The first thing the director did was order a *racetta* of my bed and possessions, although the shop wasn't searched. The two phones the *moto* had referred to were found and I was summoned to the director's office. I wasn't really worried about what would happen to me because I was already in prison. But all kinds of things could happen to José. I went into his office nervously.

'Natalie, I'm so disappointed in you for seeing José,' he said with a heavy sigh. 'You know it will never go anywhere. He doesn't really care for you. For him, it's just something to pass the time.'

'You're wrong. He really does care about me,' I replied indignantly.

'How naive you are to believe that,' he said, shaking his head sadly. I knew how disappointed he was in me because he'd done so many things for me. I sensed that my telling off was over.

'Why have you got two phones?' he asked.

I realised there was no point in lying. 'I bought one and José gave me one.'

To my surprise, he handed them back to me.

The girls in my room were not too pleased to see me return reunited with the phones. They had hoped that they were going to have some peace at last. They didn't realise that the director had a soft spot for me.

In the first couple of days after we were rumbled, José was escorted everywhere around the prison by the sub-director and I had no chance at all to see him. Both of us knew that he'd be leaving. It was just a question of when.

José paid one of the female guards to take me to the hospital one morning. He told me which female guard on the nice shift to approach with agonising stomach cramps.

José was going to be on duty at the hospital and he advised me, 'Lay the pain on thick.' My heart leapt at the prospect of having some proper time with José before he was sent away. We hadn't managed more than a few moments by ourselves up till now.

I wasn't sure what I was going to find when I went down to the hospital. The doctor sat in his office and left us alone. I presumed he'd been paid off, too. José's friend Alejandro told us to go into one of the hospital rooms. Nobody could get into or out of the hospital without José unlocking the doors, so we knew that we would be relatively safe for a while. It hadn't been confirmed that José was going but we both knew that it was inevitable. He brought me a T-shirt he'd slept in the night before so that I'd have something to remember him by. We went into this small white sterile room with just a bed in it. It couldn't have been more unromantic.

We kissed and cuddled and cried and finally made love. It should have been the most wonderful time, but instead it was sad and tear-stained because we both believed we'd never see each other again. I felt as if my heart had quite literally broken. We lay entwined on the bed and all I could think about was the terrible prospect of never seeing him again. I was overwhelmed with love for him as well as the pain of knowing that I'd experienced perfect love, and now it was all going to be snatched away from me.

José kissed my tears away and tried to make me smile. 'Let's pretend we're not here, that we're at home together,' he said softly. We were happy just to be in each other's arms. I didn't think it was possible to be any more in love, but as we lay on the bed together, my feelings became even more intense. I finally went back up to the *anexo* a few hours later.

There were so many nights when we talked for hours; sometimes I was so exhausted that I dropped off to sleep in mid-conversation. At night, we talked and talked on the phone. 'You have to fight for your benefit. You have to push for it and then we can be together,' José urged.

'Maybe I could apply for my benefit in Caracas,' I said hopefully.

'If not, I'll leave Caracas and find another job in Mérida,' he promised. I didn't really think about the details that night, I was just happy to hear that he had a plan. Until that point, I hadn't thought of things continuing after he left the prison, and anything that would allow me to carry on being with him made my heart leap. When I heard that he was leaving the following day, it was too painful to say goodbye.

While I hoped and hoped that José's plan would come to fruition, I tried to be realistic. 'This is it, it's the end. I might not get my benefit,' I said.

I tried my best to resign myself to our parting because I knew I had no choice. My heart felt like a lump of lead sinking down into the pit of my stomach. The next morning, I went up onto the wall and watched him leaving. He turned around and shouted at the top of his voice, 'I love you!'

There were a few people signing up on the wall. They gave me sympathetic looks as I wiped away my tears.

I was 150 per cent convinced that that was it. I never expected to hear from him again. Despite what he'd said on the phone the night before, it was all talk as far as I was concerned. José was free and I wasn't, and he could begin a new chapter of his life without me.

I went back to the *anexo*, climbed into bed, closed the curtain and cried and cried. Monica took over with the shop, leaving me time to mourn José twenty-four hours a day. As soon as he got to the bus station, he texted me. He said many beautiful things – that I was the air that he breathed, that I'd filled his heart. I was overjoyed to hear from him. Then his battery went dead.

I'd thought it would be so easy for him to abandon me, but he seemed to have no intention of doing that. He phoned me all the time from Caracas. He didn't ask me not to go to the men's side, but he did say some of his friends would keep an eye on me.

I stopped going out completely because I'd lost interest in everything. I didn't want to go over to the men's side. Without him, I felt there was no point in doing anything. I used to joke to Monica that José and I would run away to England together, but we never in a million years thought it would come true. Not long after he left, Monica left, too, because America signed the extradition treaty. I was devastated. She had been a great friend to me.

We had shared everything, cooked together and talked about everything under the sun. As usual with prison moves, Monica was suddenly informed that she would be leaving and within hours she was gone.

Strangely I got more sympathy when Monica left than when José did. I think that was because at the end of the day, José was a guard and I was a prisoner, and everybody assumed there was no future in the relationship. The women prisoners were better able to understand the loss of a female friendship.

Monica and I both cried a lot and promised to keep in touch. She was going to go back to INOF for a couple of days and then on to America, but everyone seemed to forget about her once she arrived there and she spent seven months in INOF. She did call me a couple of times, but then we lost contact until after I returned to England.

Without José and Monica, I was beginning to get depressed. I was sad, bored and lonely. José had told me that he was going to come and visit as a visitor, but he had been told that he wouldn't be allowed in if he tried that. One night, he called me and said, 'I can't bear it any longer, I've got to see you. I'm going mad.'

He kept phoning me from social events where he should have been enjoying himself, but instead all he could think about was me. He had a chipped phone card that never ran out of minutes and worked in certain phone boxes. I remember he went to a party one night and kept coming out of it to call me. He didn't seem to want to be anywhere that I wasn't.

Eventually, we came up with a plan. He told me to order a massive bag of sugar for the shop. Whenever I bought sugar, I needed scales to weigh it and I always went to the kitchen to get them.

'Do it when the nice shift of guards is on duty in the *anexo*,' he said. 'It'll have to be really early in the morning. As soon as anyone sees me, I'll be thrown out, but there won't be guards in the kitchen that early in the morning.'

It sounded far-fetched. I went along with it but thought I wouldn't be able to get out of the *anexo*. Penelope was my salvation. She agreed to come and get me when José arrived.

In my heart of hearts, I still didn't think the visit was going to happen. He was going to make a twenty-three-hour journey just to see me for a few minutes, then he was going to make another twenty-three-hour journey back home.

I was so excited at the prospect of seeing him again, however fleetingly, that my spirits lifted. I couldn't tell anyone apart from Penelope. We'd set a date the following week and José left Caracas as planned the day before and boarded the bus. At five o'clock, before *numero*, Penelope came to get me.

'He's here,' she whispered, grinning from ear to ear. 'He's made it. True love can carry you a long way.'

She led me out of the *anexo* towards the kitchen. Both of us crept on our tiptoes to make sure we didn't wake anybody up.

To my surprise, José jumped out from behind the wall of the *cathedral*. I could not believe that he'd really come until he held me in his arms. I clung on to him, rejoicing in the feel of his flesh and blood next to mine. It was pitch black still so we couldn't see each other properly.

Penelope kept watch for us. We passionately kissed and hugged and cried. The enormous sacrifice that he had made to come and see me took our relationship to a much deeper level. My heart was beating fast against his. I wished we could stay like that forever and never be parted again.

'I can't believe you've spent a day travelling here and you're going to spend another day travelling home again,' I whispered.

'It's because I love you so much. I hope you believe me now,' he said. All I could do was nod through my tears.

He had to go before *numero*, when guards would suddenly appear. I knew that he had to leave, but I clung desperately to him for a few more moments.

'Come, José, you must go now,' said Penelope nervously. He and I looked at each other sorrowfully, and to try and lighten the atmosphere a bit she quipped, 'You're the only guard I know who creeps around breaking into prisons.' We both laughed.

'It's only two months until you can apply for your benefit,' he said, as he reluctantly disentangled himself from my embrace. 'I know you'll get it and then we can really be together.'

He was right. I was going to do everything humanly possible to get permission for day release from the prison. I planned to focus all my time and energy on that now.

16 THE SCENT OF FREEDOM

'I hope this is going to be my last Christmas in prison. I hope that by this time next year I will have sorted out my parole and then hopefully I can get back to England the year after.

'I can't imagine what it will be like to come back to England, to speak English all the time, to be around normal people instead of the crazy psychopaths here. By the time I get back Nikita will have spent more of her life living with you than with me. I wonder if she'll even recognise me.'

Letter from Natalie to Eve, November 2003

I had some more money sent over from England and engaged a lawyer who had been recommended to me. I asked him to do whatever needed to be done to get me my benefit.

I went to the director and told him I wanted to apply for my benefit. 'Natalie, I'll help you,' he said. I was worried because I had a mark on my file for being found in possession of two mobile phones. 'I'll talk to the judge and try to get that struck out,' he said.

In order to get benefit, you need family support – someone who is prepared to go to court and take responsibility for you. You also need to have a job offer. The prison doesn't arrange that for you, you must arrange it yourself. It was impossible to organise this without someone on the outside to help you. I'd given so many people money to go to court for me, but although they pocketed the cash, they never actually turned up in front of the judge.

Vivi went out to work every day and came back to the prison every evening. Although we weren't particularly close friends, I decided to confide in her. 'I want to get out on my benefit now, but I don't know what to do. It's so difficult as a foreigner.'

She was fantastic. She promised to help me and unlike others who I'd asked but who had let me down, she stuck to her word. She sorted everything out for me: she found somebody to give me a job in a hairdressing salon, found me a lawyer and went to court to get the paperwork for me so that everyone else had to do only the minimum to move things along.

The pessimistic part of me didn't believe that I'd really get out. It all seemed like an impossible dream. I got called to court a few times but nothing much happened.

José was eager to hear every bit of news relating to my benefit. 'Let me know the minute you get it,' he said. 'I'm going to make sure you spend your first day with me.'

But still nothing happened. 'That's it now,' said Vivi, 'I've done everything that needs to be done, it's just a matter of waiting.'

I wasn't sure what to do about the shop – whether to pay someone to work there if I got benefit or whether to sell it. I decided that I was going to pass it on whether I got my benefit or not. I let all the stock run down until it was only half full and then sold it to a female prisoner from Ecuador. Then, one night the guards came up to me in the *anexo* and said casually, 'You've got court tomorrow, Natalie.'

I knew this was judgment day. Either I'd got benefit or I hadn't. I couldn't believe that I might be out walking the streets of Mérida with José soon. I called him and excitedly told him the latest development.

'I know it's going to be good news, I'm sure of it,' he said.

I'd been to court once before to apply for my benefit. The court wasn't as bad as at San Antonio and the people seemed friendlier, but maybe that was because now I was able to hold a conversation. I was led into a small room where the judge's secretary sat. 'You know you've got your benefit. The judge is going to run through the rules with you,' she said, as casually as if she was chatting about the weather.

I stayed calm. I didn't know her, and I didn't want to show any emotion. But inside I was saying to myself, *Yes, yes, yes.* I couldn't wait to tell José. We'd been seeing each other for over a year and now everything that we'd planned was coming true.

What really filled me with joy was that this was one step nearer to getting back to Nikita. While the ten years stretched endlessly ahead of me, I didn't dare think about being reunited with her, it was just too painful. But now I could tentatively begin to think about being back with my beloved little girl once more.

I knew the judge I was about to see quite well because she and other judges regularly came to the prison. The prison had a van and a budget for petrol to take prisoners to court, but often because of corruption the money was spent on other things, so when prisoners needed to get to court, they had to buy the petrol to get them there.

Rather than waiting in court all day for prisoners who didn't always turn up, the judges found it easier to travel to the prison and deal with cases there. There were four judges from the court, and they were always in demand whenever they arrived at San Juan. The male prisoners had more freedom to go and see the judges than the women did. The judges came to see specific people and brought their files with them. It sometimes took several visits before a prisoner got to see the judge.

The initial application to court was made in the prison office but if you didn't have a letter from a man called Roberto, which you had to pay him for, no application would go through. I asked Roberto if he could take the warning I received for possession of two mobile phones out of my file if I paid him. He said he was unable to do that, but I later discovered that the director had already taken it out for me.

After a few minutes of drumming my fingers on the table waiting for the judge, I was taken to her office. I'd seen her a few times in the prison. She was a nice, ordinary woman with an air of authority and a 'don't mess with me' attitude. But she was fair and if you played by her rules, you were generally OK.

She beamed and said to me almost affectionately, 'Well done, I can see you've been fighting hard for your benefit.'

Then she went through the rules with me. 'You can't start until the order has arrived at the prison. And you have to report to the probation office before you start work.'

The men on benefit didn't have to go back to the prison every night but the women had to be inside the prison gates by nine o'clock. The benefit I had was day release. The next stage on from that was where you could stay out for weekends.

'You must make sure you go to work every day and you have to present yourself at court on your first week out,' said the judge firmly.

I nodded eagerly. 'Yes, of course I will,' I said.

Excited, I could hardly breathe. Deep down, I had been sure that I'd be stuck there forever. I don't think daydreams come true often but this time my prayers had been answered.

When I arrived back at the prison, I showed no emotion to the guards because it was the *brugas* shift. I just said coolly, 'I'll be able to see my boyfriend at the weekend.'

They knew I was still in contact with José because he sometimes phoned the public phones and one of them picked it up. Sometimes, they shouted to me, 'Mrs Guedez!'

Once I got into the *anexo*, I started jumping up and down. 'I've got my benefit! I've got my benefit!' I shouted jubilantly.

I asked the guards to move me into the room where the girls on benefit stayed. That room was locked during the day but later in the evening I moved into it.

It was Friday and the order was due to come through on Monday. I didn't care about having to wait a few more days. I don't think anybody or anything could have burst my bubble.

When we were locked in, I phoned José. 'I've got it!' I yelped down the phone.

He was overjoyed. 'I'm going to leave work soon so I can be there on Monday. I'm going to wait outside the gate so I'm the first person outside that you see.'

I told him that I had to go to court and sort things out, and that it was better for me to work out what I was supposed to be doing before he arrived. Reluctantly, he agreed that this was the sensible thing to do.

I spent the whole weekend in a state of feverish excitement, desperately waiting for Monday to come. When Vivi came back from her weekend release on Sunday evening, she saw which room I'd moved into and knew straight away what had happened. She was delighted for me and hugged me tightly.

'Thank you so much, Vivi,' I cried. 'All this never would have happened without your help.'

She was going somewhere else on Monday, so she arranged for her Mexican friend Xochi to pick me up, show me the way on the bus and take me to the probation office in the town of Mérida.

The guards were really pleased for me when Monday morning came, and I got ready to board the bus to freedom.

'Is José coming to pick you up? When are you seeing him?' Penelope asked.

'Wednesday,' I said, trying to hide my excitement.

I didn't leave the prison until almost noon. When I stepped outside the jail, the feeling was indescribable. After four years behind bars, I was finally going to breathe in the air of freedom.

We had to get a bus to the nearest village and from there another bus into town. We got on a ramshackle bus which took us into a poor area. I was sure it was going to break down at any moment but fortunately it didn't. It was exciting just seeing an old woman walking down the road carrying some shopping. I'd forgotten what real life looked like. When we got to the village, there were real shops and a bakery that sold all different kinds of bread – milk bread, fruit bread, chocolate bread.

It was a completely different experience being out in the streets than it had been when I arrived in Margarita on holiday. Now I understood the currency and could speak the language. I'd also learnt the hard way what freedom meant. I felt I'd arrived on another much more pleasant planet. This was not a world I knew, but one I was much looking forward to getting to know. We boarded another bus into Mérida. When we arrived in town, we got on yet another bus to the probation office. Mérida is famous for having the biggest cable car in the world, and for being at the foot of Venezuela's highest mountain. It is a university town and I saw lots of students walking around.

I gawped at all the bright and lively colours on the streets. Lots of shops and stalls were selling *empanadas*, big pancakes stuffed with meat or chicken. Everywhere I walked, there was music, the smell of food, and people bustling. It felt surreal in the best possible way.

I went to the probation office, where it was explained to me that I'd be starting work the following day and that periodically they would come and check up on me. The probation people seemed unenthusiastic about the whole thing. As far as they were concerned, I was just another number to process, but they couldn't put a damper on my joy.

For the first time in years, I felt as if I had a future. All the time I'd been in prison, I'd tried not to think too much about going back home. I couldn't allow myself to dream that far ahead and I tried my best to take each day as it came. I hadn't really had time to mentally prepare myself for this liberation because I hadn't wanted to raise my hopes before I knew my benefit was going ahead. I was walking around the streets of Mérida like a zombie trying to take everything in.

Xochi and Vivi worked at a small sewing school. Xochi took me to the school and we met up with Vivi there. It was wonderful to see her. She hugged me. 'Welcome to freedom,' she said with a grin. 'I think you'll like it better than life in San Juan.'

'I can't believe I'm here,' I gasped. It still hadn't really sunk in that for more than twelve hours of every weekday, my life was going to be entirely my own.

The sewing school was in a flat on the second floor of a block in the town centre. There was a lounge area with some sofas and a kitchen-diner that was a hub of activity. The two bedrooms had been converted into work rooms and there were huge tables in both with women sitting at them sewing. Profi, the woman who ran it, had a big, kind heart.

Vivi and I chatted for a while and although I'd sampled a few of the delicious breads in the village bakery, I was hungry again. There was a bakery next door and, once again, it was a thrill to be able to walk into a shop and buy exactly what I wanted when I wanted it. When you're free, you take so many things for granted, but when these things are taken away from you it's awful. I started to appreciate all kinds of things that I'd never really thought of before. Vivi took me to the hairdresser's that was two blocks down from the sewing place. This was where I was to be working.

Mérida is made up of avenues and streets designed on a grid system and it's simple to grasp the system. None of the blocks or shops had numbers though, just descriptions.

The hairdresser greeted me warmly. 'It's nice to meet you.'

'It's even nicer to meet you,' I said. 'Only problem is, I can't cut hair.'

'No problem,' she replied. 'All you need to do is pass by now and again.' I got the impression that she didn't want me hanging around there too much. She'd been robbed by another prisoner she'd helped, so she was a little wary.

She cut my hair there and then, and told me about the fraudster who had conned her out of a lot of money. In prison, we'd all cut each other's hair, but this was the first proper haircut I'd had for years. Just sitting at the back having my hair washed and feeling the shampoo suds run through my hair felt so luxurious. It made me feel more like a pampered celebrity than a convicted drug smuggler.

'What would you like to do?' asked Vivi, her eyes sparkling, when my hair was finished. We both decided we were hungry again and she took me to a beautiful pizza restaurant. It was almost evening by now. The day had been a whirlwind and I hadn't had a chance to stop and catch my breath. It was so nice to get to the restaurant and sit quietly, evaluating the many joys of the day. The restaurant had a cool, pleasant courtyard. There was nice music playing and plants whose leaves made a soothing, swishing sound in the breeze. As I sat there, in the courtyard, drinking my beer, it finally sunk in that I was free. It was bliss and I felt completely relaxed.

When we arrived back in the prison, we were searched. We had to wait for a female guard to come down from the *anexo*. The national guard searched through our stuff, then two female guards told us that we had to take the bottom half of our clothes off completely, straddle a mirror and squat three times.

'Too fast, do it again,' said one of the guards who didn't like me. 'Do it again.'

It was so degrading, and it was particularly hard for some of the older women. Even though I hated having to do this, it couldn't tarnish my first day of freedom. Nothing could. Back in the *anexo*, everyone was asking me what it was like on the outside. I had spent so long watching the other girls coming back from benefit and at long last it was my turn.

José had arranged to call me on one of the public phones after nine o'clock. I sat on the floor cradling the phone and filled him in on every detail of my day. It was so nice to have something different to tell him and he was so happy for me.

'I went to the bakery and went for pizza. I had a proper beer, not *miche*; I wasn't pissed on one drink like with *miche*,' I said with a laugh.

José, of course, knew what Mérida was like, but he loved to hear about it through my eyes. 'I can't wait to be able to see you and touch you and hold you in my arms. I can't wait to be able to show you how much I love you,' he said, his voice full of longing.

The following day, Vivi took me around the town centre to help me learn my way around. José had begun his long journey from Caracas and gave me a running commentary on his progress. 'I'm at the bus station ... I'm getting on the bus ... I've reached this place ...'

Eventually, Wednesday arrived. I was more excited than I'd

ever been. José kept texting me through the night. 'Only fifteen hours to go …' Then his battery went dead. We'd arranged to meet at the bus station at eleven in the morning, but eleven came and went and there was no sign of his bus.

Suddenly, I doubted him. *Has it all been a joke, or a lie?* I thought. It was impossible that so many things would go my way. *He obviously isn't coming.* Another half hour passed and still no bus appeared. This felt like the most important moment in my life. I was wound up more tightly that a coiled spring.

Eventually, the bus pulled in at noon. I was so relieved but all I could do was scream and shout at him for being so late. 'I didn't think you were coming,' I said, starting to sob.

He took me in his arms, repeatedly saying '*mi niña*' – my girl.

He had obsessively saved up his wages so that we could have a nice time together in Mérida. 'I can't believe we're really here. I can't believe it's really happening,' we kept saying over and over.

His first task was to find a hotel. We jumped into a taxi and couldn't keep our hands off each other. We were constantly touching each other and the heat coming from both of our bodies was unbelievable. 'I'm nervous,' I told him. 'About being with you.'

'But why? We've already had time together, in the hospital.'

'I know,' I said, 'but this is different somehow.'

I bought a big bottle of whisky to calm my nerves. But we never even opened it. As soon as we arrived in the room, we kissed properly, and my nerves melted away. We made love and it was different from the time in the hospital, special and meaningful and wonderful and not in the slightest bit rushed. There was so much love between us both. Yet again, even though I didn't think it was possible, it made the relationship stronger. This man was consuming every bit of me. There was no room for anyone else in my life. He filled up every nook and cranny of my being.

We spent the whole day in the hotel, then in the evening he got the bus to the village with me. All the prisoners who sat on the bus with us couldn't believe that he'd come all this way back from Caracas just for me.

The next couple of months passed in a blur of love. José came up to Mérida whenever he wasn't working, and the rest of the time, I counted down the days, hours and minutes until I could see him again. I spent most of my time at the sewing school with Vivi and didn't spend much time at the hairdresser's.

A couple of months later, on Christmas Eve, José booked us into a beautiful hotel, which had cost him a month's wages. We went into a little village high in the mountains. Christmas in prison was a time to think about home and feel miserable, and to think about the loss of my mum.

On Christmas Day, he took me riding in the snow. It completely took my breath away. For a moment, I forgot that I was in prison in Venezuela for trafficking drugs. My mind only had space for thoughts about the horse and the mountain and the man I loved. When we got to the top of the mountain and looked down on a stunning icy lake, the beauty of the scene took my breath away. If Nikita had been there with us, it would have been the most perfect Christmas I'd ever had.

Then we came down the mountain, returned the horses and waited for the bus that would take us back to the hotel. As we waited, we saw some children who must have been around ten years old. José had a knack of being able to laugh and joke with everyone and these children were no exception.

'This is my girlfriend, what do you think of her? She's the most beautiful girl you'll ever see.' He gave them the equivalent of ten pounds to climb over a wall and go down part of the steep mountain to pick some flowers for me. My heart felt heavy when I had to return to the prison and José had to go back to Caracas.

Unsurprisingly, the long commute was taking its toll on José. The director at San Juan who had sacked José had left, and José decided to risk applying for a transfer back to San Juan. To our amazement, it was granted, and he returned to his old job.

By now, the novelty of benefit had worn off for me and I wasn't behaving well. My attitude, understandably, bred resentment among the other female prisoners. I can't believe I behaved so stupidly, but I was so besotted with José that all reason flew out of the window. On the day José returned to San Juan, we walked in together.

'See you later,' he said, grabbing me and pulling me towards him to kiss me. He just didn't care who saw.

José worked for two days, then stayed the night in the prison. He left with me in the morning and then came back in the evening with me even though he wasn't working. He tried to get as many shifts as he could guarding prisoners at the hospital in the city. If he was guarding a badly injured prisoner who wasn't likely to get up and run away, he and I could go off together. I went and sat with him at the hospital if he had to stay there.

Sometimes, we booked into the hotels where you could rent a room for two-hour periods. Our passion for each other remained strong.

Vivi and I had become close friends. Now we shared everything in the same way that Monica and I had, and, before that, Mary and I had. I used to buy food for everyone whenever I had money and took it to the sewing flat. Vivi did the same. Profi knew the whole situation and thought it was amazing what José and I were doing. She was a great believer in the adage that love conquers all. She had fallen in love with someone unsuitable and they'd abandoned everything for each other. Forty-five years on, they were happily living together with lots of kids.

Corruption is rife in Venezuelan society and now that José was back working at the prison, I got to hear about the kind of things that went on. Once, a group of guards smuggled some drugs into the prison at the behest of Che. They picked them up in the prison van bearing the insignia of the Ministry of Justice. They waited for a phone call from Che telling them where to go, then they went to a hotel and met a guy who gave them a large consignment of drugs. Various guards inside and outside the prison were paid off so that they could drive the van back into the prison without being searched. Another guard delivered the drugs to Che. He would not have dreamed of smoking crack himself, but knew exactly how to distribute it to maximise his earnings. The same method was often used by Che and the other *prangs* to get guns into the prison. Nobody batted an eyelid about this kind of arrangement. It was a way of life that people on both sides of the law simply accepted.

Carnival in Venezuela is in February. There's a tradition of water throwing, and everyone takes part, in prison as well as everywhere else. People try to keep off the streets because they are liable to get drenched by someone standing at the upstairs window of a house or in a doorway. I never discovered where this strange tradition came from or what the reasoning behind it was.

During carnival, there are floats and a travelling market selling clothes, food and lots of sunglasses. This goes on for twenty-four hours a day for four or five days.

I wanted to stay outside the prison for the duration of carnival. José had arranged to meet some of his work colleagues there. The sub-director of the prison was with us and he said he'd sort it out for me to stay out for a few days. The end of each day is marked by a street party involving lots of alcohol. It goes on until the early hours of the morning, when the police shut it down. The streets swarm with people.

I phoned up the prison with the excuse that I was sick and so couldn't return that night.

'You can't keep staying out overnight and producing fake sick notes,' the guard on the other end of the phone said grumpily.

'Well, report me to the sub-director then,' I said airily, knowing that the sub-director had promised to cover me. When the sub-director returned to the prison, he said it was fine for me to be out for three days. I got away with it, but resentment against me continued to build among both prisoners and guards.

I knew I was pushing my luck with my benefit and that a lot of the Venezuelan girls would do anything they could to get my benefit taken away from me. It was their country and they were struggling. It irked them to see that although I had no family in Venezuela, I seemed to be leading a charmed life.

Now that José and I were able to spend more time with each other, our relationship had grown even stronger and we wanted to be together more and more. We discussed whether I was going to knuckle down to my benefit for the next six years, or whether I'd try to escape with him by my side. 'Either I'll stay and set up my own business in the town as part of my benefit, or I'll run away,' I said.

Everyone dreams of escaping from prison, but I had never considered the mechanics of it.

He gave me one of his special melting looks. 'I don't want to influence you either way. Whatever you do, I'll support you,' he said. We agreed that if we stayed in Mérida, we'd find somewhere to live, as José couldn't continue using the prison as a hotel.

I emailed Shona and asked her to send me a couple of thousand pounds of my inheritance. I decided that even with José close to me, another six years in jail was too hard to bear. I didn't want to lay down roots in Venezuela, as I had Nikita back in England, and didn't want to bring her over given the poor education system there.

Escaping became an increasingly appealing option. Most importantly, it would take me back home to Nikita. I spoke often of her to José. The years I'd spent away from her had only strengthened my love for her. Every day that I was away from her felt like a month. My goal was to get back to Nikita and to start being a proper mum to her once more.

We started talking in earnest about how I could do it and decided that I'd have to go through Colombia because it was too risky to go to any airport in Venezuela. I knew I'd need a passport. I approached the British Embassy and said I needed to get a passport in order to get a better job in Mérida. I explained that the only ID I had was my prison one and I didn't want to use that.

The embassy didn't seem to think it would be a problem and I was told I'd have to send some money, some photos and various supporting documents.

I went back to the prison one evening and was talking to José when a guard referred to me as *presa*, which is an insulting word for a prisoner. José burned with rage and, before thinking through the consequences, he punched the guard in the face and said, 'How dare you speak to her like that?'

We thought that the new director might get rid of José for doing that, but she didn't, mainly because she had few allies among the guards and José was one of them, one she didn't want to lose.

Eventually, my passport arrived. José didn't have a passport and obtaining one was not easy. The number of passports distributed in Venezuela are limited and they are only given out twice a year.

One of the prisoners used to be a national guard and because of his previous job, he wasn't accepted by the rest of the prison population, so he hung out with the other national guards. He and José became good friends and José told him in confidence what our plans were and asked what the best route would be. The guy said that he knew the second in command in the passport office in Caracas. He spoke to him and got him to agree to issue José with a passport.

Overjoyed to have found a way to circumvent the system, José went to Caracas. When he arrived, the passport office was shut, but he phoned his friend at the prison, who phoned his contact, who opened the office for him and gave him the passport. I couldn't imagine bureaucracy in England being sidestepped as effortlessly as that, but in Venezuela, anything was possible. This complex process was smoothed over by the payment of a substantial sum of money to the man in Caracas.

Once José had his passport, we decided there was no going back. All our efforts were focused on finding a way to get across the border into Colombia, where I'd be relatively safe. It was a scary thing to be planning and I'd never heard of any female prisoners managing to do this before.

Every time you leave a town in Venezuela, there's a checkpoint. We pored over maps to find the route that had the fewest checkpoints. One of the conditions of my benefit was that I wasn't allowed to leave the town. We mapped out several routes.

The only other people who knew were Vivi and Alejandro. Vivi was all for it, especially as tensions were rising inside the prison. Checks were done by the probation service and it was found that I wasn't at the hairdresser's where I was supposed to be. I explained that I'd found a new job at Profi's sewing school, but I knew that the days of my benefit were likely to be numbered.

Meanwhile, José's friend, the former national guard, advised us which route was the safest one to take.

In the end, we had to leave two days earlier than we'd planned. We were in town at a plaza, sitting talking quietly. Suddenly, the national guard came up to me and told me that I was being arrested, and that José had to go along, too. I was terrified and wondered if I was being arrested for not being at work. We were taken to a national guard centre and I was told that I couldn't be with José because he was a police officer. The prison staff had become so fed up with us that they had issued instructions for us to be arrested if we were seen together. José looked irritated by the whole thing.

'You have no right to arrest me because I haven't done anything wrong,' he said.

Lisette, the prison director, came along and said, 'Oh, Guedez, why have you done this?'

José offered a passionate defence of his actions. 'If I have to choose between my job and Natalie, I'll always choose Natalie,' he said, handing over his official badge.

'Don't be hasty, let's talk about this,' said Lisette. Despite her annoyance with José for consorting with me, she still wanted to keep him as an ally.

'There's nothing to talk about. I'm not going to leave Natalie.'

I was then released from the national guard centre and we booked a hotel because we both knew that José couldn't go back to the prison that night.

We discussed escaping there and then but decided in the end

that we'd stick to our original plan to escape in a few days' time. I went back to the prison that night and went up to the *anexo*. I noticed that some of the female guards were looking smug about José's resignation.

'You can laugh as much as you like, but I'm going to have the last laugh,' I said quietly. Then I climbed into bed and fell asleep.

As I dropped off, images of José and me walking across the border of Venezuela to freedom filled my head.

The following morning, Lisette wouldn't let me out of the prison.

'You can't take my benefit away from me because I'm dating a prison guard. It's not against the rules to do that, you know,' I said.

She wanted me to sign a long statement saying I was going out with José. Reluctantly, I signed it, and then she let me go. The following day, I was out in town with José when Vivi called me on my mobile.

'Natalie, you need to get out of here fast,' she said. 'I've heard that probation are sending a request to the court tomorrow to revoke your benefit because they've had enough of you breaking the rules.'

I was staying out all the time with fake sick notes saying that I hadn't come back because I was ill. The guards knew it was all a scam and I realised I'd pushed things too far. My behaviour had been foolish and ungrateful, but it was as if my desire for José obliterated logic. At the back of my mind, I kept thinking that the sooner I escaped, the sooner I'd get back to Nikita and that if my bad behaviour speeded up my escape, it would be no bad thing.

José and I looked at each other. We'd have to move our plans forward by one day and leave at the crack of dawn the following day.

The few people who did know about our plan urged us to go immediately. I'd been taking my stuff gradually to the sewing flat. I'd sold my stereo, the shop, the phones. The idea was to get as much money together as possible. All I had left were some bits of furniture that I told Vivi she could have. That night I slept like a baby.

17 SO MUCH LUCK

'Could you please give me some advice regarding Natalie, or else tell me who I should be talking to? I gather she has fled the country and I need to know what implications that has from a legal perspective – is she 'wanted' outside Venezuela? If she comes back to the UK will she be arrested? Natalie has been sending me emails but I do not know her exact whereabouts.'

Email from Shona to a British Foreign Office official

'This is a new one on me! We will call the prison today to enquire and let you know as soon as possible.'

Email reply from Foreign Office official to Shona

I'd set my alarm for half-past five. The gates opened for people to leave for work at six. I bounded out of bed and jumped into the shower. When I heard the guards coming with the keys, I crept over to Vivi's bed and shook her gently, then hugged her, kissed her on the cheek and whispered, 'Thanks so much for everything. Goodbye.'

She whispered 'Goodbye' back and gave me a conspiratorial wink.

I was petrified. If this went wrong, I would be going back to prison, because today the probation board were applying to have my benefit taken away from me. This absolutely had to work. Having tasted freedom, the prospect of being locked up again was horrific. I knew that there could be no half-measures where escape was concerned. If I hid out in Mérida, it was just a matter of time before the national guard would catch me.

My stomach was churning, and my heart was pumping hard. Today was supposed to be the first of the rest of my life. I clutched my supply of US dollars. It had been difficult to get hold of them in Venezuela but eventually I had persuaded a tourist place to exchange some for bolívares.

At first, they hadn't been interested in doing business with me, but eventually they let me in. They shut all the doors and windows of the shop, and then they gave me the dollars. I got the rest of my dollars from a tourist hotel.

The people who sold me the dollars were European – not many Venezuelans had access to dollars. The money I'd had transferred from England had to be put into José's bank account, but when it came to withdrawing it, the bank was reluctant to hand it over.

Usually, I left the prison at around seven o'clock in the morning, in order to miss the traffic on the way into Mérida. Today, I left an hour earlier, but thankfully none of the guards queried this change in my daily routine. The prison was once again shrouded in the morning mist. I'd arrived there in mist and now I was leaving, hopefully forever, in mist. Deep down, I had nagging doubts that this wouldn't be the last time I'd ever see the prison, but I screwed my eyes tightly shut and prayed that it would be.

It had been raining all night and the roads were muddy. I didn't pay much attention to the weather conditions and it didn't occur to me that they could have disastrous consequences for my escape. It was a rare chilly day, something that I hoped would not be a bad omen. I shivered and pulled my jacket more tightly around me, then I climbed onto the bus to the village. My heart lifted as the bus started moving.

At last, I was on my way.

The plan was to meet José at the bus station in Ejido, a nearby town. It was too risky for us to meet in Mérida, particularly given our recent arrest by the national guard. From Ejido, we would catch a bus to Cúcuta, the first city inside the Colombian border. I couldn't imagine the joy I would feel if we reached Cúcuta safely.

Like me, José was incredibly nervous, but for me, not for himself. I got on a bus to Ejido. The route was through the mountains and the road was blocked because the heavy rains had caused a mudslide. I had worried and worried about being caught by national guards or stopped at one of the many checkpoints we would have to go through, but being thwarted by a mudslide had never crossed my mind.

Because of the rain, there were lots of national guards around, dealing with the effects of flash floods and avalanches. They seemed to be everywhere I looked. I put my head in my hands, convinced that my escape was now doomed to failure. I had visions of the gates of San Juan prison clanging shut behind me for six more years. I started to cry but quickly wiped my tears away because I didn't want to draw attention to myself. The mudslide had caused a huge traffic jam. Everyone was honking their horns and looking frustrated as nothing was moving.

Every second that passed, delaying my rendezvous with José in Ejido, felt like an hour. Eventually, one of the guards climbed on the bus and said to the driver, 'Turn around and go back. The road is impassable from here.'

I couldn't take this in. There seemed to be no way round this problem. I wondered what was happening to José. We'd sold our phones, so had no way of communicating with each other. I was panic-stricken and had no idea what to do. The bus turned around.

'I really need to get to Ejido,' I said, trying not to sound too desperate.

'There's another route,' one of the passengers said. I decided to get off the bus and try to find a taxi to take me the other way.

I found a taxi quite quickly and the driver agreed to try the alternative route, but because of the floods, he couldn't get through on that road, either. I got out of the taxi, desperate to speak to José.

If I can't get through, how's he going to get through? Should I go back? Should I keep trying to make it to Ejido? I asked myself. I just didn't know what to do. *Stick to the plan as far as possible*, I kept saying repeatedly. *That's what José will be doing.*

Then I got on a bus that went the same route that the taxi had tried. I thought that a big strong bus might have more chance of getting through the floods than a flimsy taxi. By now, I was hours behind schedule. The bus got through this first obstacle that the taxi hadn't been able to. I felt as if I'd been holding my breath for the past ten minutes, and when we got through the flooded road I exhaled sharply. Then we came to a river caused by the flood.

There were national guards helping people get across in four-wheel drive vehicles, although the water was reaching high up on them.

'We'll have to turn around,' said the bus driver.

I'd run out of options. I went up to the bus driver and, with tears in my eyes, begged him to go through the river.

'You don't understand. My whole life depends on this. I need to get to the other side of that river,' I cried. I was too distressed by that point to bother trying to be low key about it.

Other passengers heard, gave me sympathetic glances and said, 'Go on, give it a try.'

The bus driver must have seen the desperation in my eyes, and he went for it.

The guards were waving some people through, but they didn't seem overly keen for the bus to go through this temporary river. But now that he'd decided he was going to try to get across the river, the bus driver wasn't going to let himself be put off by the guards.

'It's my bus. Let me give it a try,' he said. The guards nodded.

I didn't want to duck down, as that would have looked too obvious, but I turned my head away from the window and fiddled with something in my bag so that I looked inconspicuous. Once again, I held my breath. My heart was pounding so loudly that I was sure the other passengers would be able to hear it.

The bus driver had been watching the four-wheel drives going through and had worked out where there were bits of higher ground. Instead of steering a straight course, he snaked his way across, miraculously avoiding sinking into the mud. When the bus reached the other side, everyone was clapping and cheering. I rejoiced and was convinced this was a sign that everything was going to be all right from now on – at least until I reached Ejido. A bit of water had seeped into the front of the bus but not too much.

My optimism soon dissipated, though, as my thoughts turned to José. I was now three hours late and was sure that I'd finally arrive in Ejido only to simply have to come back because he would no longer be there.

When we arrived at the bus station, I felt terrified. It was likely that I'd bump into national guards and, because Ejido wasn't far from Mérida, I was bound to run into a guard who would recognise me. I felt scared and alone. This place was absolutely heaving. Buses and taxis and people all tried to negotiate a space that was far too small to fit everyone in.

Even if José has made it, how the hell am I going to find him? I said to myself, but about two minutes after I got off the bus, I saw José's friend Alejandro – who had said he wanted to come with us to make sure we got across the border safely – carrying some cups of coffee. He took me straight to José, who was in a terrible state. I fell into his arms and kissed him madly. I was trying to blurt everything out. I was happy and nervous and excited.

'Don't worry, I would have waited all day for you,' he said. 'And all night.'

After our initial euphoria at finding each other, José became agitated and said we needed to get moving. He started panicking and said, 'Let's not take the bus. Let's take a taxi.'

We jumped into a taxi going to Cúcuta. Two Colombians had already got into the taxi and asked us if we wanted to share with them. They didn't have much luggage, but José and I had a huge rucksack each, which went in the boot of the car. Thankfully, there were no floods on this side of Ejido and the taxi set off.

The journey was difficult. José had always been easy-going but now I could see that the pressure was getting to him. He was completely silent and pale. Usually, he laughed and joked his way through things, but he knew how high the stakes were on this journey. I was getting more and more nervous as we started to go through checkpoints. It's much easier to get through a checkpoint on a bus than in a taxi, because the guards don't usually check buses. I wished we'd travelled by bus instead but said nothing.

I knew that I stuck out as a non-Venezuelan and decided to pretend to be asleep before we arrived at each checkpoint so that at least my blue eyes wouldn't show. I realised, though, that I couldn't do this every time. At the sixth checkpoint we were stopped. I was terrified that they might ask to open the boot and would see our rucksacks. The guard stuck his head through the window and said something to me. The taxi driver knew I could speak Spanish but said to the guard, 'Oh, you're wasting your time speaking to that gringo – she can't speak a word of Spanish.'

The guard lost interest and waved us on. I don't know why the taxi driver did that. Perhaps he was in a hurry to get to our destination and couldn't be bothered to have a big conversation with the guards. I tried to be as cool as I could. After that, even though there were more checkpoints to go through, I relaxed. I could feel José's body next to mine taut with tension.

I knew that it wasn't that much further to the border. You must get your passport stamped before you get to the border, but I didn't want to risk showing mine to any official person in Venezuela. I didn't know if there was a national computer network that would flash a warning when the name Natalie Welsh was typed in. I just couldn't take that risk.

We dropped the two Colombians off at a town before the border. I felt a bit more relaxed not having to play the role of carefree traveller anymore. The taxi driver explained to us about getting our passports stamped. 'But a lot of people who are only going to Cúcuta don't bother,' he said.

'Oh, let's not worry then – we're only going to Cúcuta,' I said, as casually as I could. José looked as if he was paralysed with fear. He hadn't uttered a single word throughout the entire journey.

The taxi driver seemed to accept our explanation and we carried on driving. My mouth felt dry as we approached the border and I became increasingly terrified. The whole place was swarming with national guards and everyone got stopped. I sat on my hands, crossed my fingers and closed my eyes. Going to sleep was the only thing I could think of to do. Unbelievably, we were waved through without any questions. Some of the colour that had drained out of José's face started to come back.

A mile down the road, we saw a sign saying '¡Bienvenido Colombia!' They were the best words I'd ever seen. I turned to José and we hugged each other.

As soon as he knew we were safe, he became his old self again. The whole mood in the car changed. The taxi driver must have picked up on this and beamed at us. José and I felt euphoric that we'd made it.

I gazed at him and said, 'This is it.' I couldn't believe it. I was still nervous just in case a national guard in Colombia did something to me, but I was free at long last. I stared gratefully around me. Cúcuta was obviously a poor area.

The taxi driver dropped us off at the bus station and told us to be careful, to put our bags in a hotel and not to leave anything valuable there. I had a money belt on me, and José and I split the cash between us. 'Don't go out late at night,' were the taxi driver's parting words. We were conscious that we would be prime targets for any gang, and we weren't on home territory now.

Alejandro decided to leave us after we'd booked into a hotel. We parted tearfully. He'd put his job on the line and he wasn't getting anything out of it. He had come with us out of pure friendship, a friendship that has endured to this day.

The hotel was disgusting. It was the cheapest one we could find – previously we'd stayed in decent accommodation but now we were on a tight budget. There was paint peeling off the walls and it was smelly and dirty. We were led down a narrow, dark corridor and left our bags in a poky room buzzing with mosquitoes. But we didn't care. This was my first night of freedom and the first night of our lives together. We vowed that we would never be separated again.

We didn't want to risk walking around the town, so we sat tight in the hotel, only venturing out to the bus station that was nearby. We bought tickets to Bogotá and sat in the terminus for a while, munching on hot dogs. Then we went back to the hotel and chatted about the future.

José was so happy for me. 'Mi niña, you're free now,' he kept on saying. He looked at me adoringly.

I had been so absorbed with the mechanics of escaping from San Juan that I hadn't thought too much about what it all meant to José. He was leaving his friends, the chance of steady employment, his beloved mother and daughter, and his language behind just so that he could run to a strange part of the world with me.

'José, I can't believe that you're prepared to give up so much for me. I know how hard it must be for you to leave behind so many people and things that you love.'

'No, no, we must be together, you are the breath of my life. I can return to Venezuela to see my family or they can come to visit us in England. Our future has to be together.' He kissed me tenderly. I felt reassured that he was not leaving his country weighed down with regrets.

I was keen to buy myself more time before they sounded the alarm back at the prison. I didn't want Vivi to have to go through an interrogation even though I knew she wouldn't say anything, so I called the prison and said I wasn't feeling well and couldn't come back that night.

Then we phoned Penelope and said, 'We've gone and we're not coming back.'

She was happy for us. 'You deserve to be free and together,' she said. 'You're young and in love and you have a right to a future.' I could sense that she was grinning broadly down the phone. The Venezuelans are a passionate people and they believe in love, and that where love is concerned, half-measures just won't do.

We also called Vivi to let her know that we were safe. She too was overjoyed for us. 'I might do the same thing myself,' she said. 'You've put ideas into my head.'

José and I fell asleep in each other's arms. The next thing I knew, he was gently shaking me awake.

We stepped out of the hotel, crossed the road and climbed onto the bus, loading our rucksacks into the boot at the side of the coach. There was a bit of bustle and noise already, with bus station shops open and quite a few coaches revving their engines. We steeled ourselves for the twenty-six-hour journey ahead.

When we got on the coach, the driver said to us, 'Have your passports ready because you will get stopped at some point on the way to Bogotá by the national guard.'

Suddenly, I was filled with panic again. I was terrified that as our passports hadn't been stamped, we'd be sent back to Venezuela because we didn't have the necessary permission to be in the country.

Every time we approached a checkpoint, I got scared. We sailed through the smaller checkpoints, but I was sure we'd be stopped at the larger ones. As we approached one, the driver said, 'You'll probably have to produce your passports here.' Unbelievably, we weren't stopped. I couldn't believe our luck and decided that God or fate or some other benign force must be on our side, and that our love was meant to be.

As we got out of the main town area, I relaxed a bit more and started to take note of the scenery. The countryside reminded me a lot of Holland, with a few more hills. All that was missing were the windmills. The scenery didn't take my breath away in the way it had in Venezuela. When we stopped, we ate *arepas* and had *café con leche*. In both Venezuela and Colombia, coffee is served in tiny little cups that you can drain in just a mouthful. Street vendors walk around with coffee urns as some of the prisoner vendors in San Juan had done.

The next morning, we finally arrived at Bogotá. Panic rose in my throat again. I thought to myself, *It's too good to be true that we've got this far.*

The coach driver shook his head and said, 'I've been driving this route for fourteen years and that's the first time we've never been stopped at a checkpoint.' José and I looked at each other. We still couldn't believe we'd been this lucky.

We got off the bus in the middle of a political demonstration. I was terrified and was desperate to get away, because there were lots of police around. I had no interest in finding out what was going on; all that mattered was getting away from the police. They were dressed in full body armour, were on horses and had massive riot shields.

We had to find a hotel before we did anything else. We hailed a taxi, explained to the driver that we wanted somewhere not too expensive but in a safe neighbourhood where we wouldn't be vulnerable to kidnapping or attack. Unfortunately, the hotel he took us to was on the edge of a violent area. After we'd checked in, we walked cautiously to a nearby telecommunications place. On our way there, we walked through a residential area. It was early evening and was growing chilly, but we saw lots of young women standing in doorways scantily clad in miniskirts and crop tops. I guessed they were prostitutes. Then we bought ourselves a cheap and unappetising meal.

At the telecommunications place, I emailed Shona apologising for lying to her about what I'd needed money for and explaining that I'd escaped from the prison and was now safely over the border in Colombia. I explained that I hadn't wanted to put her in an awkward position by informing her of our plans.

Shona was great. She was always supportive of me, was fine about the escape and said she would contact the embassy to find out what my legal status was. She said she understood that I did what I had to do and that she didn't know what she would have done in those circumstances. I also emailed my sister and she told me later that she really admired my great escape. Once again, José and I phoned Vivi and updated her.

I was feeling confident now, but there was one more hurdle still to cross. I was worried about buying a plane ticket with a passport in case my name showed up on some international 'wanted people' list. I didn't feel home and dry yet, but I felt I was on my way.

José was giving up so much to be with me. I hugged him tightly because the crunch moment had come. Our plan was to settle in Spain. One of the prisoners who had day release was Spanish and we asked him if he knew anyone who could help us find accommodation over there. He said someone would be waiting for us who had a hotel where we could stay and work for our board. The plan was to bring Nikita over when we were settled. We went into a travel agency to buy our tickets. The first flight we were told about involved changing planes at Caracas.

'No thanks,' we said in unison.

They told us the fare in dollars but said we couldn't pay in dollars and had to first change our money into the local currency.

We rushed to an exchange booth and got everything changed back into Colombian pesos. Then we bought our plane tickets for the next day. We had to show our passports, but the travel agent glanced at them without batting an eyelid. Holding the tickets in my hand felt amazing.

This flimsy piece of paper is all that's standing between me and freedom now, I said to myself. I still have the boarding pass.

We left the travel agent's and went back to our hotel. I wasn't worried about walking into an airport again because I was sure that nothing could go wrong, not now that we'd come so far. We got into the queue and a woman came and checked our passports before we reached the check-in desk.

'There's something wrong with them,' she said, and went off frowning. For some reason, I didn't feel worried. José said nothing but he also didn't look too alarmed. The woman returned with two immigration officers.

'Come with us please,' they said. I felt slightly concerned but I wasn't panicking. I was convinced that we hadn't come through this many obstacles for nothing.

Immigration wanted to know how we'd got into Colombia without a stamp.

We had a story ready: 'We came in through Venezuela.'

'Why didn't you get your passports stamped at the border then?'

We played dumb. 'What do you mean? Nobody told us. When we got to the border we just got waved through.'

'You're supposed to get it stamped before you get to the border.'

'It doesn't say that anywhere. How were we supposed to know?' I said. But the officials weren't satisfied. My heart sank. Then José and I were separated, and all our bags were searched.

I prayed that we'd make it onto the plane. Suddenly, all the memories of being arrested at Margarita in July 2001 flooded back. The immigration officials started interrogating me and said they suspected us of carrying drugs. I burst out laughing. If only they knew.

'We need to X-ray you,' they said sternly.

'Yes, that's fine. But can we go now, then we can still catch the plane,' I begged.

The story José and I had made up was that I had gone on holiday to Margarita, then gone to Caracas with friends and met José there and fallen in love with him, then we had moved to Mérida because of José's job. We stuck to the truth as far as possible. To my overwhelming relief, they believed us and abandoned the X-ray plan. I prayed that we would still be in time for our plane. We were trying to rush down the corridor when the national guard stopped us, wanting to search our bags.

'We haven't got time for this, we've just been searched,' we said, somehow managing to shake them off. We raced to the departure lounge. It was deserted because all the passengers were already on the plane. We made it on board just in the nick of time. There was a complimentary glass of champagne for everyone because this was the first direct flight to Spain this airline had made. As José and I breathlessly clinked our glasses together, we knew that we had more to celebrate than most of the other passengers.

José had always been there supporting me. He had been the wise one but now he had to put his trust and faith in me. We were entering familiar territory for me, but he was about to land in a continent which was different from his own.

On the plane, I said to him that it was highly likely that he could be interrogated when he arrived and that I probably wouldn't be questioned. 'What you have to tell them is that we're boyfriend and girlfriend and that we're on holiday for two weeks. Tell them I've always wanted to go to Colombia, so we took time off work and tried to fit Spain and Colombia all into one trip.'

The plane didn't have many people on it. I moved to four empty seats, sprawled out across them and slept and slept and slept. I felt as if all the years of stress were lifting off me. José also slept deeply. Escaping is a tiring business.

I loved José deeply but on that plane journey I wondered if we were doing the right thing. For a moment, I was scared that with José it might be like it had been with Delroy, where I thought I was madly in love but had then fallen out of love.

I was also worried for him and wondered whether he had made the right choice. I knew how hard it was to be suddenly transplanted into a strange country and I also knew how hard it was to be separated from your child.

When we landed in Madrid, I cheered under my breath. I peered out of the window of the plane, glad to see some grey European weather after years of blue skies in Venezuela. At passport control, we were separated by a couple of people. I walked straight through and the official didn't even glance at my passport.

Because the plane was coming in from Colombia, the immigration staff were vigilant. José was stopped and said simply, 'I'm with my girlfriend,' I waved to him and he was let through.

He'd never left Venezuela before, nor did he have any desire to before he met me. But because he loved me, he'd gone to two different countries in the space of a few days.

The plan was to call the contacts of the Spanish prisoner who was supposed to pick us up from the airport. We dialled the phone numbers, but they didn't work. We hadn't been expecting that at all.

'Why promise to help us if he had no intention of doing so?' I asked José. We had no idea of what to do next. *We'll have to go to England*, I thought, but I didn't feel ready yet.

We called Vivi, told her we were in Spain and asked to speak to the Spanish guy. She said he'd gone missing.

'How have they reacted to me being missing with José?'

'They aren't happy about it. They think you're still in Venezuela, that you've gone to Caracas.'

'Why would they think we'd be that stupid?'

I looked around the airport. I was overjoyed to be back on a continent with a solid infrastructure again. I wanted José to see everything – the people, the roads, the buildings – just for him to be able to see how different Europe was from South America.

The lack of anyone showing up to meet us at the airport punctured my euphoria. I pondered what to do next and then José saved the day. His guard friend who had been imprisoned had a cousin called Pedro who lived in Spain. José called him and the guard told us to ring him back in ten minutes. We were told we could go to his home in Bilbao the next day and his cousin would help us find work.

We decided to stay in Madrid for the night. We walked through the town centre to try to find a hotel. Eventually, someone recommended a place to us and took us there. José gave the person some money because that was the way things always worked in Venezuela. The man looked surprised but accepted it.

We booked into a hostel with a shared bathroom on the landing, then went out and got some food. We had to be careful with our money now as we didn't know how long it would have to last us. All our hopes were pinned on Bilbao and getting jobs there.

The next morning, we took the train to Bilbao. It was a long journey and when we arrived, we phoned Pedro. It was six or seven hours before he came to collect us, and we were convinced that he too was going to abandon us. 'We're going to have to go to England, José. We haven't got enough money to keep staying in hotels until we sort ourselves out.'

When Pedro did turn up, he gave no explanation for being so late. He hadn't been told the full story about us; he knew that José was a guard but not that I had been a prisoner. When we told him, he shrugged and seemed to accept it. The flat was comfortable, and Pedro lived there with his sister Corina. He had a spare room with no bed and one of the first things he did was phone up and order a bed for us. We gave him what we thought was the right money for a month's rent. Our plan was to save up enough money to get our own place.

Pedro was able to explain to José how things worked. 'One week's wages as a security guard are the equivalent of three months' wages in Venezuela,' he said.

José's eyes lit up. 'We'll get Nikita, and I can send money home to my mum,' José said excitedly. He saw himself as a provider and it was important to him to support his mum and his daughter, as well as me.

Finally, he called his mum. As far as she knew, he was at work in Mérida. He had told her about me and explained that that was why he'd gone back to Mérida.

'Hi Mum, I'm in Spain,' he said.

'You can't be, you haven't got a passport,' she gasped.

'I got one,' he replied. He was so excited and happy, and although she was surprised, she was happy for him. Europe is considered a good place to be in Venezuela and his mum supported his move. No doubt she hoped that, like many other migrants seeking better employment opportunities in Europe, once José got himself a good job, he'd start sending money home for her and his daughter.

Filled with nerves and excitement, I called Nikita, but didn't tell her that I'd escaped from Venezuela. How could a girl of her age understand something like that? I told her I had a boyfriend because I wanted her to meet José. 'I've told him all about you, Nikita, about what a wonderful little girl you are. He really wants to meet you.' I had planted the first seed.

'That's nice, Mummy. You sound really happy,' she said. I'd

spoken to her little on the phone because it was so expensive and difficult to get through. I had always phoned her on her birthday and at Christmas, and a couple of other times in between. I was a regular, if infrequent, phone presence in her life.

I emailed the embassy to find out what my legal status was. Nobody had even told them that I'd gone. The embassy seemed uncertain, saying that they would investigate it and report back. It was later clarified that while Venezuela would not try to extradite me, I could be rearrested and put back in jail if I ever set foot in Venezuela again. I shivered and vowed never to return.

The day after we arrived in Bilbao, we tried to find work. There was a Metro station nearby and Pedro showed us how to use it. He said he could get José a job, but time went by and no job materialised.

Our money was running out, and we were eating Pedro and Corina's food and feeling increasingly uncomfortable about it all.

José and I were used to being with each other and we weren't annoying each other, but now we needed something more than love to survive. I said that I'd try to find a job. I thought it would be easy because I could speak English and Spanish. I wanted to get a good job and decided I'd try to get a position at a travel agent. But there was nothing and nobody seemed interested in employing me. We spent the whole day looking without success.

We discovered that there had recently been a crackdown on illegal immigrants. Those who had been working for more than five years had an amnesty, but anyone caught employing people post-amnesty was fined a lot of money.

José started getting depressed. He was away from home and his family, and wanted to provide for me. He went off early one morning, saying determinedly, 'I'm not going to come back until I've found a job.' But despite searching hard, he found nothing and didn't return until late at night.

He came back feeling miserable. All he wanted was to look after me and keep himself busy. After about a month, we started running out of money. José had a serious conversation with Pedro.

'Can you get us work or not? We don't want to hang around here forever.'

'Don't worry. I'm just waiting for someone to leave and then I'll be able to get you something.'

José and I had a talk. 'This is how much money we've got left. We can keep holding out here or we can use the rest of the money to go to England,' I said. 'I will try to find a job but if I can't get one, we'll get money from the state.' José couldn't understand that – it was such an alien concept to him.

He looked defeated by events. Both of us had used so much energy reaching freedom and we had never dreamed that freedom itself would cause us problems. We decided to try to hold out a bit longer although nothing much was happening. We slept the days away – it was like being back in prison all over again.

José eventually saw the sense in what I was saying. We wrote Pedro and Corina a note saying, 'Thanks very much for your kindness and hospitality but we can't continue living like this. We're going to England.'

We packed up our belongings and decided to get a boat back, guessing that we'd have an easier time with immigration at a seaport than at an airport. We boarded a bus to Santander, to catch the ferry to Plymouth. I warned him that it wasn't going to be easy. We would have to come up with an even more elaborate story this time as, whatever happened, we didn't want the immigration officers thinking that José was coming to live in England.

The story was that we lived in Venezuela, went to Spain on holiday and were going to nip back to England to see my family for a couple of days before going back to Spain via France, because I wanted José to see as much of Europe as possible.

I wasn't expecting it at all, but we were stopped by immigration as we tried to board the boat. 'You will have to get entry clearance from the UK authorities before you can board,' said the official self-importantly. I knew that permission would never be granted.

He walked off to make a phone call to England. My heart sank and José turned pale. As we waited for an answer, I knew what it would be. We waited and waited until we were the only people left in the waiting room.

I turned to José and whispered, 'Let's go quickly. We've got nothing to lose.'

We reached passport control. I could see that the barrier to let people on to the boat was being lowered. An official looked at José's passport and shook his head.

'Oh no, we've had all this,' I said. 'They had to get permission from England. That's why we're last.'

To my amazement, he believed me. My acting skills were obviously better than I thought. 'OK, you might as well go through,' he said.

We skipped joyfully onto the boat. We had booked a cabin, as the journey was almost twenty-three hours. I love ferries and I was excited for José.

'Things will be different when we get to England, you'll see. I'll get a job and you can get work on a building site.' I was determined not to get stuck in the benefits rut.

Now that we were on our way to England, I allowed myself to think of Nikita at last. Thoughts of her took over from everything else. Until now, I hadn't let myself dare to hope that we could be reunited, but finally, after all those years away, I let myself look forward to seeing her again. It was torturous to dream about it before when any realistic prospect of seeing her was still years away. But now I was just twenty-four hours away from seeing my daughter. I began to feel incredibly nervous about what sort of reception I'd get.

We were both excited and optimistic on the ferry. José must have been absolutely terrified about going to England – my home and a country whose language he couldn't speak. I was too nervous about my own return to say too much about that, though. I thought sadly that the last time I'd been on English soil, my mum had been alive and well. I missed her terribly and would have been overjoyed if I could have seen her again just one more time.

I knew that she would have seen the change in me straight

away. I was no longer a selfish, silly child who listened to no one. I'd been through a lot and had gained maturity and, I hoped, empathy for others.

The ferry docked in Plymouth the following day. There were two queues at immigration. Behind one desk was an older man, while the other was young. I whispered, 'Let's go to the queue with the younger guy; we're less likely to get stopped by him.'

I told the passport guy the story we'd worked out and managed to convince him that both of us were overwhelmed with excitement. 'England, London, holiday,' José kept saying. I chatted on nervously and the young immigration official fell for it hook, line and sinker.

'Have a nice holiday,' he said, beaming as he waved us through.

We walked out of the building and into the street. I wanted to get down on my hands and knees to kiss the dusty pavement. I couldn't believe I was back. I'd never been a big fan of England before; I'd always felt it was boring, but I really appreciated boring now.

'I'm home,' I said at last, tears welling up in my eyes. I hadn't been able to say it in Spain, but at last I was here.

I called Eve. She couldn't believe it and said little. She was in shock. I knew that I should have prepared her, but I wasn't sure how to and so just blurted out the news. She must have been scared. I'd messed up my life, landed her with an extra child to look after and then, as suddenly as it had started, it was all about to finish. Nikita had spent more of her life with Eve than with me, and she and Eve's daughter Mara were like sisters. Caring for Nikita might have started out as a burden, but Nikita was now like a daughter to her. She probably thought I was going to come along and take Nikita off her within hours.

'It's OK,' José said soothingly. I called another friend called Simone, who told me that her boss Lesley had written countless letters to Prisoners Abroad on my behalf.

'I'm back in England, Simone,' I said.

'What do you mean you're back? Did they release you early?'

'Well, actually, I've escaped.'

'My God, you mean you dug a tunnel?'

'No, no, nothing like that. I was on day release and I just left.'

Then Simone put Lesley on the phone. By now, I was crying. 'I don't know what to do, we've got no money. Eve is in shock that I'm back.'

'Just get the train and come to us.' So, we jumped on a train back home. I was quiet on the journey. There were a lot of thoughts whizzing round my brain. José sensed this and said little.

The balance of power had shifted once we reached Spain. I was almost, but not quite, on home turf. Now the balance had shifted further. José looked around him in bewilderment. I imagined he was scrabbling around to try to find some landmarks, but he could see nothing that was familiar to him. I knew that José felt dislocated but inevitably only one word screamed and whirred around my head, *Nikita, Nikita, Nikita.*

I needed to get a job to support her. I was determined that from now on she would want for nothing and that everything I earned would be acquired legally. One thing that mercifully wasn't on my brain was crack. Usually, returning home meant rushing back to crack, but I wasn't interested in it at all. My lack of interest in the drug told me that I'd changed fundamentally. At last I'd grown up. I was really looking forward to people seeing me as me, not as a crackhead. I was no longer a skinny, scrawny addict hunched in the gutter. I had no respect from anybody when I left. Now I had put on weight; I was slim but healthy. I was in love. I was looking forward to people seeing the difference in me, watching me turn over a new leaf.

When we got off the train, I was astonished because so much had changed. Lesley's hairdressing salon was just around the corner. We had heavy bags and although we were down to our last £20, I wanted to get a taxi to get there as fast as I could.

There had been a leisure centre with a swimming pool slide outside the building when I left but that had gone. Apparently, they had got a substantial lottery grant and a big glass building had been built in its place. The road layout had been changed. Time for me had frozen but it never occurred to me that for everyone else things had moved on.

By the time we arrived at the hairdresser's, I felt like Rip Van Winkle. Simone saw the taxi pulling up outside. She was wearing a long white gypsy skirt, as they'd just come into fashion. It looked odd to me because fashions in Venezuela were so different. I didn't think that within a few months I'd be wearing one myself.

Simone and Lesley came rushing out. It was a big reunion and we were all hugging, kissing and crying. José stepped back and let me get on with it.

Lesley had got engaged to a famous hairdresser. They'd bought the shop next door and knocked it through to make one big, more upmarket salon. Not even that was familiar.

Lesley and Simone were chatting away to me but suddenly it was all too much. I hadn't prepared myself mentally. I managed to hold it all together, but I felt spaced out, as if I'd smoked some cannabis. I looked around at all these people and just didn't feel comfortable.

'Don't worry about Eve. Your sudden return has just been a bit of a shock to her,' Lesley said.

'I don't know what to do, Lesley, we've got nowhere to go.'

The last thing I expected was to come home and be homeless.

Lesley gave me some money. 'Book yourselves into a bed and breakfast and tomorrow you can go down to the DSS and get housing benefit.' My heart sank. This was everything I didn't want. I was horrified at the prospect of having to survive on handouts.

Lesley and Simone welcomed José and were warm towards him. I made sure he wasn't left out and introduced him as the love of my life and the man who had saved me. José was the person who was familiar to me, while the people I used to know no longer were. He was the only one who knew what I'd been through.

We managed to find a bed and breakfast place. The owner lived next door and rented the rooms out in the house, some on a long-term basis. It wasn't nice – damp and scruffy and not quite what I'd envisaged for my first night home.

I called Eve again. The children weren't home from school yet. I'd waited for more than three years to see my daughter and I couldn't wait any longer. 'See you at half-past three,' I said.

18 THE END OF LOVE

It was a ten-minute walk from where we were staying to Eve's house. I was feeling nervous but was also filled with huge excitement. I kept saying repeatedly to José, 'I'm so nervous, I'm so excited, I wonder what Nikita's going to be like.'

There was a truck with a trailer parked up in the street and I could see two girls playing in it. 'That's them,' said José, recognising Nikita from photos.

'No, it isn't.'

As we got closer, I realised that he was right – it was Nikita. In front of me was a little girl who was now a stranger. She was halfway through junior school and I'd missed all of it. She was beautiful and I couldn't take my eyes off her as I watched her playing happily in the trailer. It was clear that she was thriving in Eve's care.

Thank you, Eve, I said silently. *For keeping my daughter safe and happy and for looking after her so well. This is a gift too great to measure.*

Seeing Nikita again didn't feel real. It wasn't until later that it hit home. I'd been in a whirlwind from the moment I'd left Mérida and I hadn't had time to sit down and prepare myself for anything.

'What are you doing?' I said casually.

'We're playing in the truck,' Nikita said.

Nikita had no idea that I was her mother. I looked deep into her big brown eyes. It was an odd feeling to see no recognition there.

'Do you live nearby?'

'Yes.'

'Do you go to school near here?'

'Yes.'

'Do you know who I am?'

'No.'

'Well then, you shouldn't be talking to strangers.' I grinned. 'My name's Natalie.'

Nikita froze, then slowly a smile spread over her face. It was almost as if she didn't dare ask. She looked at me quizzically, then said hesitantly, 'Are you my mum?'

'Yes I am.'

Mara went screaming into the house. 'Mum, Mum!'

I held out my hand to Nikita. She took it and we walked into the house together.

It felt as if I'd last seen Eve yesterday.

'Mum, Mum, Mum, do you know my mum's back?' Nikita cried. I hadn't expected her to be calling Eve Mum, but I knew it was understandable.

Nikita hugged and kissed me. She was so open and innocent and trusting. There were no recriminations, no suspicion, just a warm and open cuddle. I introduced José to everyone. Once again, he stepped back and let me have my moment but, straight away, he was included in everything. Eve couldn't pronounce his Spanish name and said, 'I'm going to call you Jack.'

He seemed to like being given an English name. Nikita sat on my lap for a while, then she ran back outside to play. The reunion that I had sweated over she had taken completely in her stride. I couldn't believe it.

Eve explained that people kept asking why Nikita called Eve by her first name and she had said to Nikita, 'You can call me Mum if you want. It's going to be a long time before your real mum's back.'

There was no talk about Nikita coming home to me that day. It was too soon for all of that. I was relieved when we went, because it was all too much for me to deal with. I was tearful and confused as José and I walked away from Eve's house. I felt like it wasn't supposed to happen like that. It should have been like the final frame of a film with us rushing into each other's arms. Instead, it was all anticlimactic.

The following day, I went down to the DSS. It was an awful place, somewhere I'd spent so much time at before. And there were the same people scamming, trying to get Giros and loans. This was one place that hadn't changed.

I told José he couldn't come with me to my interview. While I was sat down waiting to be called, I stared hard at the girl sitting next to me and realised it was Emma, who I had known from my crack-smoking days. When I'd first met her, she had taken a lot of pride in her appearance. She had paid to have extensions in her hair and walked around with a bounce in her step. She had always dressed nicely and looked well groomed.

When I left England for Venezuela, she wasn't in as bad a state as I was. But now, she was clearly in a much worse condition than I'd ever been in. Her hair had always come first but now it was all over the place and she was wearing strange clothes that were hanging off her.

'Hello, Emma,' I said.

She couldn't focus on anything and obviously didn't recognise me. She'd been smoking, was desperate for her next fix and I guessed she was there to ask for a crisis loan.

I looked at her and thought, *Oh my God, that could have been me.*

Suddenly, I was overwhelmed with gratitude for the years I'd spent incarcerated in Venezuela. Sadly, Emma was completely gone. I saw her a few weeks later and there was a bloodstain down her jeans that I presumed was from her period. She was no longer able to take care of herself on even the most basic level.

Seeing her was a wake-up call for me. Sometimes, these chance meetings are more than coincidental. I vowed that I was going to get myself a job, any job, and work hard to make a success of my life for my own sake and for Nikita's.

Another person I bumped into from my past was Sabrina. She was sat at the back of a bus I got on one day. I didn't see her at first. There were no seats left and I walked to the back to stand up, lost in my own thoughts. Suddenly, I heard a voice calling out, 'Hey, Natalie.'

I couldn't believe it when I saw who it was. Sabrina hadn't changed at all. In all the time I'd known her, she had never had the time or money to look after her hair, and covered it with a hat. She was wearing a hat now. She'd put a bit of weight on and I wondered if she'd stopped smoking crack. She still looked rough, though, and I decided that she must still be in the grip of addiction.

Like most people I'd known at home, she'd heard that I'd escaped from jail and so wasn't surprised to see me. 'So, what was it like in Venezuela?' she asked eagerly.

'It was awful, but in some ways, it changed my life for the better. I'm off the crack now, don't want to touch the stuff ever again. And I'm going to write a book about it.'

Sabrina raised her eyebrows.

'What are you up to?' I asked in return.

She explained that she'd lost her flat and had been in and out of prison for shoplifting. I shivered, knowing that it could so easily have been me. She seemed genuinely pleased that I'd got off crack, though, and didn't appear to begrudge me my drug-free life.

I felt sorry for Sabrina because I couldn't imagine her ever changing. Once again, I thanked my lucky stars that I'd got away.

I gave her £20. In a strange kind of way, it was closure for me to be able to turn around and do that. Then I gathered up my bags to get off the bus, waved goodbye to her and walked away without looking back.

I got a place in a hostel and explained the situation with José to the landlord. He accepted it. The room was tiny, with just a single bed in it, but we didn't care. On our first night, the police turned up. We just stayed in our room, wanting to keep out of the way of any trouble. On our second day back, we spent the whole day out. I was looking for work, then we went shopping.

The landlord realised we were different from the other

occupants and offered us a bedsit in a different area. He said he didn't take housing benefit for this bedsit that was for people who worked, but that he could see I'd get a job soon so we could move in.

José got a bit of building work with a friend of mine. He was delighted to be working. He handed all the money over to me, keeping ten pounds back that he used to buy me small presents.

I got a one-day, temporary job at a recruitment agency and ended up staying there for two years. I'd only been back in the country for a month when the job was made permanent. I was overjoyed to come off benefits. I was well paid, had a lot of responsibility and, before long, we had the money to move into a beautiful apartment in a listed building with security, electronic gates and high ceilings. All the features and fittings were expensive; we had an en suite bathroom and felt as if we were staying in a nice hotel. José absolutely loved the place.

Nikita came to stay with us every weekend. Everything was going well between us. I made sure that the whole process was gradual so that it felt normal and natural for her. We went to see her and Mara every day after school. Then she visited me, but also with Mara because I didn't want to separate them. After a while, Eve said, 'I think it's time for Nikita to move back in with you.'

I was delighted that at long last I was going to get my daughter back properly. Everything felt right. We didn't talk about Venezuela at all. Nikita didn't give me a hard time about abandoning her and José made a great surrogate father. In fact, he was more of a stand-in mother because I worked such long hours.

José took Nikita to school, picked her up, cooked dinner and cleaned the house. At first, he really took pride in all of this. He was learning English and Nikita was helping him.

Everything was going unbelievably well. But then José started to get possessive and jealous. For the first time ever, we started to disagree. He must have been getting frustrated because he had no job and could not provide for Nikita and me.

The balance of power had shifted even further. He couldn't

buy things for me. He once tried to steal a bunch of flowers from the supermarket for me and got caught. Thankfully, they didn't press charges.

I was wrapped up in my job and in Nikita. José couldn't do anything because he had no legal right to work. He should have applied for a working visa in Venezuela, but it was something that had never occurred to us.

I was so preoccupied with my work that I didn't pay enough attention to how he was feeling. The demands of my job were huge and after all the things I'd failed at in my life, I was determined to make a success of this.

I had lots of business meetings in the evening, but José was convinced I was being unfaithful to him. I couldn't go out or do anything without being questioned, and he couldn't work. His suspicion about me eroded our love.

Everything became a vicious circle. I decided to buy a house and hoped that could be a new start for us. The house needed a lot of work doing on it and at first, he was happy and occupied doing the house up, but soon his frustrations returned and so did the arguments.

José desperately missed his family, his old life, his identity as a working man. He'd allowed all these facets of himself to be stripped away just so that he could be with me. Life was a real struggle for him, and England was becoming more and more of a prison to him.

'I never thought I'd miss my home so much,' he said to me despairingly one day. 'I can't tell you how much I miss my daughter and my mum and everything that's familiar to me.'

I knew exactly what it felt like to be separated from a child and put my arms around him. 'José, I'm so sorry that this isn't working out the way we planned. I wish I could fix things, really I do.'

Our relationship had been tested in Venezuela, but it was by the kind of adversity that united us and made our love stronger. Now, we were faced with much less dramatic problems and they were forcing us further and further apart. I wondered if the circumstances of high drama in which we fell in love meant that we simply couldn't withstand the normal pressures that couples face.

I couldn't believe that things had come to this, but I started to wonder how much it would cost to buy him a plane ticket home.

We spent a lot of time arguing, then we both got upset. José often cried after our rows and said, 'After everything that we've got through, I can't bear it that things are falling apart now, when our big problems are over.'

In the end, things disintegrated so far that with rivers of tears from both of us and many words of love and sadness, José boarded a flight home to Venezuela in September 2006.

EPILOGUE (2009)

I had been convinced that my relationship with José would last until the day one of us died. He was my soulmate and we had been through so much together. My time in Venezuela was an extraordinary period of my life with many highs and lows, and because José had been involved with so much of it, he could understand what I'd been through in a way that friends and family back in England never could.

I was sad when he left. As well as being my lover, he had been my best friend, my confidant, my rock and a father figure for Nikita. But at the same time, I now felt truly free. He had become increasingly possessive, probably because he felt lost and insecure in England and that caused many different problems. Without him, I could go where I wanted, when I wanted, without having to justify myself to anyone or ask permission from them, neither guards nor José.

When I said a tearful goodbye to him at the airport, I felt I was saying farewell to a whole chapter of my life. I loved him with all my heart, but having him by my side was a constant reminder not only of Venezuela but also of my crime. I know that I will never be able to escape from the terrible and stupid mistake that I made, but I feel I deserve a chance for a new start, this time making different choices. When I met new people, I had to explain José to them and why I can speak fluent Spanish. I longed to be normal and not to have to tell new people about my past.

With hindsight, I can see that there were just too many factors stacked against us. In the early heady days of passion, practical obstacles only served to intensify our feelings for each other, but when that initial excitement had settled down to something more measured, real life started to get in the way. Bringing José over here was like transplanting a rare tropical bloom into arctic soil and hoping that it would thrive. Uprooting him from his friends, family, job, culture and language, and expecting to avoid an earthquake, was too much to expect.

Perhaps if we had organised a UK work permit for José before we left Venezuela, things might have turned out differently. Even so, it would have been hard.

The culture in Venezuela is a macho one and José felt that if he couldn't provide for the woman he loved, then he was a failure. Our whole relationship had been founded on drama and adversity and adventure, and even without the issue of José being an unemployed illegal immigrant, I believe that the adaptation to normal, everyday life was too great a transition for our relationship to withstand.

I continued to work and be successful in recruitment, and am proud of the way I have transformed my life from those days of surviving on benefits and limping from one fix of crack to the next.

When I boarded the plane in Holland to Venezuela, fully expecting to be back home in a couple of weeks' time, I scorned conventional life. I was looking for thrills and excitement, and the thought of holding down a steady job, having a nice house in suburbia with a husband and a couple of kids was as appealing as forcing down a bowl of congealed porridge.

But I've changed. By the time I'd returned from Venezuela, I felt that I'd had enough excitement to last three lifetimes. I had long since stopped using crack and I had no desire to go back to the stuff. I felt as if it was something that belonged in the past and was now over and done with for the rest of my life.

The thought of meeting a partner and settling down suddenly became appealing. I met and fell in love with Jason a couple of years ago. He is a hard-working man with a job at a garage. He is a wonderful father to Nikita and to our son Brandon, who was born in 2008. We live happily in a village in the middle of some stunningly beautiful countryside. It is a tranquil, friendly place and could not be more different from my life in various prisons.

I learnt a lot about the meaning of true friendship while I was in Venezuela. My three close friends, Mary, Monica and Vivi, helped me more than I can say at the various stages of my time there. All three of them gave a lot of themselves. I feel that the deep bonds I forged with them will last a lifetime.

Watching Nikita grow up brings me incredible joy. She is a beautiful, polite girl who works hard at school and has lots of friends. Thankfully, she has no memory of her brief visit to Venezuela and still only knows scant details about what happened.

She is still too young to understand, but I'll talk to her properly about it when she's older. We have a close and open relationship, and I hope she will forgive me for my stupid mistake, for which I paid a high price. I know people will criticise me for taking a four-year-old on a drug run to a Latin American country I knew nothing about, and I readily accept their criticisms. All I can say in my defence is that addiction is an ugly and wretched business that prevents rational decision-making. In my crack-addled state, it never once entered my head that I wouldn't be boarding the plane home two weeks after Nikita and I arrived in Margarita.

I feel sorry for people who smuggle drugs and am disgusted by the people at the top who organise the illegal trade. The smugglers, like me, don't appreciate the real risks of what they're doing and the reality of having to spend years behind bars in a foreign jail.

The mules are bearing most of the risk, yet they get paid a pittance in comparison with the dealers. Smugglers are just pawns in a complex game of chess. They are regarded as completely expendable and no consideration is given by the dealers to how one smuggling run can destroy their lives forever. I have a child who suffered because of what I did but the dealers don't care about things like that. Unlike the smugglers, they are fully aware of the risks and dangers, and that's why they don't do the dirty deed themselves.

Drugs are ruining people's lives all over the country. Many people who could have made something of their lives have been reduced to complete wrecks because of their insatiable thirst for one addictive substance or another. I sometimes see addicts in the street now and wonder what they would be doing if they hadn't developed a drug habit. I've seen people's lives destroyed. I've watched them go from having good homes, jobs and families to sleeping rough, begging and shoplifting. People who meet them in the street have no idea of what they used to be. All they see is the shell that's left.

I know that it is thanks to my good friend Eve that Nikita is as happy and well-adjusted as she is. Eve was a struggling single mother on benefits, but without hesitation took Nikita in when she returned from Venezuela and brought her up as her own daughter. I will never be able to repay Eve in words or deeds for keeping my precious daughter safe and happy while I was away.

My heart breaks when I think about my mum's death. I know that the life I was leading before I went to Venezuela and the choices I made caused her enormous distress. I wish with all my heart that she was still alive to see that I kept the promise I made to her from San Juan prison the day before she died, that I'd turn my life around and make her proud of me. If spirits do float around after our bodies have breathed their last, then I hope that hers is looking down on me from somewhere and smiling.

I had many dark times during my years in jail in Venezuela, but I wouldn't exchange that experience for the world. I'm certain that if I'd remained at home, gorging myself on crack, that I would, sooner or later, have lost Nikita, probably my liberty and maybe even my life. In Venezuela, I grew up and started to understand what matters in life: love and loyalty and hard work. Now, I wake up in the morning, hug Jason and my beloved children and get ready for a day's work, feeling that I'm the luckiest woman on the planet. I've been given a second chance at life.

AFTERWORD (2020)

When I first published this book, my goal was to inspire people who were in dark places. I wanted to share my story and for you to know that no matter how dire your situation, with the right frame of mind there is always a way to turn around your life; to never give up, because as long as you believe, you can make the impossible possible; and there is always light beyond the tunnel as long as you persevere to the end and don't quit before you get there.

While I was in Venezuela, my gran died, and my mum and I received an inheritance. I invested every penny of that, plus my initial payment from this book and my salary, into the deposit on a house, hoping to secure a stable future for myself and my kids. Things were going great.

To my surprise, after the book's first publication, I was asked to resign from my job. On a good salary, I had been working in financial services for the clergy. I had a mortgage and a family. Having changed my life, I naively believed that my job was safe because the Church is about forgiveness, and I thought that they would have viewed me as a productive member of society with an empowering testimony.

I was wrong! Local media attention at the time of publication led to my forced resignation and sabotaged my further attempts to gain employment. Having paid my taxes, I assumed the government would help, only to be told by the Job Centre that no assistance would be forthcoming because I had a mortgage. For them to even consider offering help, I would have to lose my house and be homeless with my children. Then, I would probably be relocated to a different area, where I would be housed in a variety of bed-and-breakfast establishments sufficiently long enough to be eligible to claim benefits.

I felt broken again. I couldn't bear the thought that my family had worked their whole lives to leave an inheritance to establish my future, only for it to be wiped out. It wasn't fair – when I had built a new successful life in accordance with society's rules.

I was upset and stressed, and my relationship was breaking down with my partner. I felt like I had been let down again by a system that was supposed to help vulnerable people. I couldn't stand the thought of having to put my children through the process of losing their home, their friends and school. I was in a bad place and just didn't know what to do. Angry, I thought: *what's the point of trying to do right when you just get screwed over at the first opportunity?* In my misguided justifications to cling onto the life I had created for us all, I stupidly involved myself with drugs again in an attempt to pay my bills.

But being involved in drugs is never going to be a normal life, no matter what the intentions are behind it. My world came crashing down when I was sentenced to six years and nine months in prison in the UK for new drug charges, followed quickly by a proceeds-of-crime case, which led to the confiscation of my property, bank accounts, car and daughter's savings account. The outcome was even worse than the government's offer. I lost my house, possessions and my children, who ended up having to move from the area where they had settled, and worst of all: their mum was in prison again. I would have been better off had I accepted the bed-and-breakfast establishment route. Another hard lesson and I had no one else to blame but myself.

I now live on the road with little money, travelling around in a van. It is extremely difficult to maintain a normal lifestyle because of the proceeds-of-crime case that followed my last conviction. I would need to win the lottery to pay it off before I am able to own a property again. So, I have chosen a different lifestyle. Outside the UK, I have a beautiful life, although not always easy. I am free of having to try to conform to the expectations of society that it seems I never live up to. After surviving Venezuelan prison, I can get through anything, and I hope this book has shown that you can, too.

Natalie Welsh

To contact Natalie, please email Gadfly Press at gadflypress@outlook.com

If you have enjoyed this book, we would appreciate you leaving a review on Amazon or Goodreads.

Gadfly Press Socials
  https://gadflypress.com/
  https://www.facebook.com/gadflypressuk/
  https://twitter.com/GadflyPressUK

OTHER BOOKS BY GADFLY PRESS

English Shaun Trilogy
Party Time
Hard Time
Prison Time

War on Drugs Series
Pablo Escobar: Beyond Narcos
American Made: Who Killed Barry Seal? Pablo Escobar or George HW Bush
The Cali Cartel: Beyond Narcos
Clinton Bush and CIA Conspiracies:
From the Boys on the Tracks to Jeffrey Epstein

Un-Making a Murderer: The Framing of Steven Avery and Brendan Dassey
The Mafia Philosopher: Two Tonys
Life Lessons

Pablo Escobar's Story (4-book series)

Pablo Escobar: Beyond Narcos
War on Drugs Series Book 1

The mind-blowing true story of Pablo Escobar and the Medellín Cartel beyond their portrayal on Netflix.

Colombian drug lord Pablo Escobar was a devoted family man and a psychopathic killer; a terrible enemy, yet a wonderful friend. While donating millions to the poor, he bombed and tortured his enemies – some had their eyeballs removed with hot spoons. Through ruthless cunning and America's insatiable appetite for cocaine, he became a multi-billionaire, who lived in a $100-million house with its own zoo.

Pablo Escobar: Beyond Narcos demolishes the standard good versus evil telling of his story. The authorities were not hunting Pablo down to stop his cocaine business. They were taking over it.

American Made: Who Killed Barry Seal?
Pablo Escobar or George HW Bush
War on Drugs Series Book 2

Set in a world where crime and government coexist, *American Made* is the jaw-dropping true story of CIA pilot Barry Seal that the Hollywood movie starring Tom Cruise is afraid to tell.

Barry Seal flew cocaine and weapons worth billions of dollars into and out of America in the 1980s. After he became a government informant, Pablo Escobar's Medellin Cartel offered a million for him alive and half a million dead. But his real trouble began after he threatened to expose the dirty dealings of George HW Bush.

American Made rips the roof off Bush and Clinton's complicity in cocaine trafficking in Mena, Arkansas.

"A conspiracy of the grandest magnitude." Congressman Bill Alexander on the Mena affair.

The Cali Cartel: Beyond Narcos
War on Drugs Series Book 3

An electrifying account of the Cali Cartel beyond its portrayal on Netflix.

From the ashes of Pablo Escobar's empire rose an even bigger and more malevolent cartel. A new breed of sophisticated mobsters became the kings of cocaine. Their leader was Gilberto Rodríguez Orejuela – known as the Chess Player due to his foresight and calculated cunning.

Gilberto and his terrifying brother, Miguel, ran a multi-billion-dollar drug empire like a corporation. They employed a politically astute brand of thuggery and spent $10 million to put a president in power. Although the godfathers from Cali preferred bribery over violence, their many loyal torturers and hit men were never idle.

Clinton Bush and CIA Conspiracies:
From the Boys on the Tracks to Jeffrey Epstein
War on Drugs Series Book 4

In the 1980s, George HW Bush imported cocaine to finance an illegal war in Nicaragua. Governor Bill Clinton's Arkansas state police provided security for the drug drops. For assisting the CIA, the Clinton Crime Family was awarded the White House. The #clintonbodycount continues to this day, with the deceased including Jeffrey Epstein.

This book features harrowing true stories that reveal the insanity of the drug war. A mother receives the worst news about her son. A journalist gets a tip that endangers his life. An unemployed man becomes California's biggest crack dealer. A DEA agent in Mexico is sacrificed for going after the big players.

The lives of Linda Ives, Gary Webb, Freeway Rick Ross and Kiki Camarena are shattered by brutal experiences. Not all of them will survive.

Pablo Escobar's Story (4-book series)

"Finally, the definitive book about Escobar, original and up-to-date" – UNILAD

"The most comprehensive account ever written" – True Geordie

Pablo Escobar was a mama's boy who cherished his family and sang in the shower, yet he bombed a passenger plane and formed a death squad that used genital electrocution.

Most Escobar biographies only provide a few pieces of the puzzle, but this action-packed 1000-page book reveals everything about the king of cocaine.

Mostly translated from Spanish, Part 1 contains stories untold in the English-speaking world, including:

The tragic death of his youngest brother Fernando.

The fate of his pregnant mistress.

The shocking details of his affair with a TV celebrity.

The presidential candidate who encouraged him to eliminate their rivals.

The Mafia Philosopher

"A fast-paced true-crime memoir with all of the action of Good-fellas" – UNILAD

"Sopranos v Sons of Anarchy with an Alaskan-snow backdrop" – True Geordie Podcast

Breaking bones, burying bodies and planting bombs became second nature to Two Tonys while working for the Bonanno Crime Family, whose exploits inspired The Godfather.

After a dispute with an outlaw motorcycle club, Two Tonys left a trail of corpses from Arizona to Alaska. On the run, he was pursued by bikers and a neo-Nazi gang blood-thirsty for revenge, while a homicide detective launched a nationwide manhunt.

As the mist from his smoking gun fades, readers are left with an unexpected portrait of a stoic philosopher with a wealth of charm, a glorious turn of phrase and a fanatical devotion to his daughter.

Party Time

An action-packed roller-coaster account of a life spiralling out of control, featuring wild women, gangsters and a mountain of drugs.

Shaun Attwood arrived in Phoenix, Arizona, a penniless business graduate from a small industrial town in England. Within a decade, he became a stock-market millionaire. But he was leading a double life.

After taking his first Ecstasy pill at a rave in Manchester as a shy student, Shaun became intoxicated by the party lifestyle that would change his fortune. Years later, in the Arizona desert, he became submerged in a criminal underworld, throwing parties for thousands of ravers and running an Ecstasy ring in competition with the Mafia mass murderer Sammy 'The Bull' Gravano.

As greed and excess tore through his life, Shaun had

eye-watering encounters with Mafia hit men and crystal-meth addicts, enjoyed extravagant debauchery with superstar DJs and glitter girls, and ingested enough drugs to kill a herd of elephants. This is his story.

Hard Time

"Makes the Shawshank Redemption look like a holiday camp" – NOTW

After a SWAT team smashed down stock-market millionaire Shaun Attwood's door, he found himself inside of Arizona's deadliest jail and locked into a brutal struggle for survival.

Shaun's hope of living the American Dream turned into a nightmare of violence and chaos, when he had a run-in with Sammy the Bull Gravano, an Italian Mafia mass murderer.

In jail, Shaun was forced to endure cockroaches crawling in his ears at night, dead rats in the food and the sound of skulls getting cracked against toilets. He meticulously documented the conditions and smuggled out his message.

Join Shaun on a harrowing voyage into the darkest recesses of human existence.

Hard Time provides a revealing glimpse into the tragedy, brutality, dark comedy and eccentricity of prison life.

Featured worldwide on Nat Geo Channel's Locked-Up/Banged-Up Abroad Raving Arizona.

Prison Time

Sentenced to 9½ years in Arizona's state prison for distributing Ecstasy, Shaun finds himself living among gang members, sexual predators and drug-crazed psychopaths. After being attacked by a Californian biker in for stabbing a girlfriend, Shaun writes about the prisoners who befriend, protect and inspire him. They include T-Bone, a massive African American ex-Marine who risks his life saving vulnerable inmates from rape, and Two Tonys, an old-school Mafia murderer who left the corpses of his rivals from Arizona to Alaska. They teach Shaun how to turn incarceration to his advantage, and to learn from his mistakes.

Shaun is no stranger to love and lust in the heterosexual world, but the tables are turned on him inside. Sexual advances come at him from all directions, some cleverly disguised, others more sinister – making Shaun question his sexual identity.

Resigned to living alongside violent, mentally-ill and drug-addicted inmates, Shaun immerses himself in psychology and philosophy to try to make sense of his past behaviour, and begins applying what he learns as he adapts to prison life. Encouraged by Two Tonys to explore fiction as well, Shaun reads over 1000 books which, with support from a brilliant psychotherapist, Dr Owen, speed along his personal development. As his ability to deflect daily threats improves, Shaun begins to look forward to his release with optimism and a new love waiting for him. Yet the words of Aristotle from one of Shaun's books will prove prophetic: "We cannot learn without pain."

Un-Making a Murderer:
The Framing of Steven Avery and Brendan Dassey

Innocent people do go to jail. Sometimes mistakes are made. But even more terrifying is when the authorities conspire to frame them. That's what happened to Steven Avery and Brendan Dassey, who were convicted of murder and are serving life sentences.

Un-Making a Murderer is an explosive book which uncovers the illegal, devious and covert tactics used by Wisconsin officials, including:

– Concealing Other Suspects

– Paying Expert Witnesses to Lie

– Planting Evidence

– Jury Tampering

The art of framing innocent people has been in practice for centuries and will continue until the perpetrators are held accountable. Turning conventional assumptions and beliefs in the justice system upside down, *Un-Making a Murderer* takes you on that journey.

HARD TIME BY SHAUN ATTWOOD
CHAPTER 1

Sleep deprived and scanning for danger, I enter a dark cell on the second floor of the maximum-security Madison Street jail in Phoenix, Arizona, where guards and gang members are murdering prisoners. Behind me, the metal door slams heavily. Light slants into the cell through oblong gaps in the door, illuminating a prisoner cocooned in a white sheet, snoring lightly on the top bunk about two thirds of the way up the back wall. Relieved there is no immediate threat, I place my mattress on the grimy floor. Desperate to rest, I notice movement on the cement-block walls. *Am I hallucinating?* I blink several times. The walls appear to ripple. Stepping closer, I see the walls are alive with insects. I flinch. So many are swarming, I wonder if they're a colony of ants on the move. To get a better look, I put my eyes right up to them. They are mostly the size of almonds and have antennae. American cockroaches. I've seen them in the holding cells downstairs in smaller numbers, but nothing like this. A chill spread over my body. I back away.

Something alive falls from the ceiling and bounces off the base of my neck. I jump. With my night vision improving, I spot cockroaches weaving in and out of the base of the fluorescent strip light. Every so often one drops onto the concrete and resumes crawling. Examining the bottom bunk, I realise why my cellmate is sleeping at a higher elevation: cockroaches are pouring from gaps in the decrepit wall at the level of my bunk. The area is thick with them. Placing my mattress on the bottom bunk scatters them. I walk towards the toilet, crunching a few under my shower sandals. I urinate and grab the toilet roll. A cockroach darts from the centre of the roll onto my hand, tickling my fingers. My arm jerks as if it has a mind of its own, losing the cockroach and the toilet roll. Using a towel, I wipe the bulk of them off the bottom bunk, stopping only to shake the odd one off my hand. I unroll my mattress. They begin to regroup and inhabit my mattress. My adrenaline is pumping so much, I lose my fatigue.

Nauseated, I sit on a tiny metal stool bolted to the wall. *How will I sleep? How's my cellmate sleeping through the infestation and my arrival?* Copying his technique, I cocoon myself in a sheet and lie down, crushing more cockroaches. The only way they can access me now is through the breathing hole I've left in the sheet by the lower half of my face. Inhaling their strange musty odour, I close my eyes. I can't sleep. I feel them crawling on the sheet around my feet. *Am I imagining things?* Frightened of them infiltrating my breathing hole, I keep opening my eyes. Cramps cause me to rotate onto my other side. Facing the wall, I'm repulsed by so many of them just inches away. I return to my original side.

The sheet traps the heat of the Sonoran Desert to my body, soaking me in sweat. Sweat tickles my body, tricking my mind into thinking the cockroaches are infiltrating and crawling on me. The trapped heat aggravates my bleeding skin infections and bedsores. I want to scratch myself, but I know better. The outer layers of my skin have turned soggy from sweating constantly in this concrete oven. Squirming on the bunk fails to stop the relentless itchiness of my skin. Eventually, I scratch myself. Clumps of moist skin detach under my nails. Every now and then I become so uncomfortable, I must open my cocoon to waft the heat out, which allows the cockroaches in. It takes hours to drift to sleep. I only manage a few hours. I awake stuck to the soaked sheet, disgusted by the cockroach carcasses compressed against the mattress.

The cockroaches plague my new home until dawn appears at the dots in the metal grid over a begrimed strip of four-inch-thick bullet-proof glass at the top of the back wall – the cell's only source of outdoor light. They disappear into the cracks in the walls, like vampire mist retreating from sunlight. But not all of them. There were so many on the night shift that even their vastly reduced number is too many to dispose of. And they act like they know it. They roam around my feet with attitude, as if to make it clear that I'm trespassing on their turf.

My next set of challenges will arise not from the insect world, but from my neighbours. I'm the new arrival, subject to scrutiny about my charges just like when I'd run into the Aryan Brotherhood prison gang on my first day at the medium-security Towers jail a year ago. I wish my cellmate would wake up, brief me on the mood of the locals and introduce me to the head of the white gang. No such luck. Chow is announced over a speaker system in a crackly robotic voice, but he doesn't stir.

I emerge into the day room for breakfast. Prisoners in black-and-white bee-striped uniforms gather under the metal-grid stairs and tip dead cockroaches into a trash bin from plastic peanut-butter containers they'd set as traps during the night. All eyes are on me in the chow line. Watching who sits where, I hold my head up, put on a solid stare and pretend to be as at home in this environment as the cockroaches. It's all an act. I'm lonely and afraid. I loathe having to explain myself to the head of the white race, who I assume is the toughest murderer. I've been in jail long enough to know that taking my breakfast to my cell will imply that I have something to hide.

The gang punishes criminals with certain charges. The most serious are sex offenders, who are KOS: Kill On Sight. Other charges are punishable by SOS – Smash On Sight – such as drive-by shootings because women and kids sometimes get killed. It's called convict justice. Gang members are constantly looking for people to beat up because that's how they earn their reputations and tattoos. The most serious acts of violence earn the highest-ranking tattoos. To be a full gang member requires murder. I've observed the body language and techniques inmates trying to integrate employ. An inmate with a spring in his step and an air of confidence is likely to be accepted. A person who avoids eye contact and fails to introduce himself to the gang is likely to be preyed on. Some of the failed attempts I saw ended up with heads getting cracked against toilets, a sound I've grown familiar with. I've seen prisoners being extracted on stretchers who looked dead – one had yellow fluid leaking from his head. The constant violence gives me nightmares, but the reality is that I put myself in here, so I force myself to accept it as a part of my punishment.

It's time to apply my knowledge. With a self-assured stride, I take my breakfast bag to the table of white inmates covered in neo-Nazi tattoos, allowing them to question me.

"Mind if I sit with you guys?" I ask, glad exhaustion has deepened my voice.

"These seats are taken. But you can stand at the corner of the table."

The man who answered is probably the head of the gang. I size him up. Cropped brown hair. A dangerous glint in Nordic-blue eyes. Tiny pupils that suggest he's on heroin. Weightlifter-type veins bulging from a sturdy neck. Political ink on arms crisscrossed with scars. About the same age as me, thirty-three.

"Thanks. I'm Shaun from England." I volunteer my origin to show I'm different from them but not in a way that might get me smashed.

"I'm Bullet, the head of the whites." He offers me his fist to bump. "Where you roll in from, wood?"

Addressing me as wood is a good sign. It's what white gang members on a friendly basis call each other.

"Towers jail. They increased my bond and re-classified me to maximum security."

"What's your bond at?"

"I've got two $750,000 bonds," I say in a monotone. This is no place to brag about bonds.

"How many people you kill, brother?" His eyes drill into mine, checking whether my body language supports my story. My body language so far is spot on.

"None. I threw rave parties. They got us talking about drugs on wiretaps." Discussing drugs on the phone does not warrant a $1.5 million bond. I know and beat him to his next question. "Here's my charges." I show him my charge sheet, which includes conspiracy and leading a crime syndicate – both from running an Ecstasy ring.

Bullet snatches the paper and scrutinises it. Attempting to pre-empt his verdict, the other whites study his face. On edge, I wait for him to respond. Whatever he says next will determine whether I'll be accepted or victimised.

"Are you some kind of jailhouse attorney?" Bullet asks. "I want someone to read through my case paperwork." During our few minutes of conversation, Bullet has seen through my act and concluded that I'm educated – a possible resource to him.

I appreciate that he'll accept me if I take the time to read his case. "I'm no jailhouse attorney, but I'll look through it and help you however I can."

"Good. I'll stop by your cell later on, wood."

After breakfast, I seal as many of the cracks in the walls as I can with toothpaste. The cell smells minty, but the cockroaches still find their way in. Their day shift appears to be collecting information on the brown paper bags under my bunk, containing a few items of food that I purchased from the commissary; bags that I tied off with rubber bands in the hope of keeping the cockroaches out. Relentlessly, the cockroaches explore the bags for entry points, pausing over and probing the most worn and vulnerable regions. *Will the nightly swarm eat right through the paper?* I read all morning, wondering whether my cellmate has died in his cocoon, his occasional breathing sounds reassuring me.

Bullet stops by late afternoon and drops his case paperwork off. He's been charged with Class 3 felonies and less, not serious crimes, but is facing a double-digit sentence because of his prior convictions and Security Threat Group status in the prison system. The proposed sentencing range seems disproportionate. I'll advise him to reject the plea bargain – on the assumption he already knows to do so, but is just seeking the comfort of a second opinion, like many un-sentenced inmates. When he returns for his paperwork, our conversation disturbs my cellmate – the cocoon shuffles – so we go upstairs to his cell. I tell Bullet what I think. He is excitable, a different man from earlier, his pupils almost non-existent.

"This case ain't shit. But my prosecutor knows I done other shit, all kinds of heavy shit, but can't prove it. I'd do anything to get that sorry bitch off my fucking ass. She's asking for something bad to happen to her. Man, if I ever get bonded out, I'm gonna chop that bitch into pieces. Kill her slowly though. Like to work her over with a blowtorch."

Such talk can get us both charged with conspiring to murder a prosecutor, so I try to steer him elsewhere. "It's crazy how they can catch you doing one thing, yet try to sentence you for all of the things they think you've ever done."

"Done plenty. Shot some dude in the stomach once. Rolled him up in a blanket and threw him in a dumpster."

Discussing past murders is as unsettling as future ones. "So, what's all your tattoos mean, Bullet? Like that eagle on your chest?"

"Why you wanna know?" Bullet's eyes probe mine.

My eyes hold their ground. "Just curious."

"It's a war bird. The AB patch."

"AB patch?"

"What the Aryan Brotherhood gives you when you've put enough work in."

"How long does it take to earn a patch?"

"Depends how quickly you put your work in. You have to earn your lightning bolts first."

"Why you got red and black lightning bolts?"

"You get SS bolts for beating someone down or for being an enforcer for the family. Red lightning bolts for killing someone.

I was sent down as a youngster. They gave me steel and told me who to handle and I handled it. You don't ask questions. You just get blood on your steel. Dudes who get these tats without putting work in are told to cover them up or leave the yard."

"What if they refuse?"

"They're held down and we carve the ink off them."

Imagining them carving a chunk of flesh to remove a tattoo, I cringe. He's really enjoying telling me this now. His volatile nature is clear and frightening. *He's accepted me too much. He's trying to impress me before making demands.*

At night, I'm unable to sleep. Cocooned in heat, surrounded by cockroaches, I hear the swamp-cooler vent – a metal grid at the top of a wall – hissing out tepid air. Giving up on sleep, I put my earphones on and tune into National Public Radio. Listening to a Vivaldi violin concerto, I close my eyes and press my tailbone down to straighten my back as if I'm doing a yogic relaxation. The playful allegro thrills me, lifting my spirits, but the wistful adagio provokes sad emotions and tears. I open my eyes and gaze into the gloom. Due to lack of sleep, I start hallucinating and hearing voices over the music whispering threats. I'm at breaking point. Although I have accepted that I committed crimes and deserve to be punished, no one should have to live like this. I'm furious at myself for making the series of reckless decisions that put me in here and for losing absolutely everything. As violins crescendo in my ears, I remember what my life used to be like.

PRISON TIME BY SHAUN ATTWOOD

CHAPTER 1

"I've got a padlock in a sock. I can smash your brains in while you're asleep. I can kill you whenever I want." My new cellmate sizes me up with no trace of human feeling in his eyes. Muscular and pot-bellied, he's caked in prison ink, including six snakes on his skull, slithering side by side. The top of his right ear is missing in a semi-circle.

The waves of fear are overwhelming. After being in transportation all day, I can feel my bladder hurting. "I'm not looking to cause any trouble. I'm the quietest cellmate you'll ever have. All I do is read and write."

Scowling, he shakes his head. "Why've they put a fish in with me?" He swaggers close enough for me to smell his cigarette breath. "Us convicts don't get along with fresh fish."

"Should I ask to move then?" I say, hoping he'll agree if he hates new prisoners so much.

"No! They'll think I threatened you!"

In the eight by twelve feet slab of space, I swerve around him and place my property box on the top bunk.

He pushes me aside and grabs the box. "You just put that on my artwork! I ought to fucking smash you, fish!"

"Sorry, I didn't see it."

"You need to be more aware of your fucking surroundings! What you in for anyway, fish?"

I explain my charges, Ecstasy dealing and how I spent twenty-six months fighting my case.

"How come the cops were so hard-core after you?" he asks, squinting.

"It was a big case, a multi-million-dollar investigation. They raided over a hundred people and didn't find any drugs. They were pretty pissed off. I'd stopped dealing by the time they caught up with me, but I'd done plenty over the years, so I accept my punishment."

"Throwing raves," he says, staring at the ceiling as if remembering something. "Were you partying with underage girls?" he asks, his voice slow, coaxing.

Being called a sex offender is the worst insult in prison. Into my third year of incarceration, I'm conditioned to react. "What you trying to say?" I yell angrily, brow clenched.

"Were you fucking underage girls?" Flexing his body, he shakes both fists as if about to punch me.

"Hey, I'm no child molester, and I'd prefer you didn't say shit like that!"

"My buddy next door is doing twenty-five to life for murdering a child molester. How do I know Ecstasy dealing ain't your cover story?" He inhales loudly, nostrils flaring.

"You want to see my fucking paperwork?"

A stocky prisoner walks in. Short hair. Dark eyes. Powerful neck. On one arm: a tattoo of a man in handcuffs above the word OMERTA – the Mafia code of silence towards law enforcement. "What the fuck's going on in here, Bud?" asks Junior Bull – the son of "Sammy the Bull" Gravano, the Mafia mass murderer who was my biggest competitor in the Ecstasy market.

Relieved to see a familiar face, I say, "How're you doing?"

Shaking my hand, he says in a New York Italian accent, "I'm doing alright. I read that shit in the newspaper about you starting a blog in Sheriff Joe Arpaio's jail."

"The blog's been bringing media heat on the conditions."

"You know him?" Bud asks.

"Yeah, from Towers jail. He's a good dude. He's in for dealing Ecstasy like me."

241

"It's a good job you said that 'cause I was about to smash his ass," Bud says.

"It's a good job Wild Man ain't here 'cause you'd a got your ass thrown off the balcony," Junior Bull says.

I laugh. The presence of my best friend, Wild Man, was partly the reason I never took a beating at the county jail, but with Wild Man in a different prison, I feel vulnerable. When Bud casts a death stare on me, my smile fades.

"What the fuck you guys on about?" Bud asks.

"Let's go talk downstairs." Junior Bull leads Bud out.

I rush to a stainless-steel sink/toilet bolted to a cement-block wall by the front of the cell, unbutton my orange jumpsuit and crane my neck to watch the upper-tier walkway in case Bud returns. I bask in relief as my bladder deflates. After flushing, I take stock of my new home, grateful for the slight improvement in the conditions versus what I'd grown accustomed to in Sheriff Joe Arpaio's jail. No cockroaches. No blood stains. A working swamp cooler. Something I've never seen in a cell before: shelves. The steel table bolted to the wall is slightly larger, too. *But how will I concentrate on writing with Bud around?* There's a mixture of smells in the room. Cleaning chemicals. Aftershave. Tobacco. A vinegar-like odour. The slit of a window at the back overlooks gravel in a no-man's-land before the next building with gleaming curls of razor wire around its roof.

From the doorway upstairs, I'm facing two storeys of cells overlooking a day room with shower cubicles at the end of both tiers. At two white plastic circular tables, prisoners are playing dominoes, cards, chess and Scrabble, some concentrating, others yelling obscenities, contributing to a brain-scraping din that I hope to block out by purchasing a Walkman. In a raised box-shaped Plexiglas control tower, two guards are monitoring the prisoners.

Bud returns. My pulse jumps. Not wanting to feel like I'm stuck in a kennel with a rabid dog, I grab a notepad and pen and head for the day room.

Focussed on my body language, not wanting to signal any weakness, I'm striding along the upper tier, head and chest elevated, when two hands appear from a doorway and grab me. I drop the pad. The pen clinks against grid-metal and tumbles to the day room as I'm pulled into a cell reeking of backside sweat and masturbation, a cheese-tinted funk.

"I'm Booga. Let's fuck," says a squat man in urine-stained boxers, with WHITE TRASH tattooed on his torso below a mobile home, and an arm sleeved with the Virgin Mary.

Shocked, I brace to flee or fight to preserve my anal virginity. I can't believe my eyes when he drops his boxers and waggles his penis.

Dancing to music playing through a speaker he has rigged up, Booga smiles in a sexy way. "Come on," he says in a husky voice. "Drop your pants. Let's fuck." He pulls pornography faces. I question his sanity. He moves closer. "If I let you fart in my mouth, can I fart in yours?"

"You can fuck off," I say, springing towards the doorway.

He grabs me. We scuffle. Every time I make progress towards the doorway, he clings to my clothes, dragging me back in. When I feel his penis rub against my leg, my adrenalin kicks in so forcefully I experience a burst of strength and wriggle free. I bolt out as fast as my shower sandals will allow and snatch my pad. Looking over my shoulder, I see him stood calmly in the doorway, smiling. He points at me. "You have to walk past my door every day. We're gonna get together. I'll lick your ass and you can fart in my mouth." Booga blows a kiss and disappears.

I rush downstairs. With my back to a wall, I pause to steady my thoughts and breathing. In survival mode, I think, *What's going to come at me next?* In the hope of reducing my tension, I borrow a pen to do what helps me stay sane: writing. With the details fresh in my mind, I document my journey to the prison for my blog readers, keeping an eye out in case anyone else wants to test the new prisoner. The more I write, the more I fill with a sense of purpose. Jon's Jail Journal is a connection to the outside world that I cherish.

Someone yells, "One time!" The din lowers. A door rumbles open. A guard does a security walk, his every move scrutinised by dozens of scornful eyes staring from cells. When he exits, the din resumes, and the prisoners return to injecting drugs to escape from reality, including the length of their sentences. This continues all day with "Two times!" signifying two approaching guards, and "Three times!" three and so on. Every now and then an announcement by a guard over the speakers briefly lowers the din.

Before lockdown, I join the line for a shower, holding bars of soap in a towel that I aim to swing at the head of the next person to try me. With boisterous inmates a few feet away, yelling at the men in the showers to "Stop jerking off," and "Hurry the fuck up," I get in a cubicle that reeks of bleach and mildew. With every nerve strained, I undress and rinse fast.

At night, despite the desert heat, I cocoon myself in a blanket from head to toe and turn towards the wall, making my face more difficult to strike. I leave a hole for air, but the warm cement block inches from my mouth returns each exhalation to my face as if it's breathing on me, creating a feeling of suffocation. For hours, my heart drums so hard against the thin mattress I feel as if I'm moving even though I'm still. I try to sleep, but my eyes keep springing open and my head turning towards the cell as I try to penetrate the darkness, searching for Bud swinging a padlock in a sock at my head.

PRISONERS ABROAD

Prisoners Abroad is the only charity providing practical support to British people in prisons throughout the world. Every year, we support thousands of people just like Natalie, who are held far from their homes and families. We help them to get food, clean water, medicine and bedding.

We help people to stay in touch with their families, and send books and magazines to help alleviate the damaging boredom and loneliness of imprisonment. Guilty or innocent, convicted or awaiting trial, we simply work with the people who need us.

Since 1978, we have helped thousands of Britons survive in terrible circumstances. We also provide help after release, making sure that reoffending isn't the only option left to someone who has returned to the UK with nothing.

You too can help, by donating. Without the support of people like you, we simply could not exist, and many people like Natalie would have nobody at all. You can reach people that the rest of society has forgotten, people who are truly desperate for help. Even a small donation can go a long way and have a genuinely positive effect on someone in an overseas prison.

You can find out more about our work and donate at www.prisonersabroad.org.uk

Alternatively, call 020 7561 6820 or send a cheque to:
Prisoners Abroad
89–93 Fonthill Road
London N4 3JH
United Kingdom
Registered charity number: 1093710.

Lightning Source UK Ltd.
Milton Keynes UK
UKHW010831281020
372376UK00016B/1220